IMAGES
of America

DETROIT
THE BLACK BOTTOM COMMUNITY

On the cover: Please see page 27. (Courtesy of the Walter P. Reuther Library at Wayne State University.)

IMAGES *of America*

DETROIT

THE BLACK BOTTOM COMMUNITY

Jeremy Williams

ARCADIA PUBLISHING

ISBN 978-0-7385-7710-4

Published by Arcadia Publishing
Charleston, South Carolina

Printed in the United States of America

Library of Congress Control Number: 2009933632

For all general information contact Arcadia Publishing at:
Telephone 843-853-2070
Fax 843-853-0044
E-mail sales@arcadiapublishing.com
For customer service and orders:
Toll-Free 1-888-313-2665

Visit us on the Internet at www.arcadiapublishing.com

To the former residents, movers, and shakers of Black Bottom.
To Robert Hayden (1913–1980) and Dudley Randall (1914–2000).

CONTENTS

Acknowledgments

Several people provided indispensable aid and support in the writing of this book. Elizabeth Clemens, audio-archivist for Walter P. Reuther Library at Wayne State University; Mark Patrick, coordinator for special collections at Detroit Public Library; and Karen L. Jania, division head for Bentley Historical Collections at University of Michigan, gave me their prompt service and undivided attention. Thanks to my editor, Anna Wilson, for her unending guidance and direction. Special thanks to my eternal friend Maia Bass for her gracious hospitality during those chilly winter months spent in Detroit and Dearborn conducting research for this book. Super thanks to former Black Bottom resident Ms. Billie Jimerson, for inviting me into her home for coffee, cigarettes, and reminiscences on good times in Black Bottom. Extra thanks to Mary Patterson at Cup O Karma Café in Mesa, Arizona. Thanks to Bernadette Nellum. See you at Venice Beach!

I thank my family and friends, Taji, Mal, Elon, John, Lisa, Helen, Sharonda, LJ, Sparkle, Larry Lucido, Seven, Dee, Kevin, Dwayne, and Chyna for lending time and attention to my random discussions and rants on Black Bottom history.

Lastly, a great amount of recognition is due to the "vicious circle": Glenda, Erick, Michelle, Dean, Rowena, Janine, Misty, Yvonne, and Dee Wilkins. Your insightful blogs and fruitful discussions helped me to sharpen my wits, expand my ideas, and deepen my historical perspectives.

The images in this volume appear courtesy of the Walter P. Reuther Library at Wayne State University (WRL), the Burton Historical Collections at the Detroit Public Library (BHC), the Detroit Urban League records, and Bentley Historical Library at the University of Michigan (BHL).

Introduction

Today, driving through the tattered and busted remains of the lower east side of Detroit, one would perhaps never realize that there was once a place there called Black Bottom where blacks lived, struggled, and prospered. It was located on Detroit's lower east side and was bounded by Gratiot Avenue, Brush Street, Vernor Highway, and the Grand Trunk railroad tracks. Its main commercial strips were on Hastings and St. Antoine Streets, an adjacent neighborhood known as Paradise Valley. The two were not, however, the same neighborhood. To the world-renowned Paradise Valley, one went for a fancy dinner and an elegant evening of top-notched entertainment. However, it would be these types of challenges confronting the Black Bottom community that would become part of the cohesive element that turned Black Bottom into a strong and viable community.

Notwithstanding historical debate, Black Bottom was particularly unique in how it was formed and shaped into a community and why it ultimately collapsed, leaving its residents to continue their search for answers as to why Black Bottom was given such a grim and unjust fate. It has been nearly half a century since the demise of Black Bottom, but many of Black Bottom's former residents cannot seem to reconcile why "they [urban planning officials] broke up the community. They broke up the business," according to former Black Bottom resident Billie Jimerson.

This book offers a visual history of Black Bottom during the formative years between 1914 and 1951, because by this time Black Bottom had both changed its racial composition significantly and had received a significant economic charge due to the first war. After several decades of struggling to make a life for themselves, the Black Bottom community had reached its social, cultural, and political zenith. The year 1941 would mark the point of decline for this once-bolstering arena, when Mayor Edward Jeffries would mark the area for demolition and urban renewal.

Between 1914 and 1920, Detroit's African American population rose from 5,751 to 41,532. Before the war demand of labor, blacks had been unable to obtain employment in certain northern occupations, due to racism and discrimination. However, employment agencies now found it difficult to find black labor (partly because the majority of the total population still resided in the South).

However, by 1927 the importance of black labor diminished. In Detroit there were only 14,454 blacks employed, compared to 20,404 the previous year. (It was not as though blacks could logically return to the agricultural fields of the South because the labor shortages in the South were soon replenished by white labor.) This economic spin ushered in the Depression for Black Bottom residents, most who obviously depended on the economic security of Henry Ford's lucrative and alluring promise.

The countrywide collapse of the open stock market in October 1929 would shake the economic base of Black Bottom's working-class community even more. The once-stable black employment rate plummeted, sending Black Bottom residents into a depression and to the city relief offices, while industry analysts theorized the effects of the stock market crash and whether or not "our normal purchasing power [had] been appreciably impaired," one *Detroit Free Press* article reported. By November of that year, employment bureaus throughout the nation reported a significant decline in the number of applicants that applied for employment with the ones that actually obtained employment. Industrial plants in Chicago sent workers home daily. Although blacks were typically the first to suffer any employment crisis, whites too found themselves joining the ranks of the dispossessed and unemployed.

By 1930, there were 120,066 blacks reported in the city of Detroit, most who were settled in a 30-square-block area east of Woodward Avenue called Paradise Valley. According to Robert Weaver, in 1932 newly elected Franklin D. Roosevelt's New Deal offered hope for African Americans by "promising to put [them] to work." According to Christopher G. Wye's essay "The New Deal and the Negro Community: Toward a Broader Conceptualization," the New Deal also purported to include blacks into "programs designed to relieve the special problems created by the Depression." For example, the Sojourner Truth Homes would help ease the tension in Black Bottom's housing crisis. But two years later, Detroit's department of public welfare reported that 29.6 percent of its black population was on the welfare rolls.

By 1940, the annual report of the Detroit Urban League approximated Detroit's black population at 145,000. World War II, as well as economic and social tensions in the South, would continue to send black southerners to the North in search for a better way of life. The Northern factories offered the kind of wages that most blacks would never receive in the South. Although the workplace was often a hazardous environment for the black migrant worker, it was the financial rewards coupled with the steady and consistent work schedule that made blacks leave the South. "One [black man] from the North recently returned with $600 dollars. He paid his debts; paid the rent in advance for his parents; and took his own family back North," observed Dr. Robert R. Morton in a lecture titled, "Effects of Negro Migration on the South." Detroit's burgeoning war industries offered the kind of employment opportunities that provided blacks enough money for a decent living and to purchase a home. As Detroit's "emerging black industrial working class" continued to grow, this inevitably meant that the Black Bottom community would increase, creating the need for extra housing. Because of unchecked discrimination in housing in Detroit, black social and cultural organizations became inundated with the demands of migrants seeking accommodations in employment and housing.

With Black Bottom's population growing rapidly as a result of the burgeoning war industries, black leadership faced the challenge of facilitating the transformation of the rural uneducated southern agricultural worker into the expanding urban industrial metropolis. The black church served as a vital resource center for Detroit and Black Bottom's black community. Detroit's black migration dilemma encouraged some black ministers to start churches. Therefore, any examination of black social, political, and cultural strivings must begin with the church. By 1941, Detroit's Bethel African Methodist Episcopal Church (AME), Second Baptist Church, and the Detroit Urban League would prove to be major resource centers for the Black Bottom community.

There were many issues that affected blacks migrating to Black Bottom between 1914 and 1951. As early as 1905, socially minded men and women in New York City organized the National Urban League and began to grapple with the unavoidable issues affecting black migrants. Since the 1850s, the black church had established itself as an exemplary institution of social, political, and cultural progress in the Black Bottom community. But institutions assisted other local social agencies with matters of housing, employment training, recreational needs, "the protection of young black girls coming from the South for domestic training," and the "industrial adjustment" of black migrants in Black Bottom, according to the Detroit Urban League.

Life as a factory worker gave Black Bottom residents the blues. The factories were sweaty, filthy, and dangerous. Hastings Street became an escape route for Black Bottom residents looking to ease the humdrum ghetto lifestyle. Since Hastings Street ran from the west end of Black Bottom through Paradise Valley to the north, essentially, Black Bottom and Paradise Valley were not exclusive of one another because both inhabited the social, cultural, and economic dimensions of African American life. Black Bottom was the residential area, and Paradise Valley served as the commercial district.

Hastings Street in Paradise Valley was the main thoroughfare of black happenings, both commercial and entertainment, as well as crime and vice.

In 1941, as the United States prepared for imminent war in the Pacific Theater, black newspapers proliferated with stories of blatant discrimination in the defense industry that had a direct impact on the Black Bottom community. Many war plants refused to hire blacks. Those plants that did so would only hire them as janitors. "It is the company policy not to employ them as mechanics and aircraft workers," explained the general manager of North American Aviation. Standard Steel officials told the Urban League, "We have not had a Negro working in 25 years and do not plan to start now." It did not matter to the heads-of-industry that most of the black applicants were experienced machinists who were trained work mechanics, tool and die makers, and sheet metal workers, but that "it [was] not the policy of [the] company to employ other than of the Caucasian race."

Disenchantment and frustration quickly moved civil rights leaders to challenge the rampant discrimination that permeated the defense industry. While traveling through the Deep South visiting the Sleeping Car Brotherhood Divisions with colleague Milton Webster, A. Phillip Randolph proposed a march on Washington, D.C. President Roosevelt realized that the civil rights leaders were adamant about the protest movement. President Roosevelt, knowing that his wife held much deeper trust and support within the black community than he did, turned to her for help. Eleanor feared that the black movement, in a city manned by a southern-bred police force, could possibly end in violence and bloodshed. She agreed to write a letter to Randolph urging him to halt the protest. Randolph refused, and President Roosevelt agreed to meet with Randolph and Walter White on June 18.

After seven days of Eleanor refereeing the order issue, the president signed Executive Order 8802. President Roosevelt's policy assured "non-discrimination in defense employment with an executive order setting up machinery to insure that Negroes will be given equitable treatment in seeking work." The *Chicago Tribune* reported that "the order followed a memorandum the President sent to the [Office of Production Management] last week declaring many complaints had reached him that Negroes especially were being barred from armament work and ordering that agency to see to it that full utilization of the nation's man power was made."

Low morale within the Black Bottom community received a boost when their complaints and grievances had ended in victory. In other words, according to historian Doris Kearns Goodwin, "when the President signed the executive order, faith in democracy which Negroes had begun to feel had strayed from its course was renewed throughout the nation."

By 1942, the tension of racism and discrimination was at a boiling point. At this point, blacks still led the race in unemployment and of the 160,000 blacks in Detroit, 8 percent were on public welfare. With a total white population of 1,600,000, only 10,744 were on welfare. To make matters worse, the housing crisis continued to confine restrict blacks to the cramped and congested area of Black Bottom. The controversy over blacks' access to a public housing project stirred the public debate. Whites violently protested the inclusion of black war workers in the Sojourner Truth Housing Project and eventually convinced the Federal Housing Administration to restrict the housing project to white families. As soon as Eleanor resigned from the Office of Civilian Defense, she became entangled in further controversy, a brutal battle between blacks and whites over the occupancy of a newly built federal housing project in Detroit. The 200-unit development had been developed for black defense workers by Eleanor's friend at the Federal Works Agency, Clark Foreman, a liberal southerner who felt that blacks were entitled to enjoy the benefits of the public housing boom necessitated by the war.

On Wednesday, April 29, 1942, seven months after the federal government had contracted the construction of the projects "for Black war workers and their families," black families moved into the Sojourner Truth Housing Project, under police protection. The *Detroit Free Press* reported "14 Negro families were moved into the Sojourner Truth Defense Housing Project at Fenelon and Nevada . . . under the protection of State troops and battalions of city and State police."

The riots of 1943 had been forewarned by many who saw the dangerous mixture of race, housing, and unemployment as a harbinger of what was to come. "The Negro factor in Detroit is a keg of powder with a short fuse and any one of many possible incidents, fairly insignificant in themselves, may be the match put to the fuse," warned *Detroit News* reporter A. M. Smith. Detroit leaders, city officials, and industrialists scurried for answers and analysis to "the Negro Problem." Some blamed idleness (due to lack of employment) in young black youth as the source of the problem. Charles C. Diggs said "we shall never make the proper approach to the Negro problem here or anywhere else in the North until we take fully into account the basically different social and economic systems of the North and the South; make proper allowances in recognition of this difference, and set up proper aids to the Negro in making the change."

Almost a month after the riots, Black Bottom still bore the effects of the riots. Many merchants continued to try to put their businesses (and lives) back together, boarding up broken windows and replacing the vast amounts of merchandise that had been looted during the riots. Exacerbating black problems, Mayor Edward Jeffries's 1946 Detroit Plan targeted Black Bottom as the ideal site for so-called slum clearance. When the Detroit Plan was issued in its final form in 1951, 140,000 blacks lived in Black Bottom. As expected, many middle-class blacks rushed to move to the more prominent neighborhoods of La Salle Boulevard, Chicago Boulevard, Boston-Edison, and Arden Park.

The death knell, it seems, was struck by urban renewal, which transformed Black Bottom into Lafayette Park. According to a *Detroit News* article, as early as 1941 "the first concrete plan aiming at ultimate rehabilitation of the area within the Grand Boulevard circle was under consideration by Jeffries' blight committee. The plan, embracing 20 square blocks bounded by Hastings, Dequindre, and Larned streets and Monroe Avenue" had sealed the fate of Black Bottom and Paradise Valley. The 1943 riots would only provide reason and logic for what was to come. The Chrysler Freeway took Hastings. Stroh's took over St. Antoine. Hudson's took Brush and Beaubien. Some residents jokingly called urban renewal "Negro removal." And when one considers these claims, from a historical perspective, it is plausible. Many believe that possibly all of the above factored into the inevitable end of Black Bottom.

Mayor Edward Jeffries and the Detroit City Plan Commission in 1946 had destroyed a community. Black Bottom and Paradise Valley were devastated by highway construction. The Oakland-Hastings (later Chrysler) Freeway barreled through these former black enclaves. The Hastings Street commercial district in Paradise Valley felled many of Detroit's most prominent black institutions, from jazz clubs to the St. Antoine branch of the YMCA. The John C. Lodge Freeway ripped through the increasingly black area around Twelfth Street and Highland Park. It seemed as though a crime had been committed.

The aftermath was not much more than a "no man's land of deterioration and abandonment," wrote noted historian Thomas Sugrue. Actual construction had been delayed, and for 10 years after Jeffries Detroit Plan, Black Bottom lay dormant, and the city did nothing to help business owners or black residents to relocate. Shopkeepers had no real reason to invest in improvements, as condemned buildings were buried under asphalt and cement. While statistics show that, by 1950, 423 residences, 109 businesses, 22 manufacturing plants, and 93 vacant lots had been condemned for the first three-mile stretch of the Lodge Freeway from Jefferson to Pallister, the *Michigan Chronicle*'s 1951 front page story, "Progress Has Been Rapid for Negroes in Motor City," seemed propagandist, at best. By 1958, the Lodge Freeway displaced 2,222 buildings. Destruction continued to make way for the Edsel Ford Expressway with the demolition of approximately more 2,800 buildings.

Eventually homes and businesses were replaced with apartments and townhouses such as those in Lafayette Park, which many of the former residents could not afford. Hastings Street became Chrysler Freeway. The rise of new office buildings and the development of a large network of expressways whimsically cut through what was once a testament of African American socioeconomic success. Black Bottom was obliterated, but the black ghetto simply moved to the Twelfth Street area, forgotten until it became the center of the 1967 riot. Twelfth Street had been the Jewish area; the Jews were now living in Huntington Woods, Southfield, and other suburbs. Middle-class blacks moved to the more prominent neighborhoods of La Salle Boulevard, Chicago Boulevard, Boston-Edison, and Arden Park. Black Bottom was gone.

One

EUROPEAN IMMIGRANTS

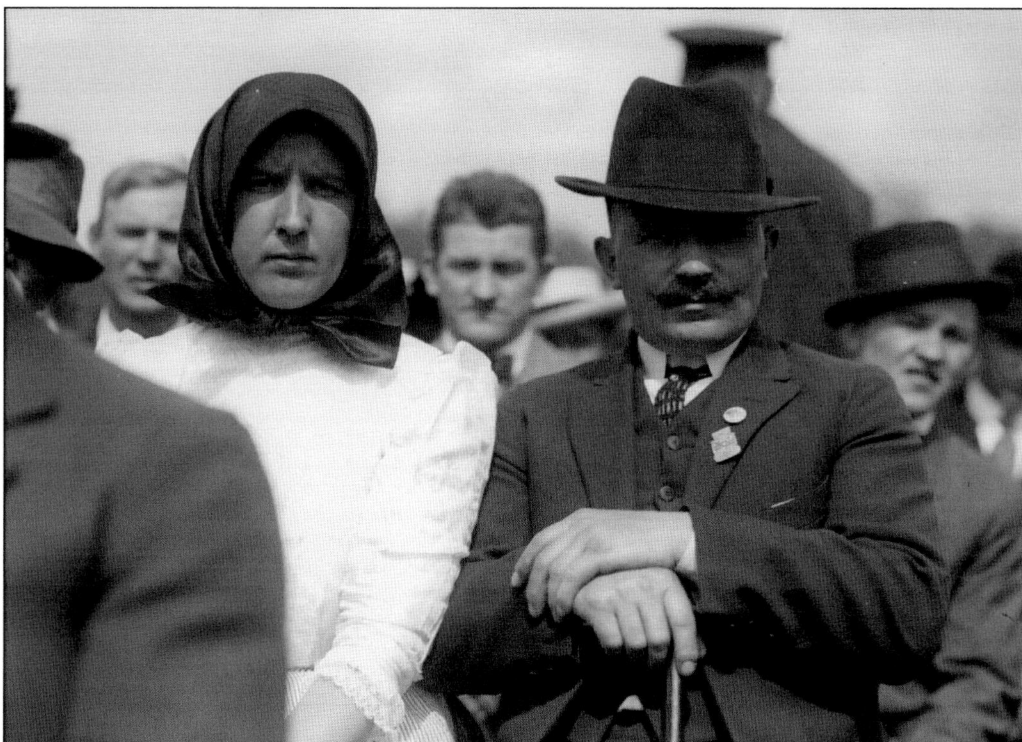

Before African Americans began to migrate to Black Bottom in large numbers, the area was an ethnic hodgepodge, home to Irish, Italian, German, Romanian, and Russian Jews living in overlapping colonies. Many of Black Bottom's early immigrant community arrived in Detroit via the 15-minute ferry ride from Ontario. The view of the industrial riverfront excited new arrivals looking for employment and stability. With the exception of the hidden slums and impoverished peoples, America was everything the foreigners expected. Chance and opportunity lay waiting. (WRL.)

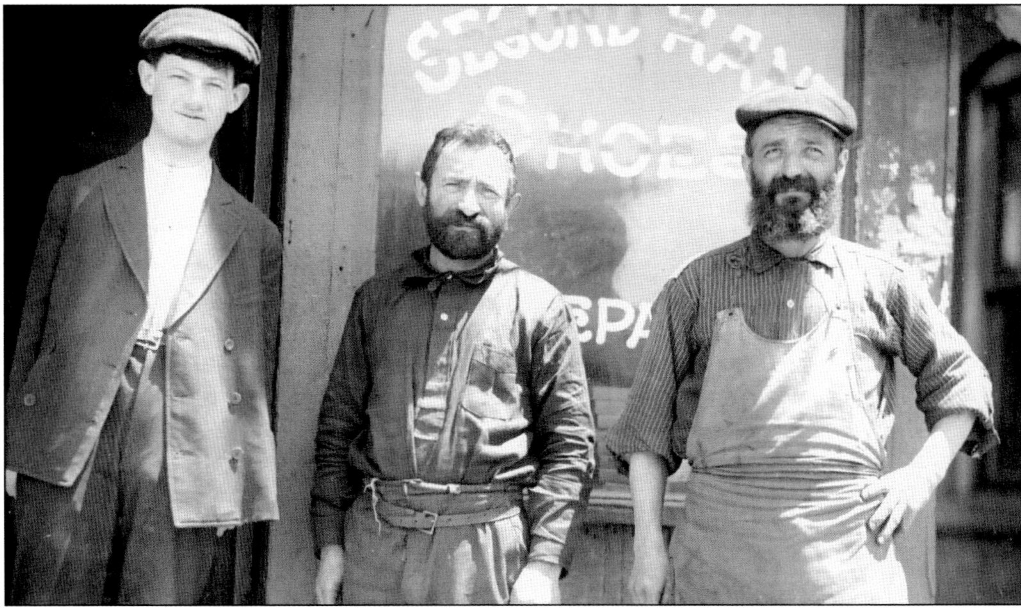

By the late 19th century, Jewish immigrants had settled around St. Antoine, Hastings, and Rivard Streets north of Gratiot Avenue. Near the beginning of the 20th century, Russian and Polish Jews began to arrive, while the more affluent Jews eventually moved toward the Grand Boulevard area. The Jewish community remained a close-knit community. (WRL.)

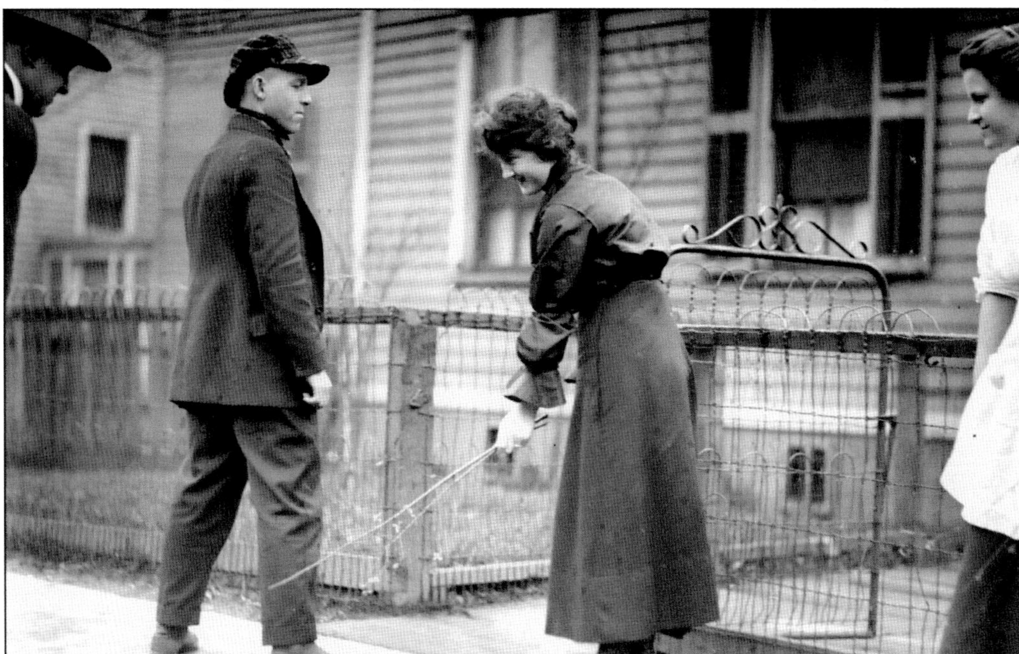

Upon arrival, ethnic groups typically disbursed themselves into many different ethnic and racial neighborhoods. Many moved to communities bonded by birth, culture, and language. African Americans occupied the St. Antoine district; Italians clustered around Paradise Valley; Germans moved toward the Gratiot area; and the Polish and Russian Jews settled the Hastings Street division. In this photograph, a Polish woman playfully taps a man with a switch. (WRL.)

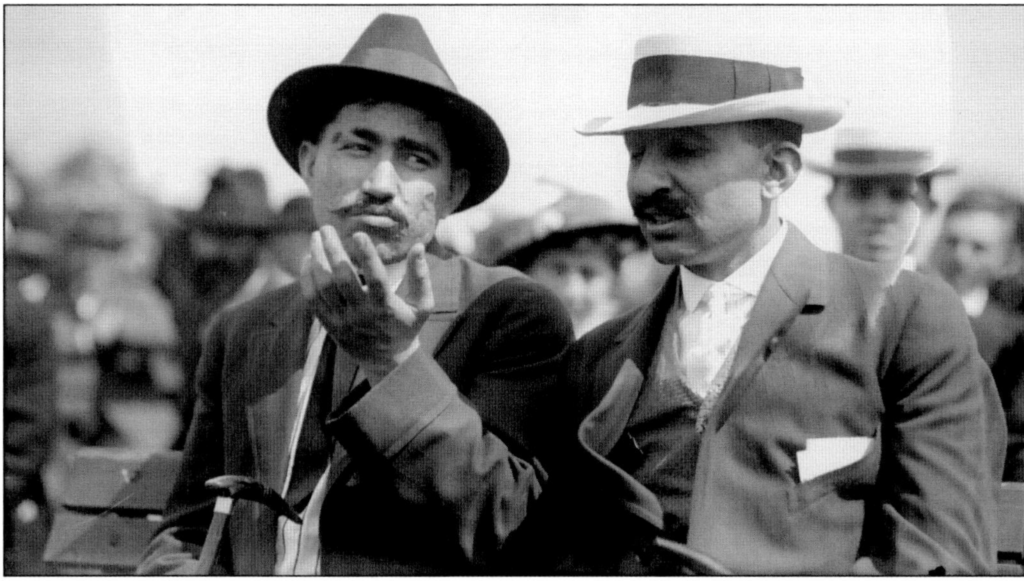

The German population quickly became the largest and assimilated into the American way of life. They were upwardly mobile and quickly established themselves in the Black Bottom community, though most Germans lived around Gratiot Avenue (also known as Little Berlin), the center of German life. Between 1870 and 1900 the German population constituted one-third of the foreign population. The second generation of German Americans became successful tradesmen and professionals and eventually moved into the upper-echelons of society. (WRL.)

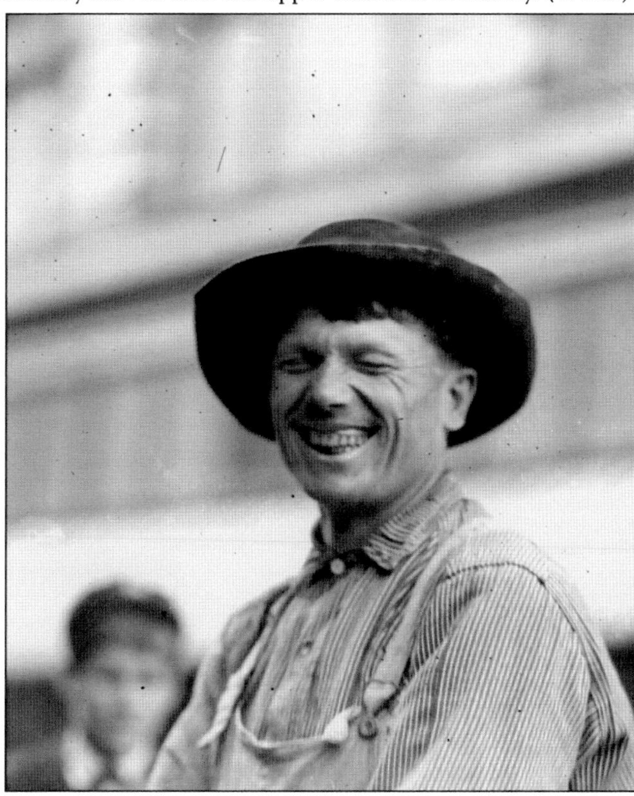

Italians migrated to Detroit's Paradise Valley in significant numbers during the 1890s. A decade later a second colony emerged north of Gratiot Avenue. As Italian migration increased, the two areas merged. Many Black Bottom residents note the Italian business community for playing a major role in the development of black-owned businesses. Many also credit the Jewish community for playing an instrumental role in the entrepreneurial uplift of the black community. (WRL.)

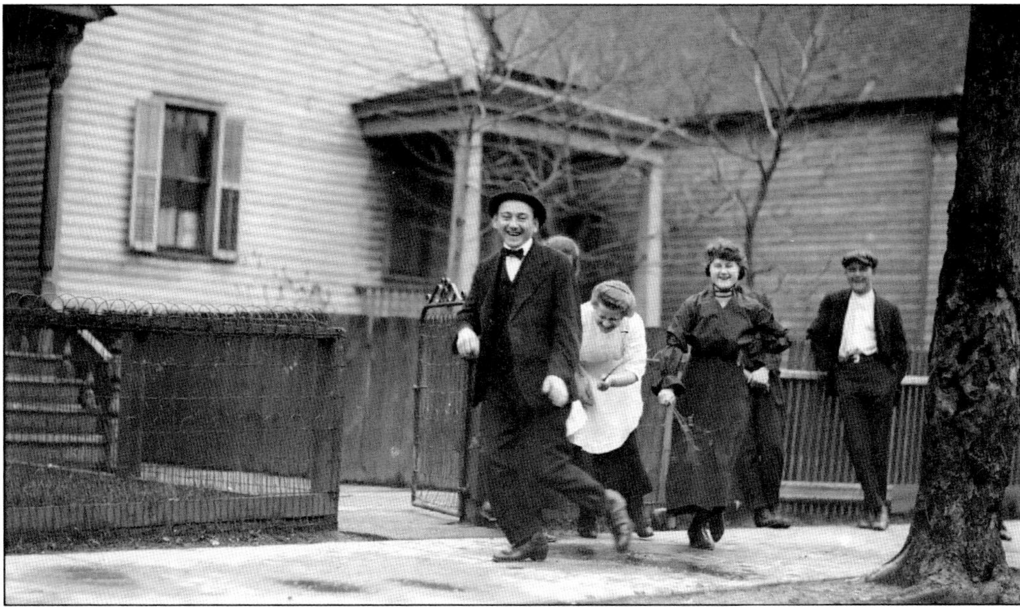

By the 1880s, many Poles lived around the St. Antoine Street and Hastings Street areas; they had become the most visible immigrant group in Detroit. The Poles first worked as unskilled laborers in the construction business, then moved into the railroad industry, and eventually to the automobile industry. Polish immigrants and blacks often lived side by side in small frame houses in what was then known as the Kentucky district in Black Bottom. The poor Polish and blacks lived in relative racial harmony. (WRL.)

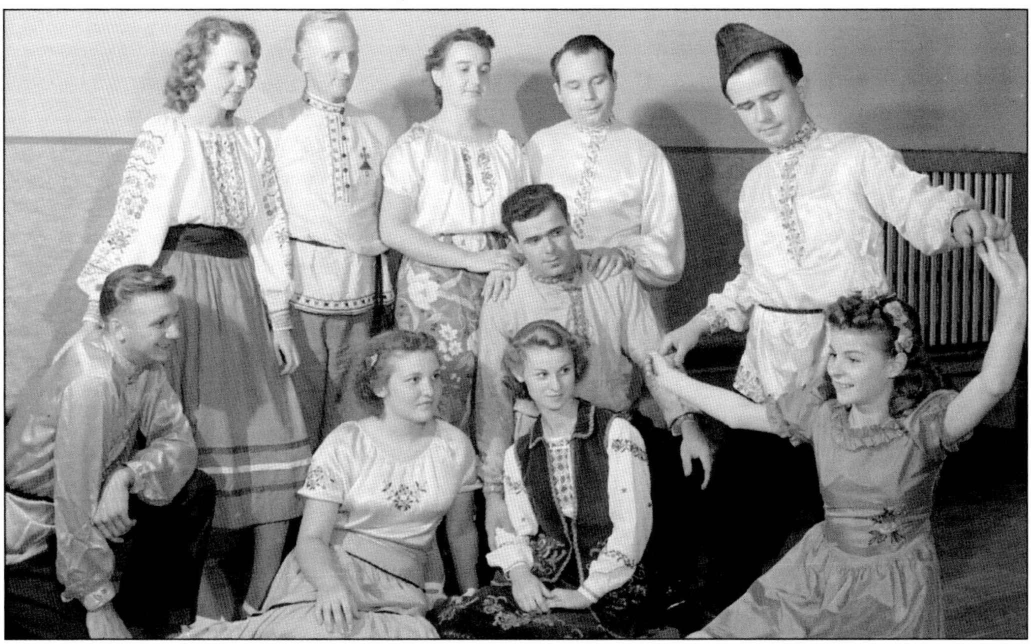

Russian immigration increased significantly around 1910. A 1930s photograph shows Russian dancers performing in Detroit, from left to right, (first row) Harry Kuzmich, Luba Pukolenko, Zena Omelianoff, John Rubin, and Olga Olmelianoff; (second row) Jean Kondratsky, Nick Kurtz, Vera Tarashoff, Victor Tarashoff, and George Werem. (WRL.)

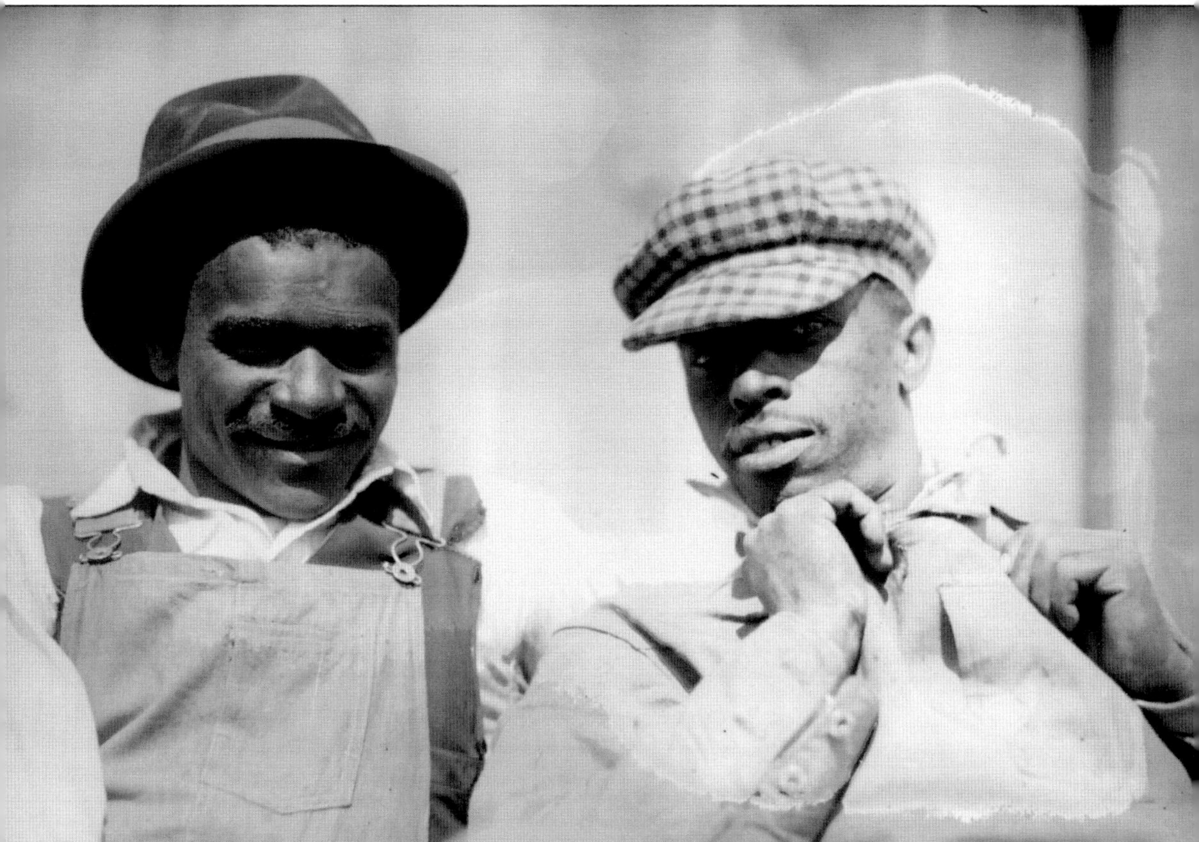

African American history in Detroit reaches back to shortly after 1701, when Antoine Laumet de La Mothe, sieur de Cadillac, along with 100 French soldiers and traders, built Fort Ponchartrain near the river. During the early 18th century, blacks occasionally appeared in Detroit as both freemen and slaves. The first significant black migration into Michigan began about 1840. From 193 blacks in Detroit and 707 blacks in Michigan in 1840, the number grew to 587 in Detroit and 2,583 in Michigan in 1850. African Americans from southern and border states fled north seeking shelter from slavery, discrimination, prejudice, and white terrorism. Skilled artisans and tradesmen migrated to Michigan in the late 1830s and 1840s to escape Virginia's black codes. By 1850, many free blacks and ex-slaves had settled in rural southwestern Cass County, but urban Detroit boasted the largest black population in Michigan. Before the Civil War, blacks began to settle in the Kentucky district, and by 1870, blacks had settled north of the Gratiot Avenue and Hastings Street area, in the neighborhood that would later be known as Black Bottom. (WRL.)

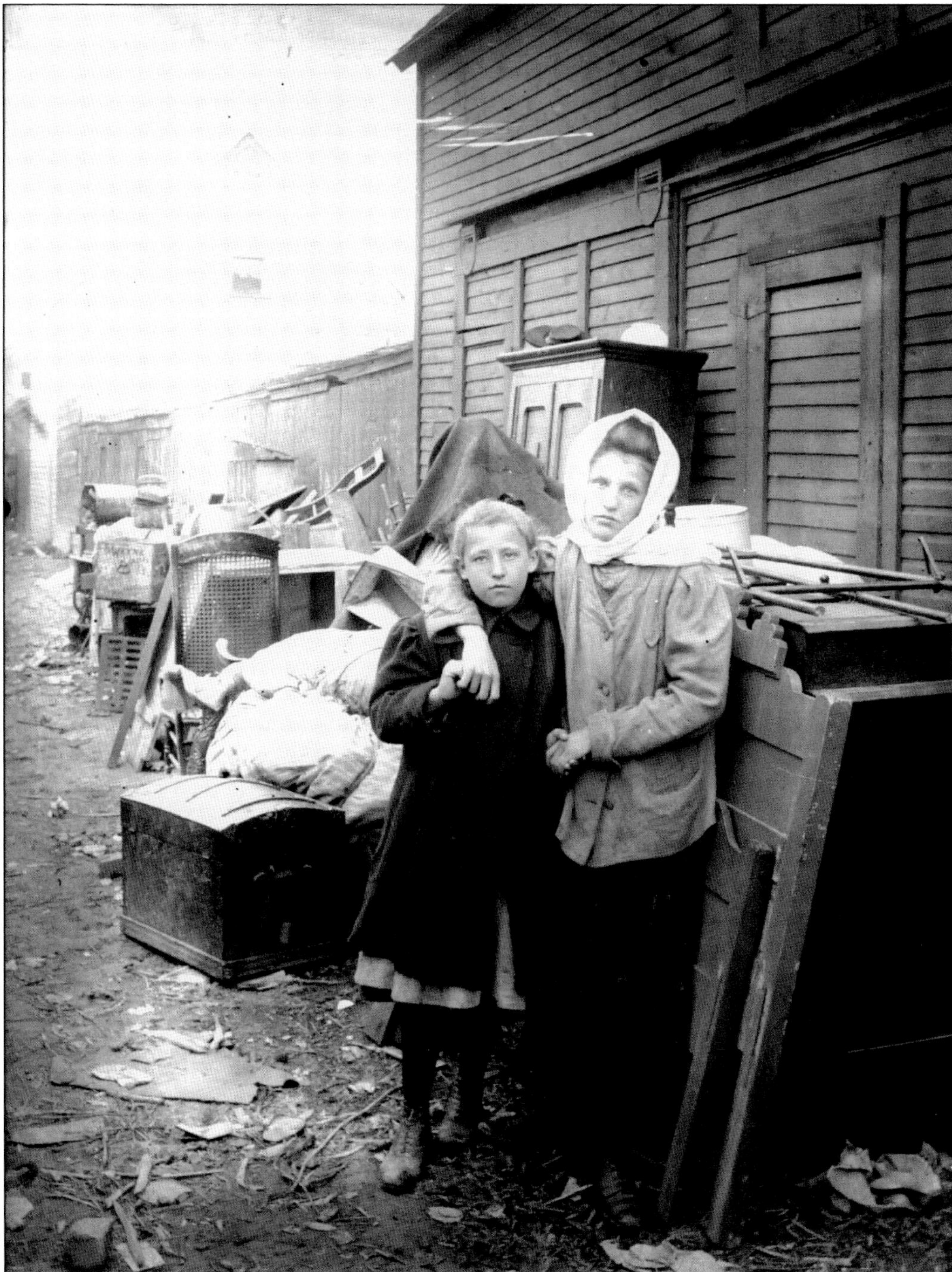

Due to the scarcity of jobs and the lack of skills and education among the immigrant classes, the unemployed and poor immigrants often suffered eviction from homes they could no longer afford. To make matters worse, some immigrants were slow to assimilate and to learn the language, which cast them further into the margins of dispossession and poverty. This c. 1910 photograph shows the eviction of a family with furniture placed out on the street. (WRL.)

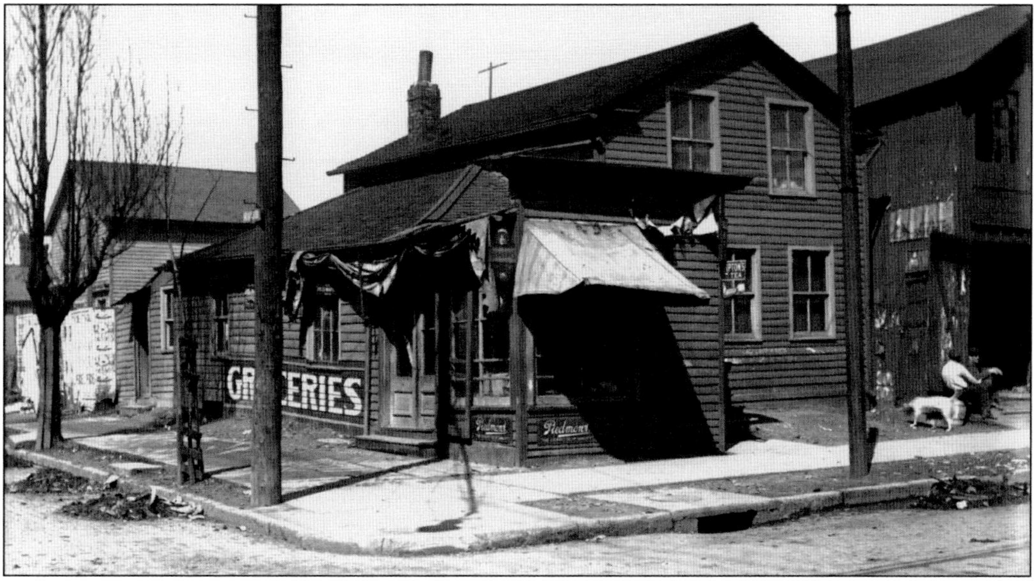

By 1920, blacks owned 350 businesses in Detroit, including a movie theater, the only African American–owned pawnshop in the United States, a co-op grocery, and a bank. The community included 17 physicians, 22 lawyers, 22 barbershops, 13 dentists, 12 cartage agencies, 11 tailors, 10 restaurants, 10 real estate dealers, 8 grocers, 6 drugstores, 5 undertakers, 4 employment offices, a few service-stations, and a candy maker. This 1920s photograph shows an African American–owned grocery store located at the corner of Rivard and Fort Streets. Beneath the shingled window is an advertisement for Piedmont cigarettes and Straight's cigarettes. The store is connected to a house standing next to a two-story wooden, warehouselike building. (BHC.)

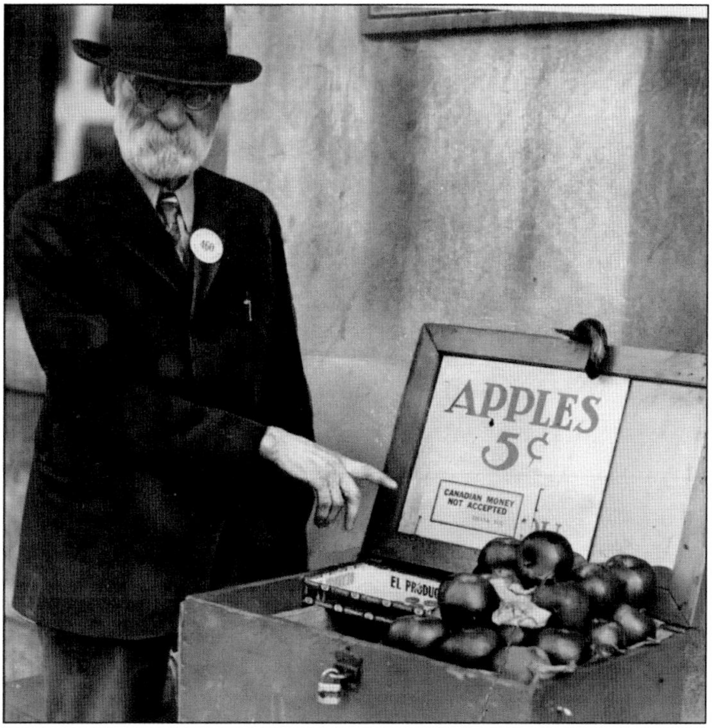

In 1929, the stock market crashed. Companies folded, and banks went bankrupt. Factories closed, sending thousands of Detroiters to the breadlines. Families lost jobs, homes, and life's savings. With no social safety net of unemployment benefits, public assistance, food stamps, or social security, those without jobs survived only by their wits—or they starved. This 1930 photograph depicts a scene common in Detroit during the Depression; this gentleman is selling apples for a nickel. (WRL.)

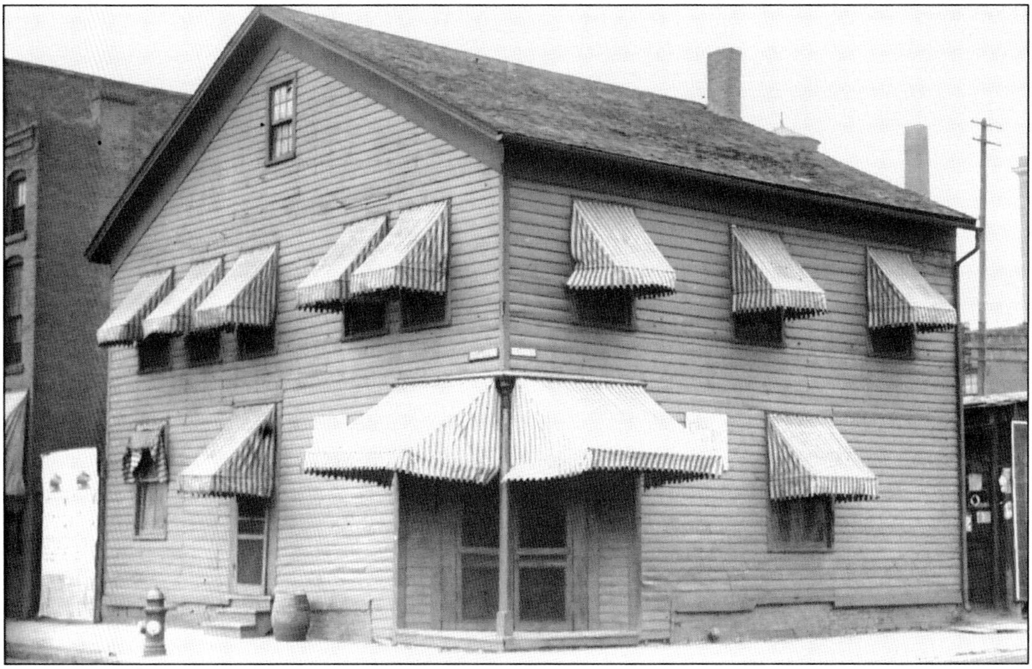

The Bucket of Blood on Hastings and Clinton Streets was a two-story wood-sided saloon. It was owned by Billy Boushaw. According to *The Detroit Almanac: 300 Years of Life in the Motor City*, "The Bucket . . . was widely regarded as a tough town's toughest joint at the turn of the century, an all-night saloon with an integrated clientele, the often-crowded Bucket was the scene of card games, crap games, dice games, open prostitution, so-called 'wild music' and considerable knife and gun play." (WRL.)

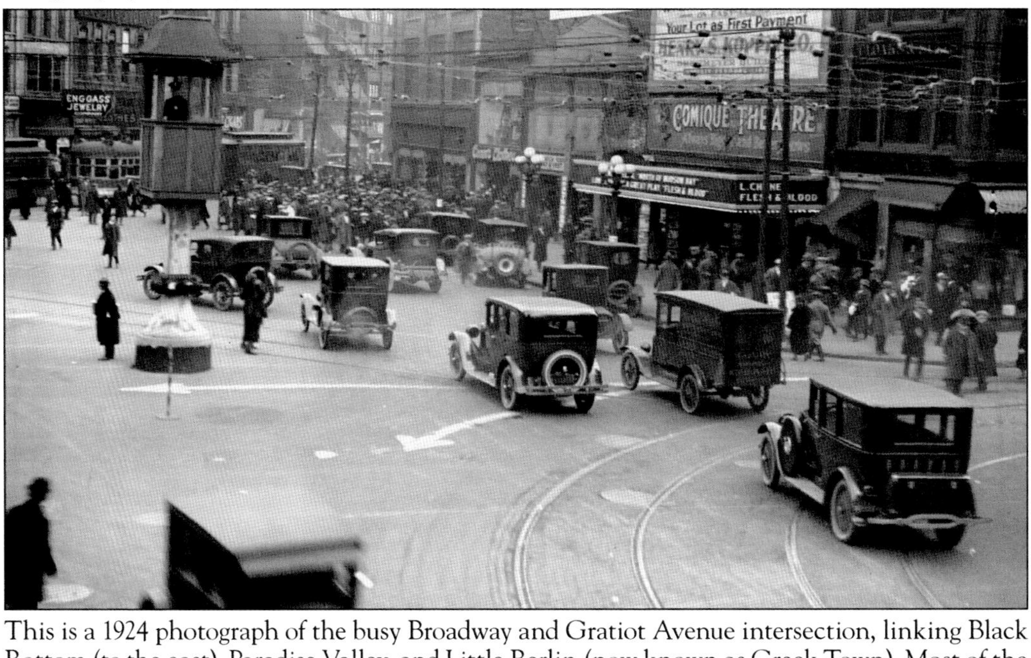

This is a 1924 photograph of the busy Broadway and Gratiot Avenue intersection, linking Black Bottom (to the east), Paradise Valley, and Little Berlin (now known as Greek Town). Most of the black and foreign-born families settling Black Bottom lived and worked in this area. (WRL.)

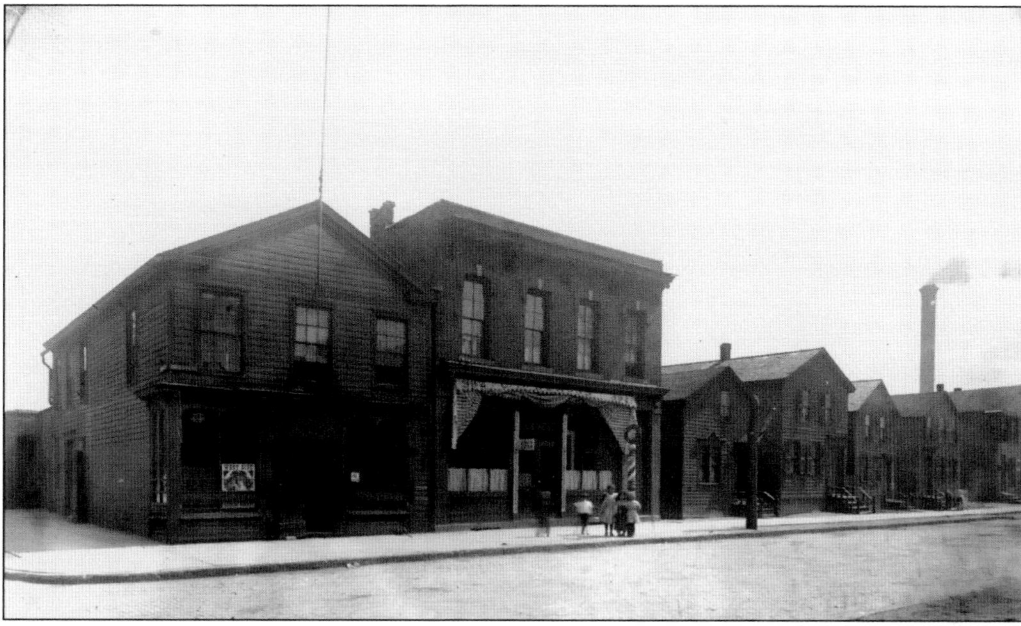

Seen as thrifty and industrious merchants in the beer and lager business, Germans were welcome residents in many parts of the city. They operated successful saloons such as this one located on Orleans Street near Franklin Street, photographed around the 1920s with children standing out front next to a line of wood frame homes. (WRL.)

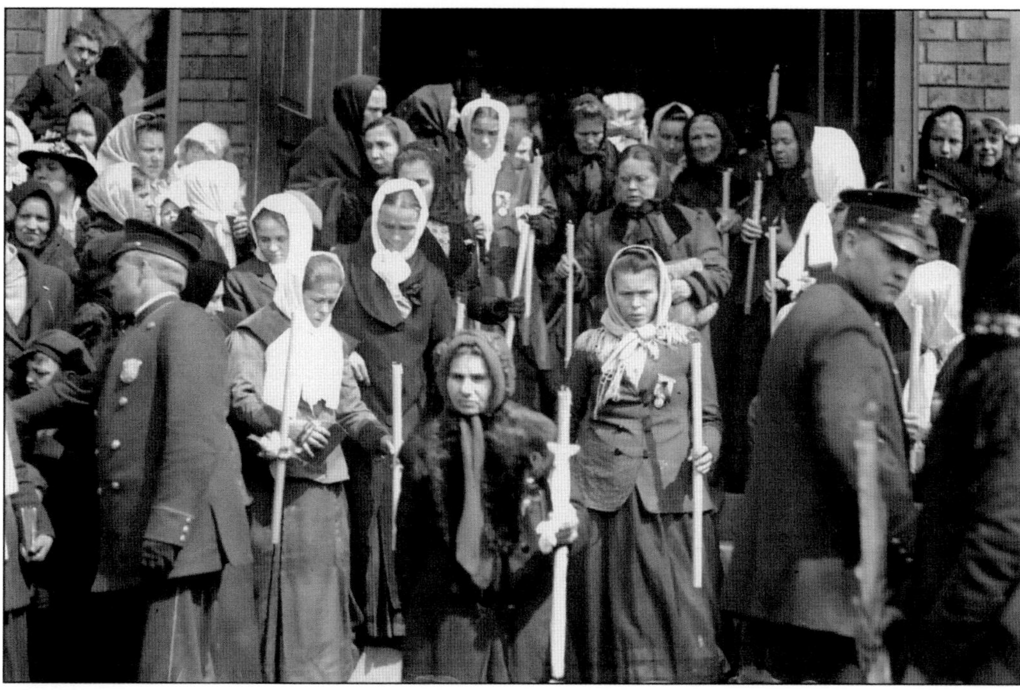

Churches provided the community with spiritual guidance and leadership. Some offered educational opportunities and food for the poor. Many churches acted as benevolent societies and charitable organizations serving Black Bottom's impoverished and unemployed. This *c.* 1910 photograph appears to show a catholic funeral in progress. (WRL.)

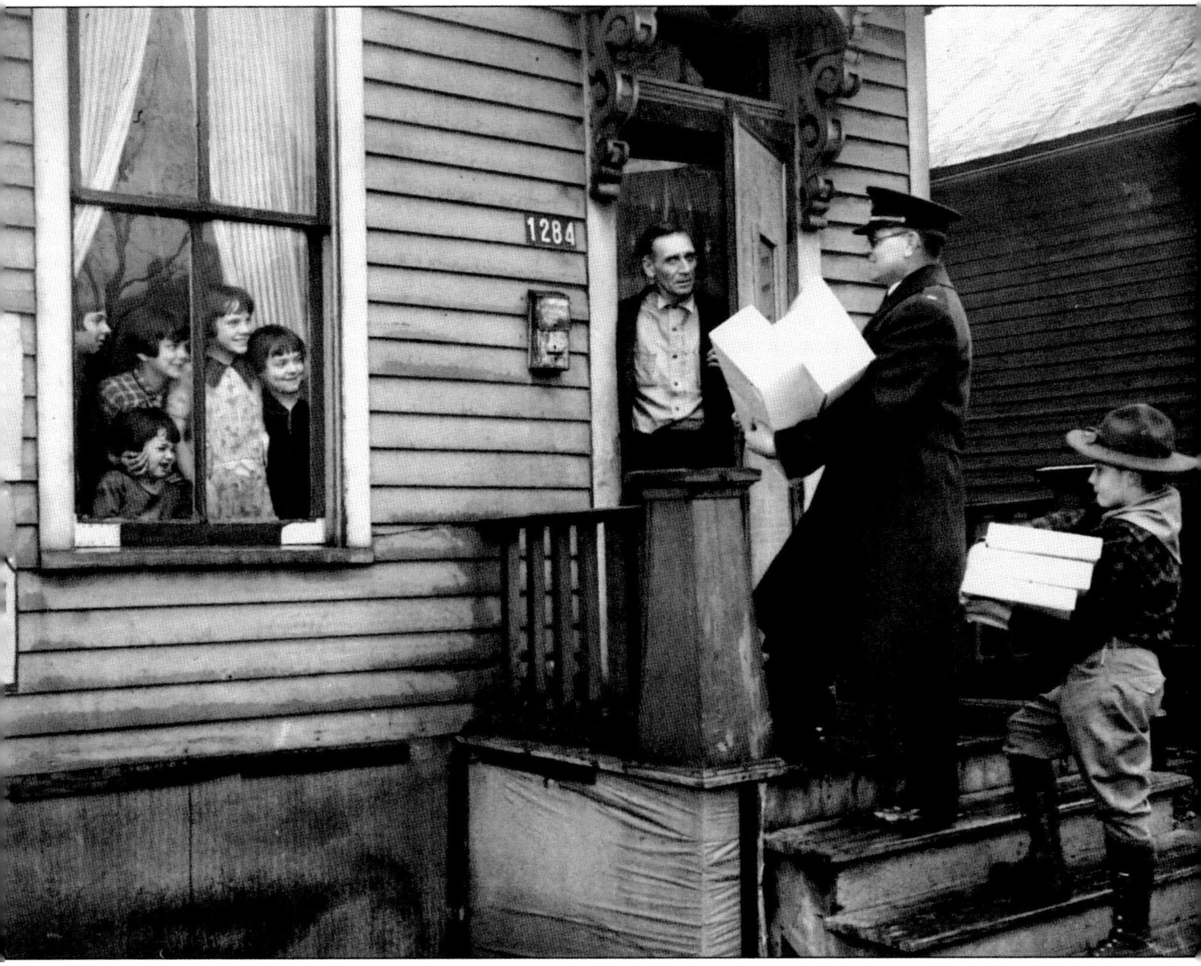

According to the America's Charities Web site, James J. Brady founded the Old Newsboys' Goodfellow Fund of Detroit (Detroit Goodfellows) in 1914. Along with a small group of Detroit-area businessmen, Brady sold newspapers on the street corners of Detroit to raise money to purchase Christmas gift packages for underprivileged children. Many of Black Bottom's poorest families welcomed the generosity and concern of the Goodfellow Fund. This photograph was taken on Christmas Eve 1932. (WRL.)

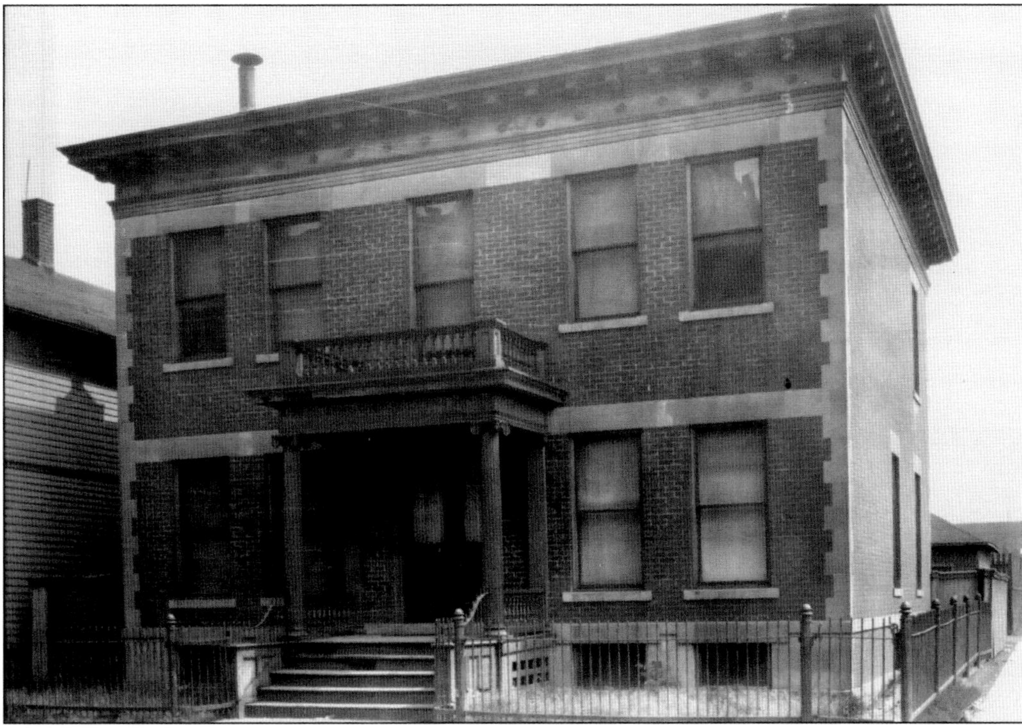

The Little Sisters of the Poor Roman Catholic religious order for women was founded by Jeanne Jugan in France to serve and care for the impoverished elderly. The order operated at 1804 Scott Street in Detroit, offering food, clothing, and employment referrals to any Black Bottom resident in need of help. This photograph was taken in 1926. (WRL.)

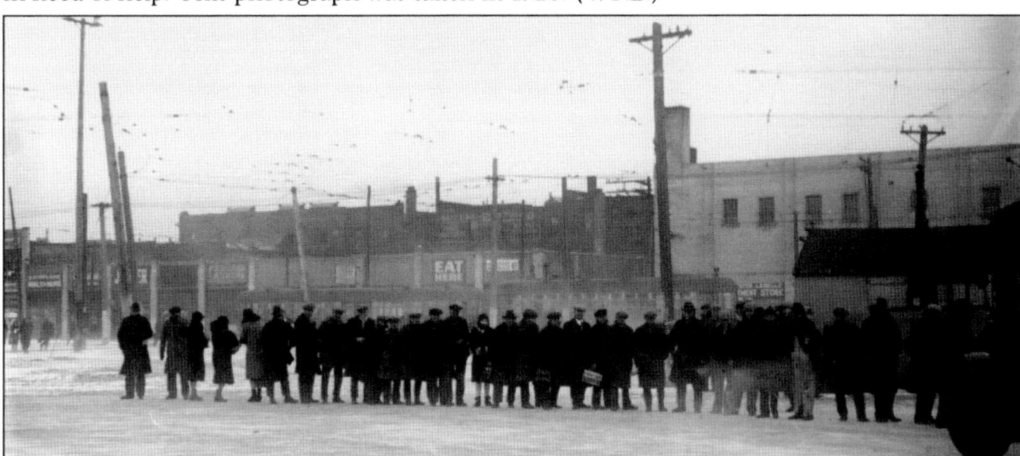

The early-20th-century automotive industry required more labor, and the immigration wave filled this need. Between 1890 and 1910, Detroit's factory workers were mostly comprised of foreigners. Many plants hired specific ethnic groups for specific jobs. For example, the Dodge Brothers employed Polish workers almost exclusively. The entry of black workers into Detroit factories, however, would have only a slight effect on a seemingly fixed occupational structure. Most black workers had to start at the bottom rung of the employment ladder and remained the lowest paid employees in the industries. This photograph shows immigrant employees going to work around 1929. (WRL.)

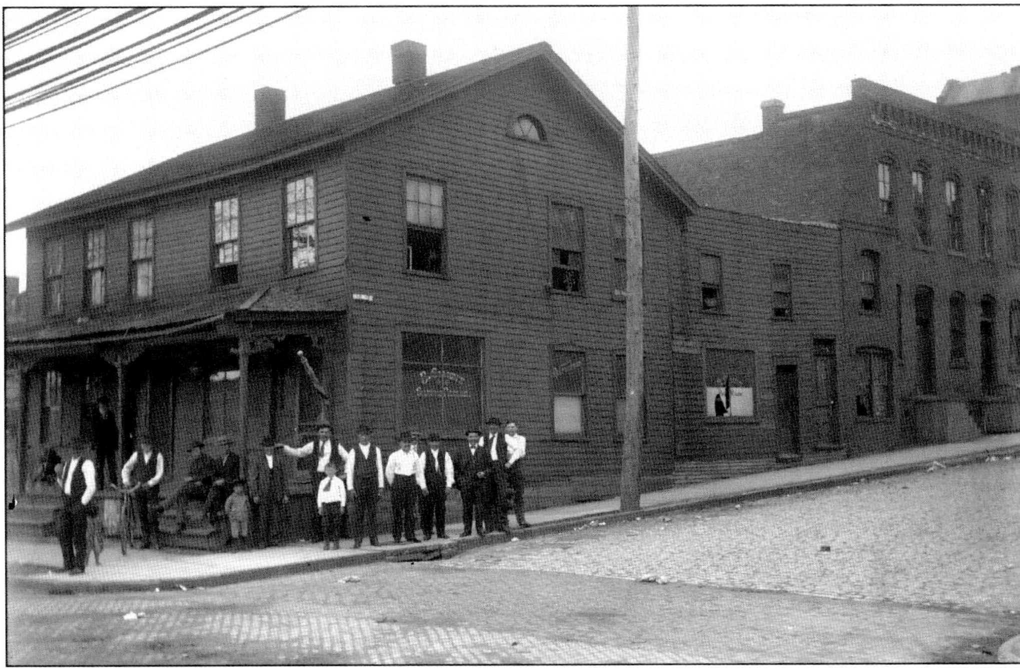

In this *c.* 1905 photograph, men and boys stand in front of B. Simon's Shaving Parlor on the corner of Hastings Street. Hastings Street became a busy thoroughfare of business and commerce. By the 1930s, it became known as Paradise Valley because of its popular entertainment district of pool halls, bars, dance clubs, good food, and top-notch entertainment. (WRL.)

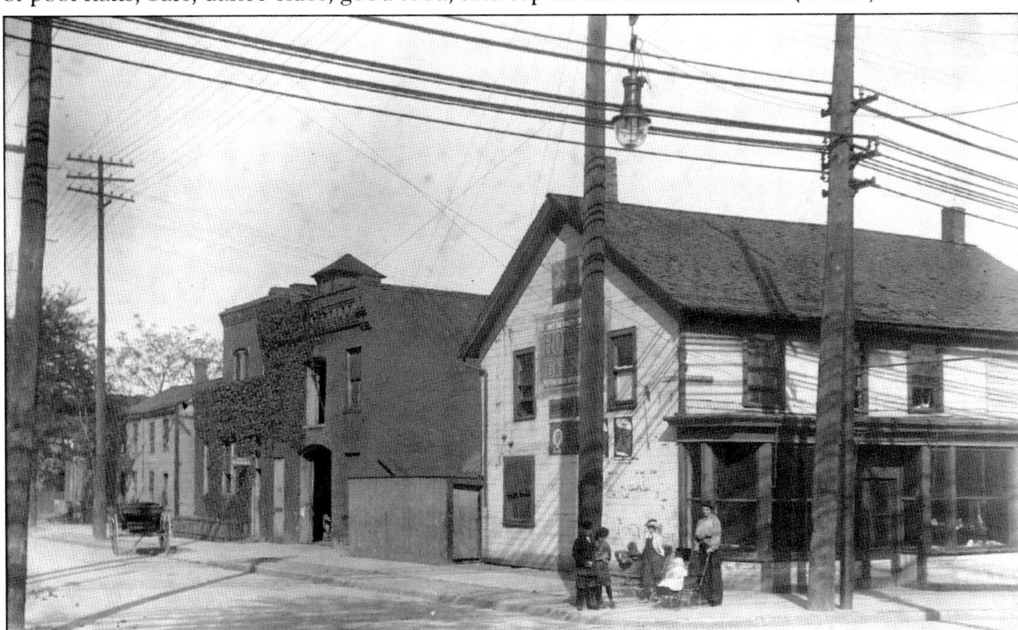

The area around Woodbridge and Riopelle Streets formed an extension of Black Bottom, mostly inhabited by foreigners and foreign-owned businesses. In this *c.* 1910 photograph, a woman and her children walk past the general store. Some stores extended credit to community residents, black and white. (WRL.)

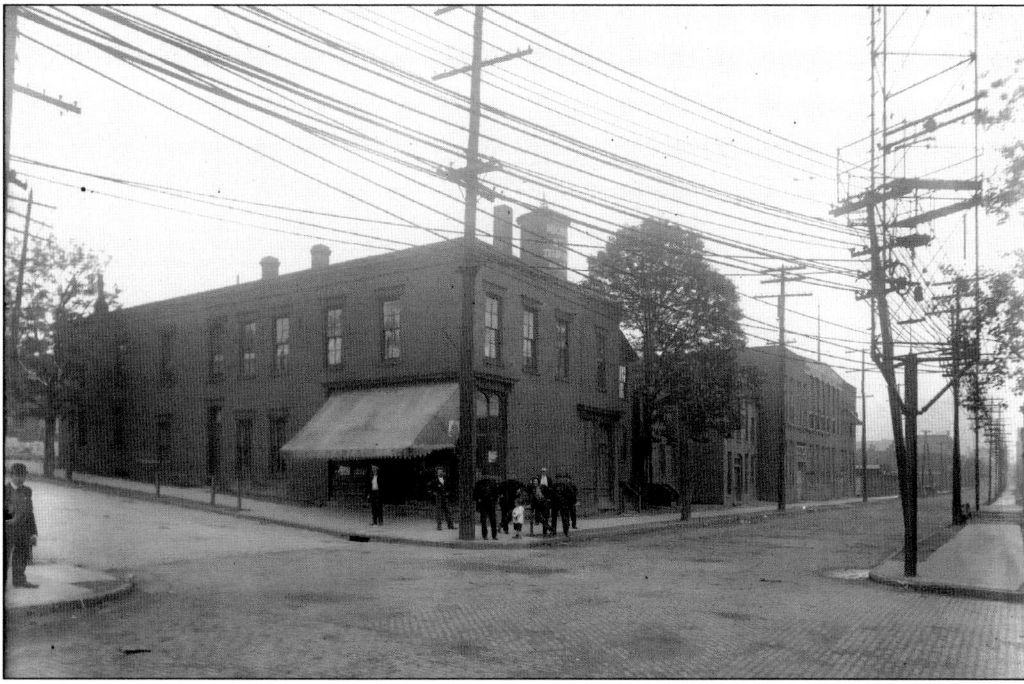

In this 1920s photograph, men and a boy stand on the corner of Rivard and Franklin Streets in front of the J. H. Barlage grocery store. This vice district, also known as the Potomac Quarter, was known for its flophouses, brothels, and saloons. It later became a popular social center for people of all colors. By the end of the decade, the area entertainments were slowly replaced by small factories and businesses. (WRL.)

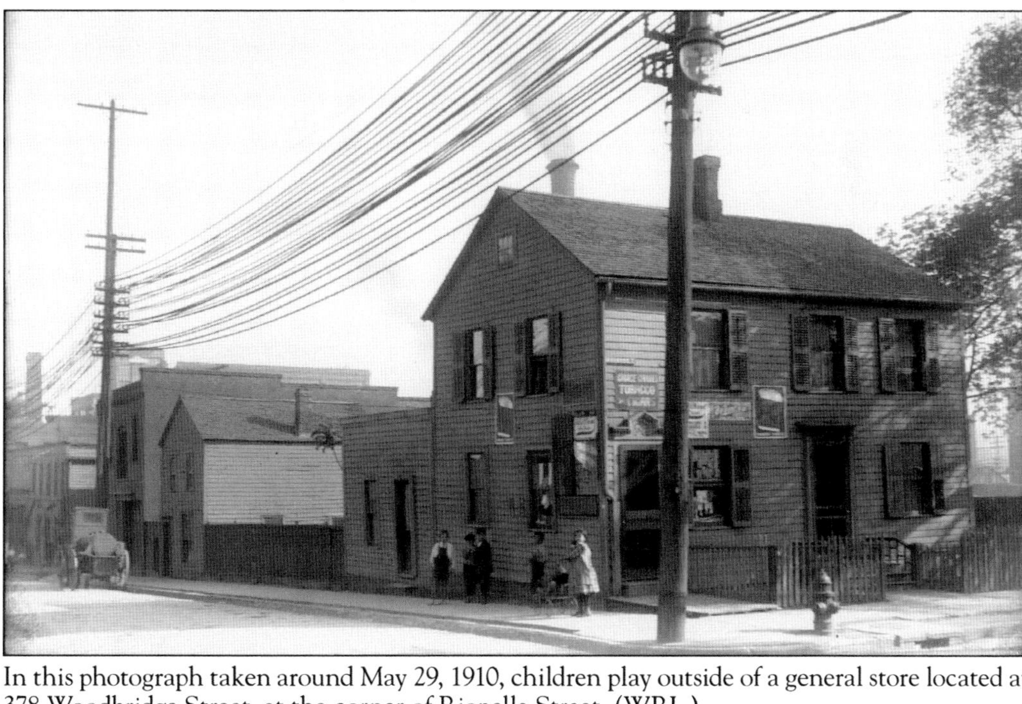

In this photograph taken around May 29, 1910, children play outside of a general store located at 378 Woodbridge Street, at the corner of Riopelle Street. (WRL.)

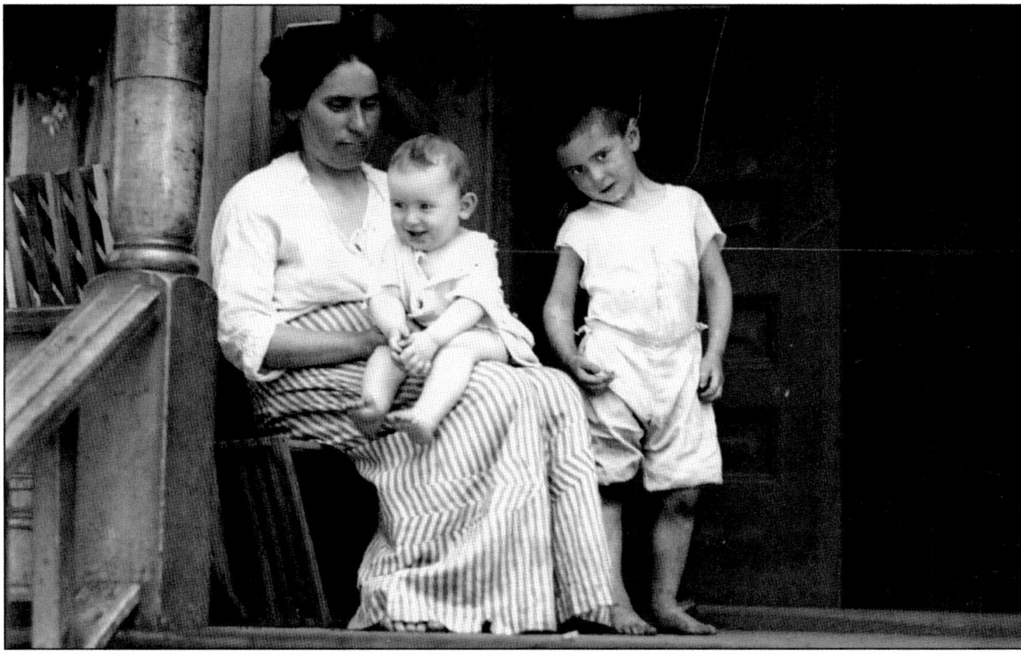

During the Depression many white women were employed as domestic workers. Domestic servants did housework as well as errands for the family. Russell McLauchlin grew up on Alfred Street in Black Bottom. He stated that, "Every family, however lowly in the financial scale, had a hired girl." The "girls" were required to wash; clean, iron, and mend clothing; cook meals; and assist with child rearing. This photograph was taken around 1910. (WRL.)

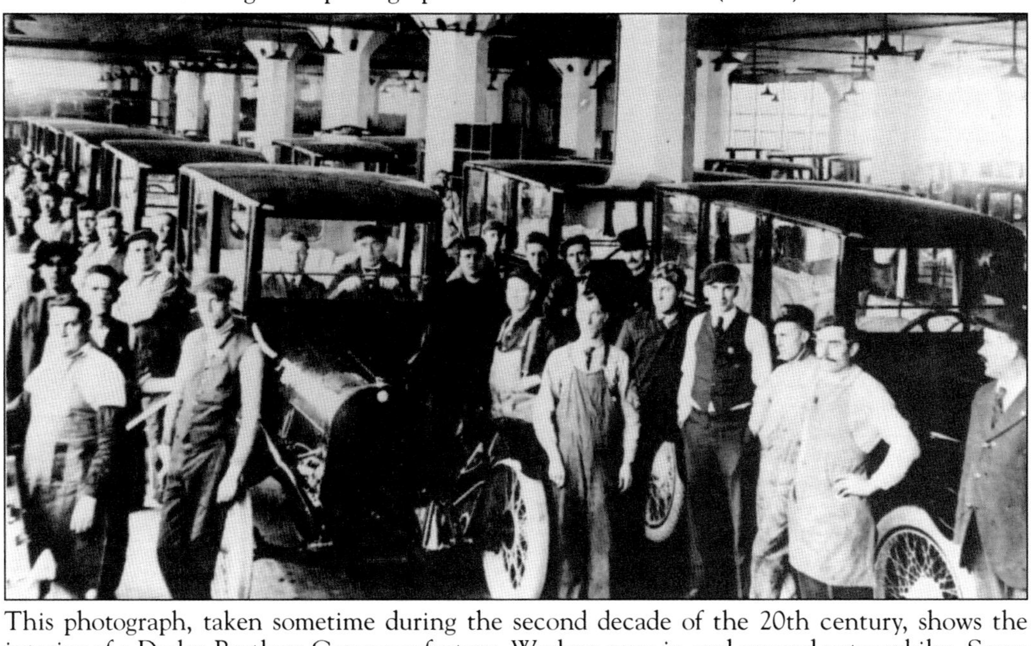

This photograph, taken sometime during the second decade of the 20th century, shows the interior of a Dodge Brothers Company factory. Workers pose in and around automobiles. Some factories employed both black and white residents of Black Bottom. Racial discrimination did not become a serious issue in Detroit factories until the first great migration, when many white workers began to fear that the southern migrants would take their jobs. (BHC.)

Two

African Americans in Black Bottom

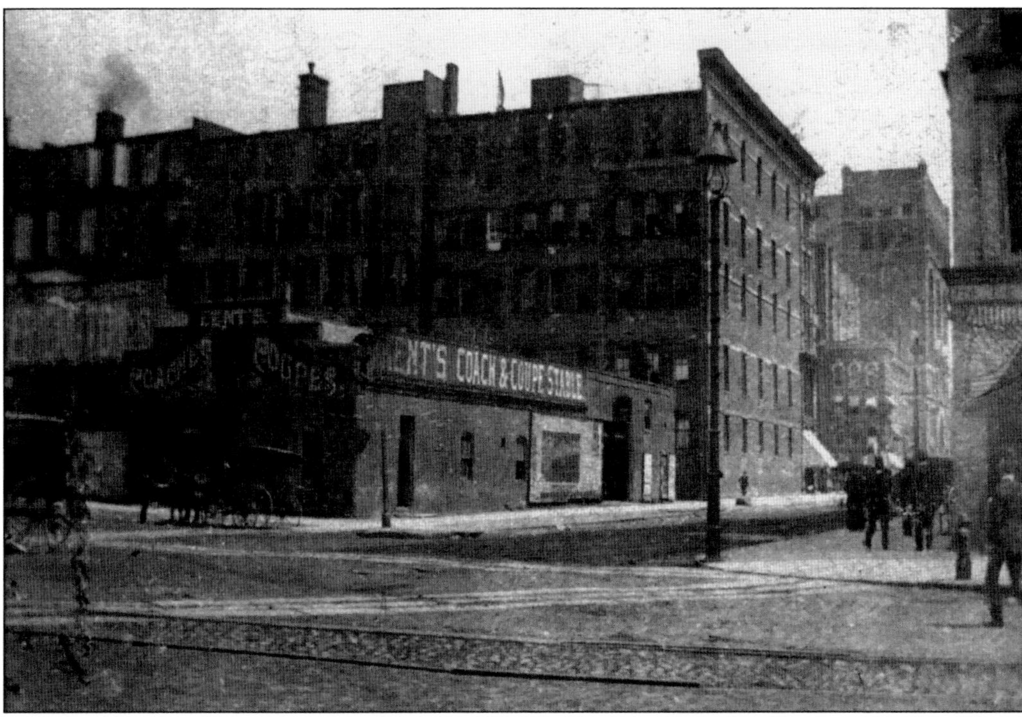

The first significant blacks-in-Black Bottom migration into Michigan began about 1840. The number of black residents grew from 193 in Detroit (707 in Michigan) in 1840, to 587 in Detroit (2,583 in Michigan) in 1850. Blacks fled to the north seeking shelter from slavery, discrimination, prejudice, and white terrorism. By 1850, with free blacks and ex-slaves settling in southwestern rural Cass County, Detroit boasted the single-largest black population in Michigan. This old barn, photographed around the 1890s, was a refuge for slaves escaping into Canada via the Underground Railroad. (WRL.)

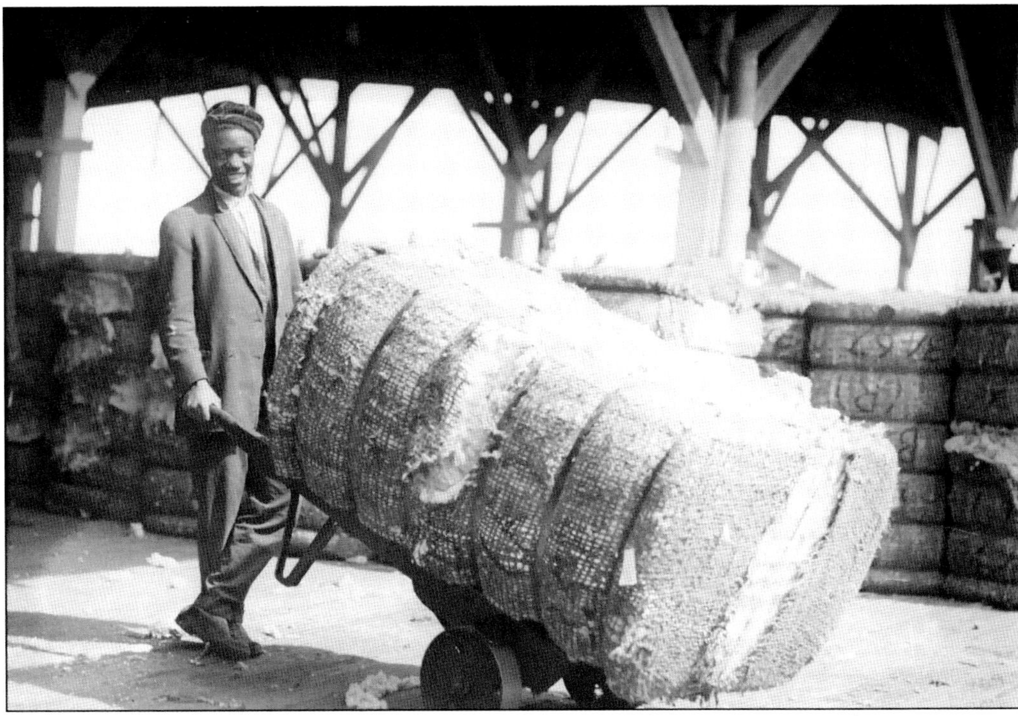

African American workers were attracted to dock work because it required no training or experience. When other work was unavailable, it was fairly easy to secure at least half a day's work on the docks. Workers arrived early in the morning to await the arrival of ships, hoping to get hired by a boss, and working in gangs until a job was complete. This photograph was taken during the second decade of the 20th century. (WRL.)

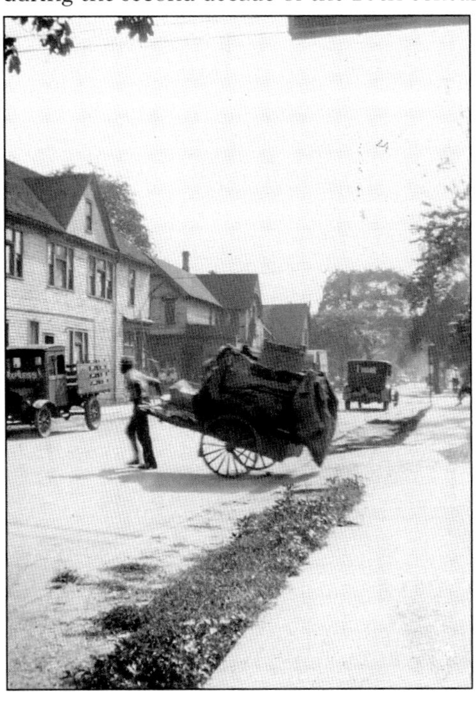

A black man pulls a cart through the streets of Black Bottom looking for saleable junk in the second decade of the 20th century; junk men were considered by some to be human scavengers. African American men were employed as stewards, bellmen, domestics, cooks, laborers, porters, barbers, dressmakers, and few worked as lawyers, engineers, and sailors. When black men could not find employment, they had to create their own sources of income. (WRL.)

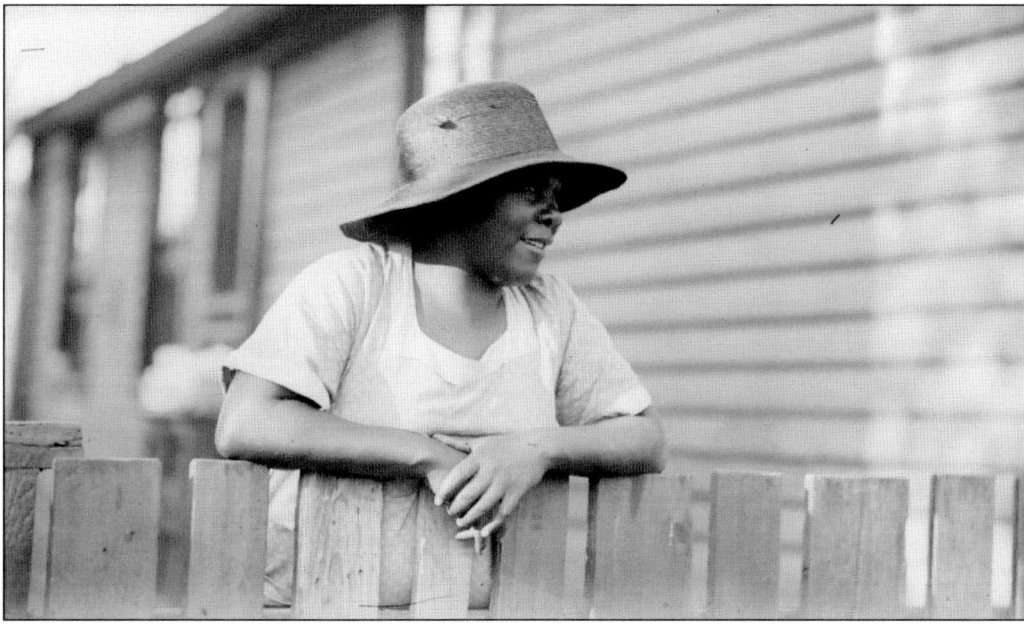

Most black women in Black Bottom worked as domestic servants. The hours were long and laborious with only one day off per week. Domestics usually lived in isolation with little companionship and little to no time for social engagement. This domestic worker, pictured in the second decade of the 20th century, is probably taking a midday break to chat with another servant working at the next residence. (WRL.)

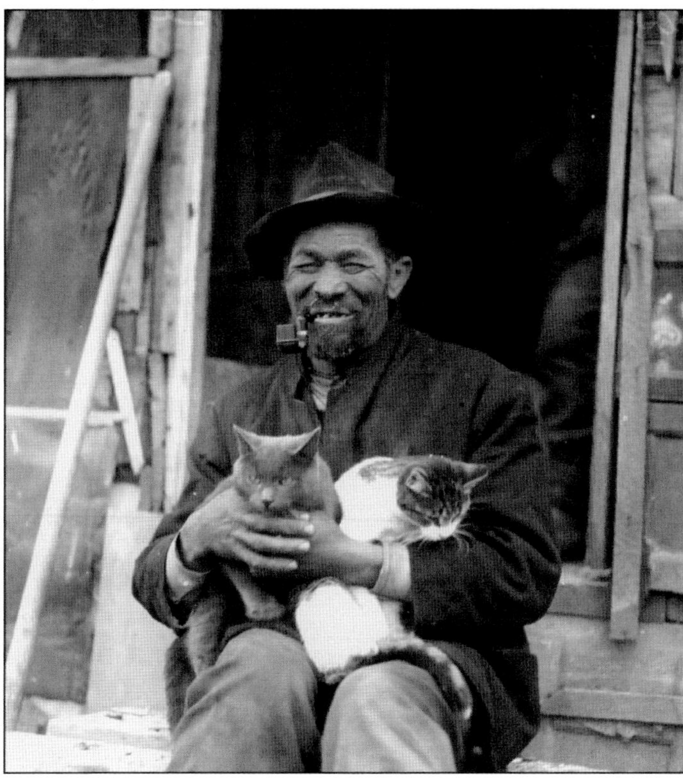

By the 1890s, blacks struggled to compete with immigrants for decent employment. Although many foreigners lacked skills and education and spoke little or no English, they enjoyed greater housing and employment opportunities. In a *Detroit News* article dated May 24, 1891, an African American whitewasher observed, "First it was de Irish, den it was de Dutch, and now it's de Polacks as grind us down. I s'pose when dey [the Poles] gets like de Irish and stands up for a fair price, some odder strangers'll come over de sea 'nd jine de family and cut us down again." This photograph was taken sometime during the second decade of the 20th century. (WRL.)

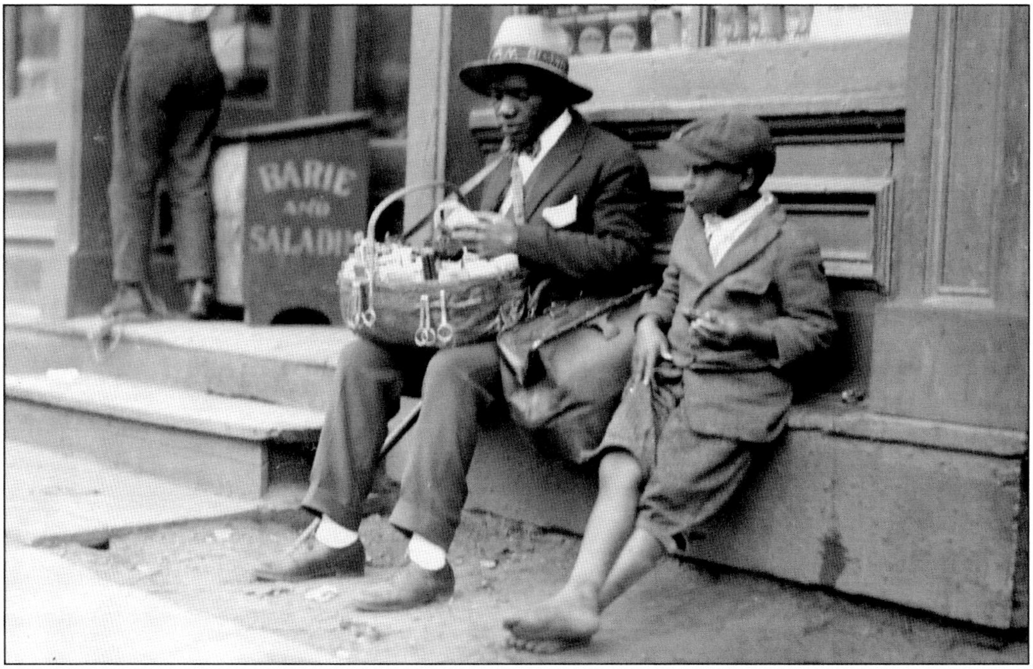

During the migration of southern blacks into the Detroit area, George Edmund Haynes observed "[African Americans] desire a fair chance to get work and to hold work on the same conditions and with the same pay as other workers; education of all kinds; removal of race discriminations in public courts . . . We wants to help say who governs us; self development and happiness." A Black Bottom peddler rests on a stoop during the 1920s or 1930s. (WRL.)

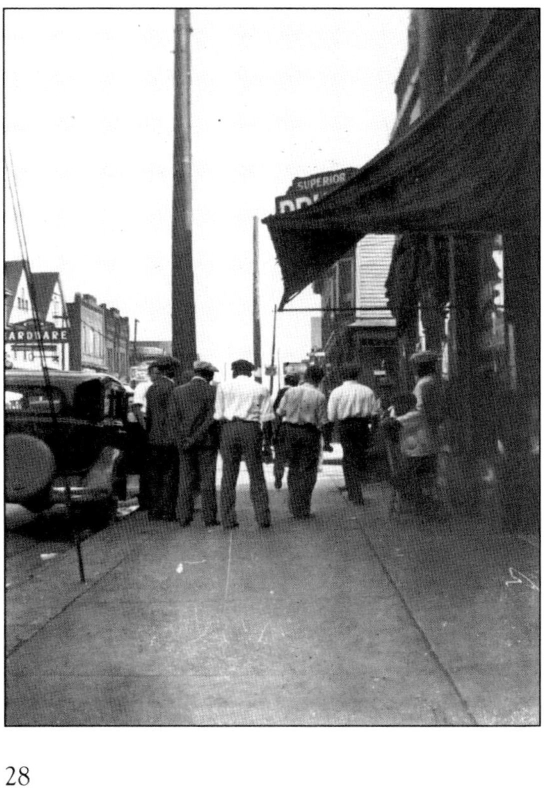

Men share laughs outside a pool hall around 1930. After a hard day on the docks, men enjoyed drinking, food, music, and other entertainments on Hastings Street in Paradise Valley. As blacks continued to move into Black Bottom, xenophobes found ways to contain them within the district. With limited access to entertainment further afield, Paradise Valley became a mecca for black entertainment. Earl Hines, the Inkspots, Ethel Waters, Pearl Bailey, Billie Holiday, Dinah Washington, Ella Fitzgerald, and many more started their careers in Paradise Valley. (WRL.)

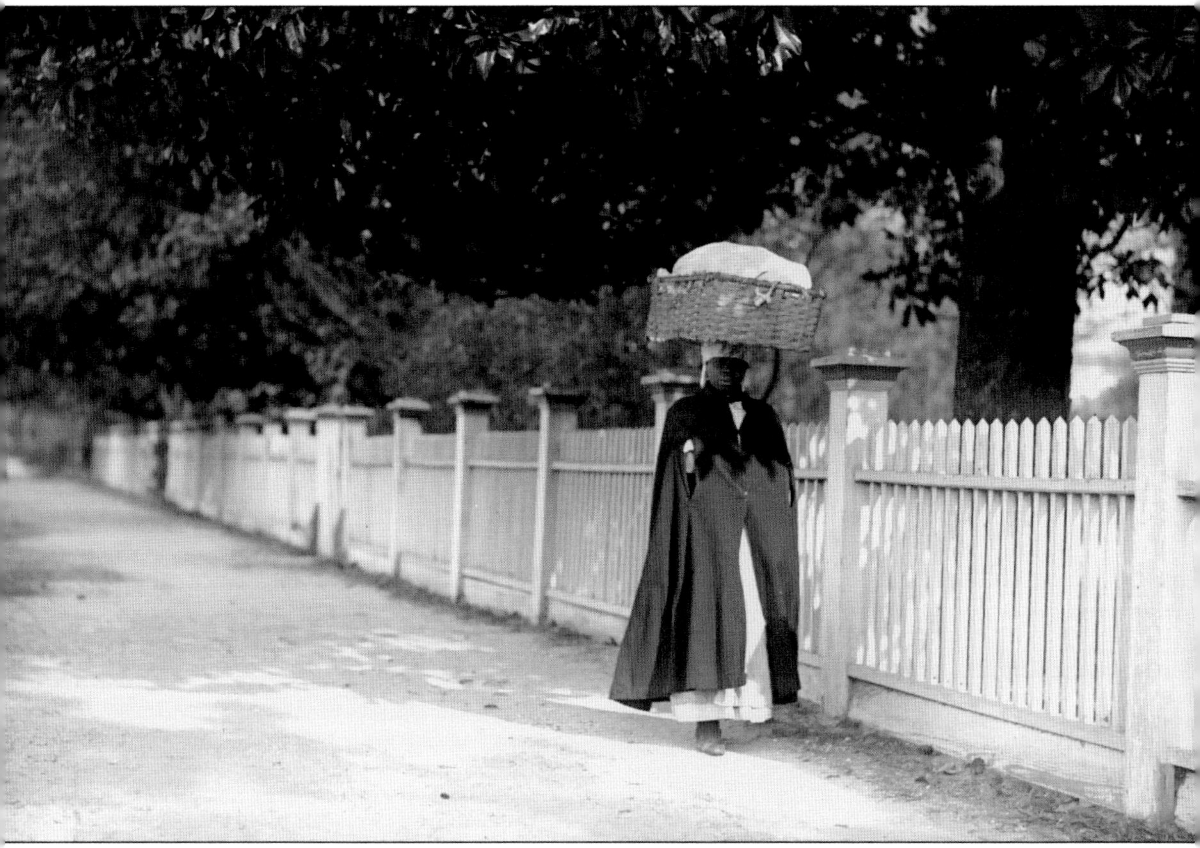

African American women in Detroit during the Great Migration faced tough job prospects. Largely barred from the formal economy, most had little choice beyond domestic service. A small number of fair-skinned African American women secured factory and white-collar jobs or started businesses. Darker-skinned women were relegated to domestic work. Every morning, housewives visited the Eastern Market near Gratiot Avenue, where women lined up for selection by potential employers. More desirable jobs usually went to white servants, whereas more laborious tasks and those involving less intimate relationship with the employing family were commonly reserved for blacks. By the 20th century, foreign-born servants were generally preferred, considered to be of a "better class" than the native-born blacks. This photograph was taken around 1920. (WRL.)

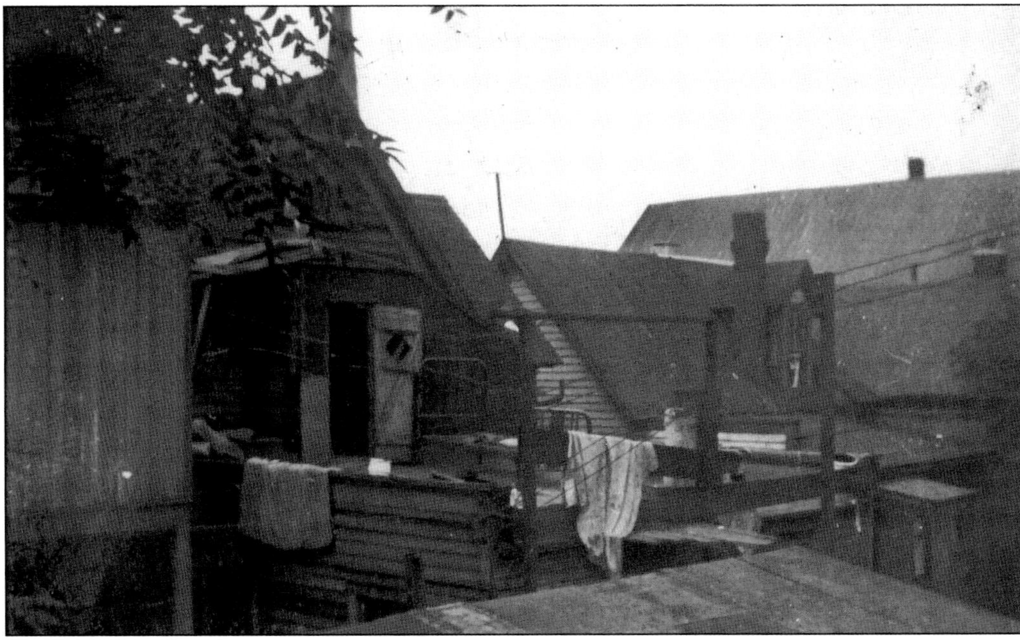

Thousands of black migrants flooded the train depots of urban Detroit looking for jobs. They slept on depot floors and benches and on park benches until the police department forced them to move on. The migrants shared overcrowded rooming houses and were often exploited by unethical landlords. The lucky few found refuge with friends. This photograph was taken around the 1920s. (WRL.)

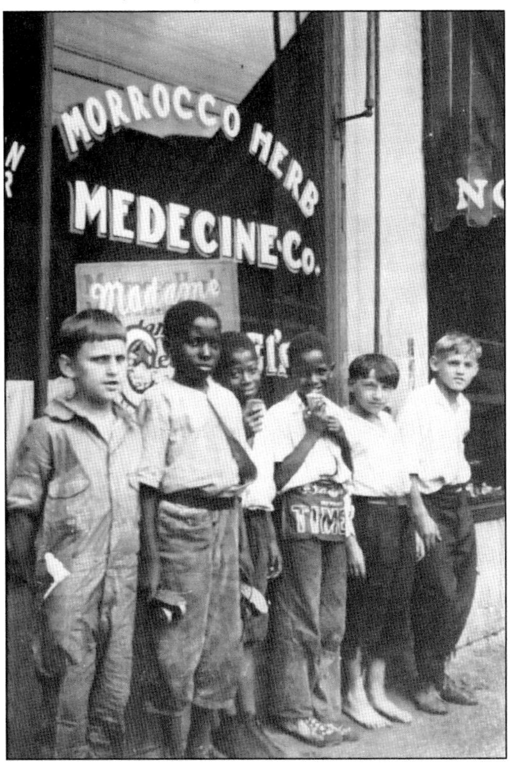

In this photograph, children pose on Hastings Street. The area was known for vice and most parents kept their children away from the area. Sometimes, the pimps and prostitutes shooed wayward children away from the strip, often simply threatening to tell their parents. When poorer children ventured down Hastings Street to earn money by carrying groceries, running errands, shoveling snow, or raking leaves, they were under the watchful eye of a concerned community. (WRL.)

The Depression took its toll on the working-class poor. Poor families faced humiliating evictions even in Black Bottom. This *c.* 1929 photograph shows a displaced family along with their furniture out in the front of the alley shack where they had lived. (WRL.)

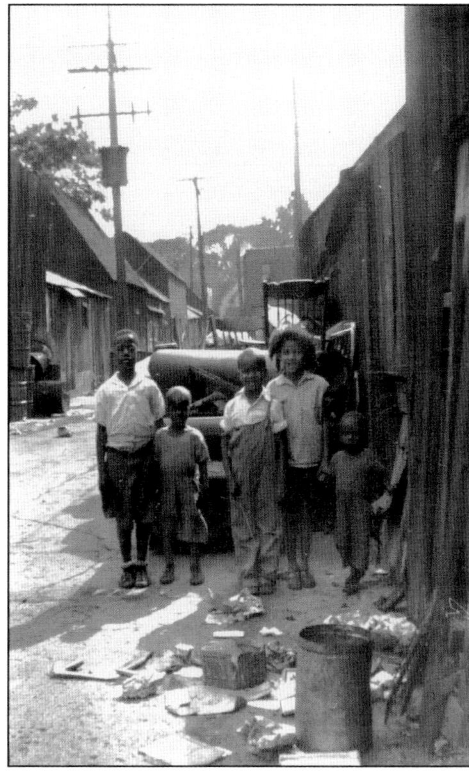

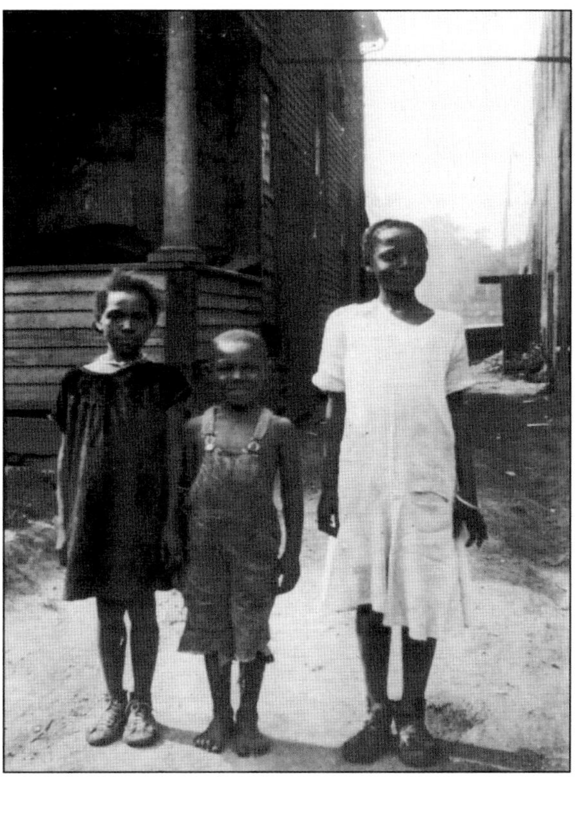

The Detroit Urban League dealt with issues affecting life in Black Bottom. The Detroit Urban League took on the role of family mediator, social worker, and relief agency. In 1926, Florence Williams's husband deserted her and her five children. Williams was forced to move in with her mother and two sisters at 3749 Riopelle Street in Black Bottom. The Detroit Urban League sent a social worker to help Williams find food and clothes for her school-aged children and employment. This photograph was taken around the 1930s. (WRL.)

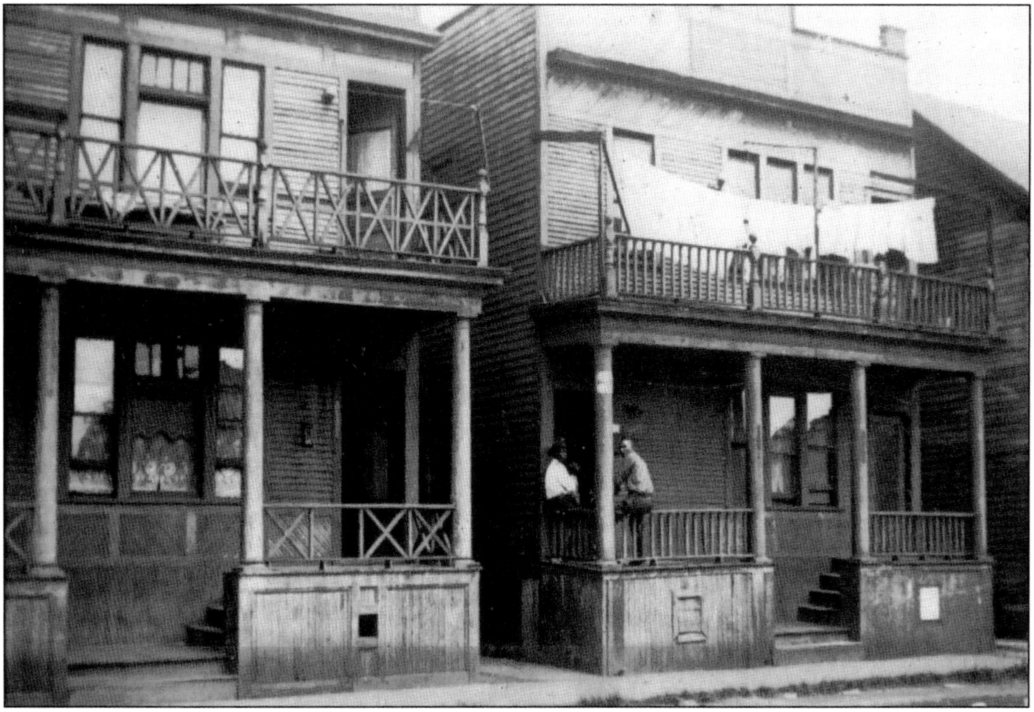

Housing for poor blacks slowly became available as the east side district expanded to the east and south. Eventually this district, in which 313,600 people were "huddled together as closely as it is possible for humans to exist," extended all the way to the Detroit River. The southernmost blocks became known as Black Bottom. In this 1930s photograph, two men sit on the porch of a crowded boardinghouse in the blighted Hasting Street district in Black Bottom. Boardinghouses provided shelter but crowding bred vice and misery. (WRL.)

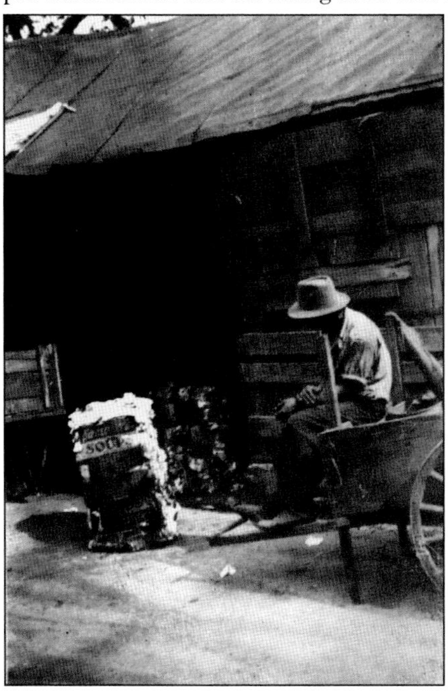

In this 1930s photograph, a man known as "Hustle Man" salvages junk in a Black Bottom alleyway. (WRL.)

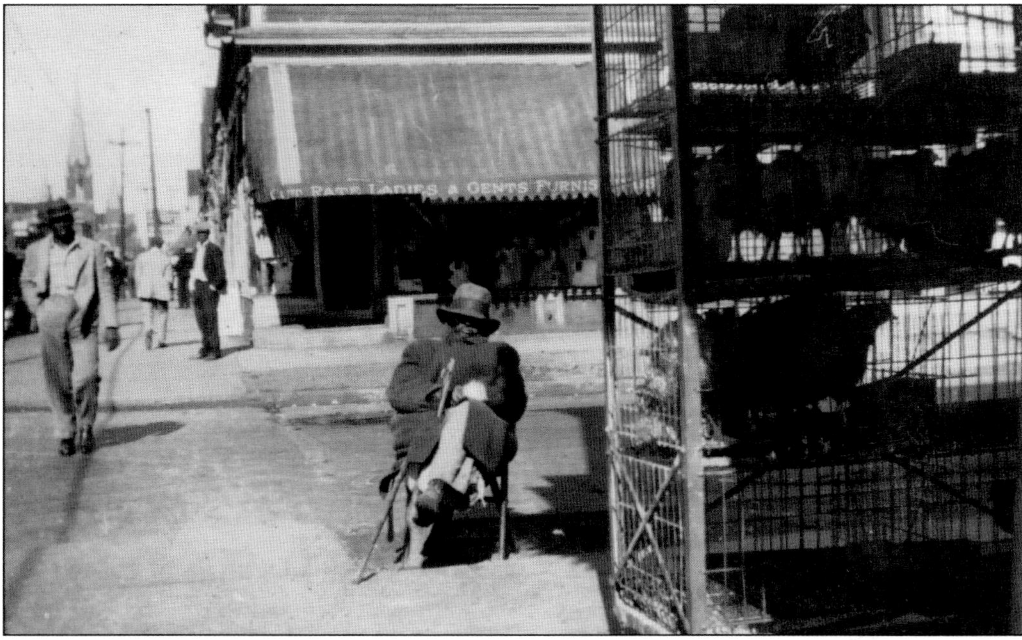

Hastings Street ran parallel to Woodward Avenue, one block east of St. Antoine Street. During the late 19th century, Jewish peddlers and shopkeepers established a thriving commercial area selling meat, groceries, milk, and cigars. By the 1930s, this popular strip along Hastings Street had become a center for black social life with grocery stores, pool halls, bowling alleys, hotels, restaurants, nightclubs, and music stores. In this 1930s photograph, a Paradise Valley vendor sells poultry on Hastings Street. (WRL.)

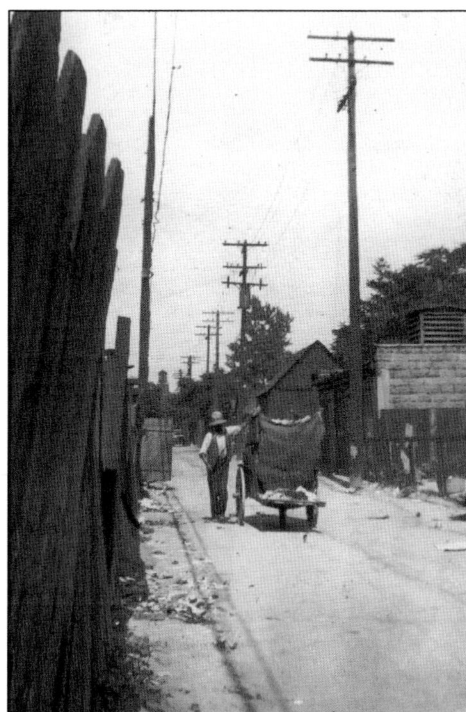

Junk collectors were denigrated by the social work establishment; one social scientist wrote "During out most prosperous days the alleys of our great cities are filled with thousands of these human scavengers, who go from rubbish pile to rubbish pile, sort out paper, rags, or anything they might sell for a few pennies . . . What price the future will pay for our present social stupidity, what anemic, deformed human derelicts we are grinding out to be the fathers and mothers of tomorrow." (WRL.)

"OUR GROWING INDUSTRIAL SCRAP HEAP."

The high speed of a modern industrial plant wears out machinery and men at an ever increasing pace. When a machine is worn out or obsolete it goes back to the smelting furnace to repeat the production cycle, but, when a man is worn out or broken down, he is thrown upon the fast growing INDUSTRIAL SCRAP HEAP of human wreckage.

Every city has its heap of human derelicts who bear the scars of industrialism.

This view shows a blind and one legged victim of the modern industrial slogan "PRODUCTION AT ANY PRICE." This man is forced to sit on the street and beg a few pennies from other workers who any day may find themselves on the same industrial scrap heap.

At times the cry of the blind, the maimed and the destitute becomes so loud that those who glut in wealth throw them a few crumbs. If one of the industrial lords throws crumbs at regular intervals he is given the saintly title of Philanthropist.

"Philanthropy,"as Scott Nearing states it, "may be defended as conscience balm, or as social fire insurance."

This victim of vicious greed and exploitation is a mocking echo of the saying, "CAPITAL BEARS THE RISK."

This message printed around the 1930s demonstrates the contemporary attitude toward Black Bottom's poor and homeless men and women. Single male migrants traveling to Detroit to work in the automobile industry often started out with little money and no prospects for shelter. Black churches often provided some money and references for boardinghouses located in Black Bottom. (WRL.)

"SISTERS IN VICE"

Two sister prostitutes who were found working the side streets off Hastings Street. The youngest girl is but 14 years of age and already a professional and veteran at the trade. The cringing hand of vice reaches into the cradle of poverty for its victims. "The ranks of prostitution are recruited from among the daughters of the poor." In the most prosperous of times thousands upon thousands of girls in their early teens are engulfed in the vicious whirlpool of vice. The depression with its resulting unemployment and economic insecurity has forced thousands of young women to sacrifice themselves on the alter of vice and prostitution. Reliable social workers report that the depression has made competition so keen that girls, both white or black can be secured for 25¢ in the Hastings Street District. On a saturday night in an hours time one will be approached by from 20 to 25 women. As high as 8 girls have been found to working the same corner at the same time.

These girls not only sell themselves to keep their own body and soul together, but many are shouldering the burden of supporting their unemployed fathers and the entire family.

The Illinois Senate Committee's report on vice, states:

1 Poverty is the principle cause direct and indirect, of prostitution
2 Thousands of girls are driven into prostitution because of the shear inability to keep body and soul together on the low wages received by them.
3 Low wages on the part of the father, inadequate schooling and

A 1930s caption attached to the photograph at the top of page 35, along with the title "Sisters in Vice," reveals the pervasive sentiments of the establishment toward what was perceived to be the lower class of society. During the Depression, prostitution thrived in Black Bottom and Paradise Valley. The practice was somewhat accepted within the community, providing income for black women whose families depended on them. (WRL.)

The 1930s photograph shows sisters working as prostitutes on Hastings Street in Paradise Valley. In *African American Women in Interwar Detroit*, Victoria Wolcott discusses that some black women rejected notions of "bourgeois respectability," turning prostitution into a necessary evil that "provided employment opportunities for African American women." The informal economy—including the numbers racket and prostitution—helped sustain the Black Bottom community during the Depression era. (WRL.)

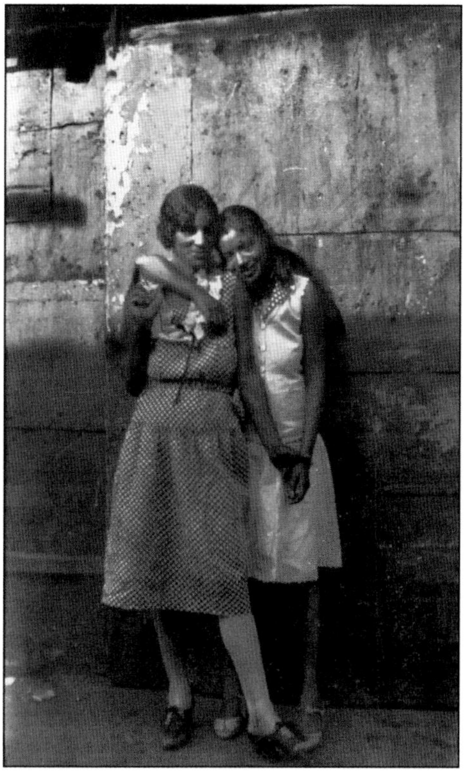

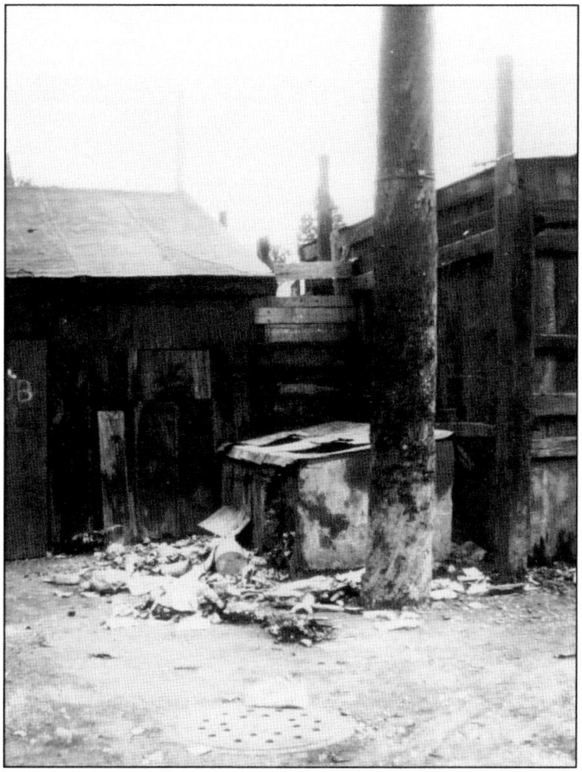

Many Black Bottom residents lived in squalid, infested slums with no plumbing and no sanitation services. (WRL.)

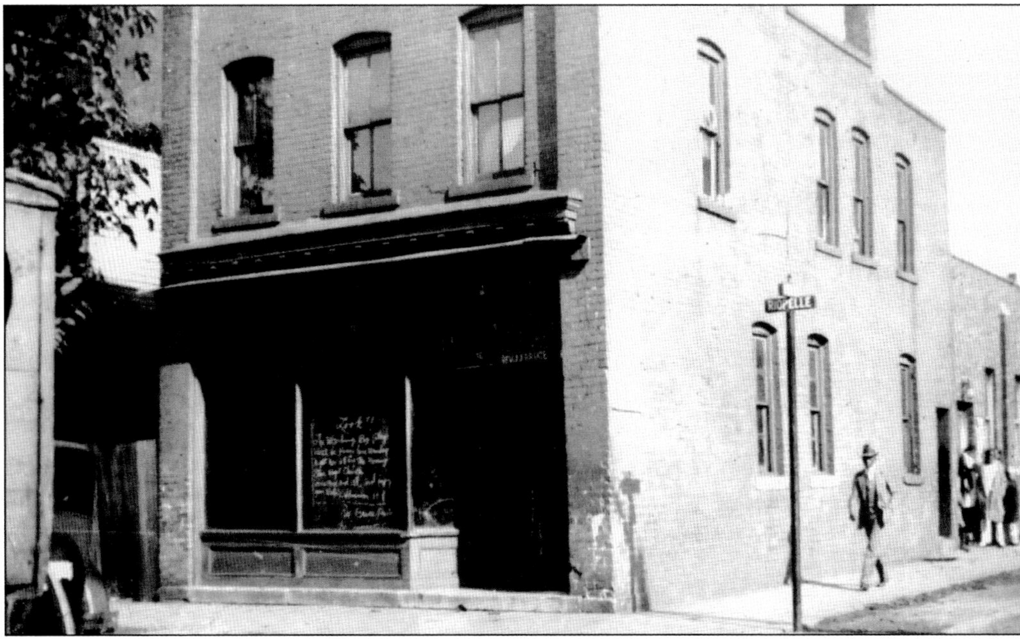

The board of health condemned a growing number of houses and other buildings during the Depression. The city cited plans to revitalize blighted areas through construction of new playgrounds and other public spaces. However, the board failed to rebuild on demolished properties. In this 1930s photograph, a man walks alongside an abandoned building at the corner of Riopelle Street. (WRL.)

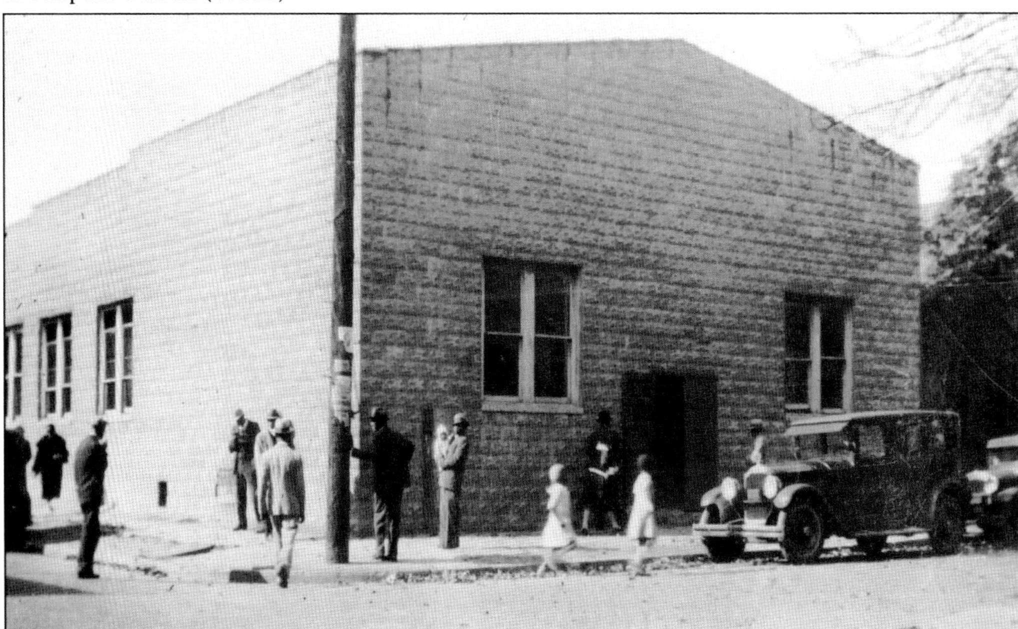

When immigration slowed, the St. Antoine district became known as the "East Side Colored District." Because the city's business district lay to its west, the St. Antoine district could not expand in that direction to accommodate its residents. This photograph was taken around the 1930s. (WRL.)

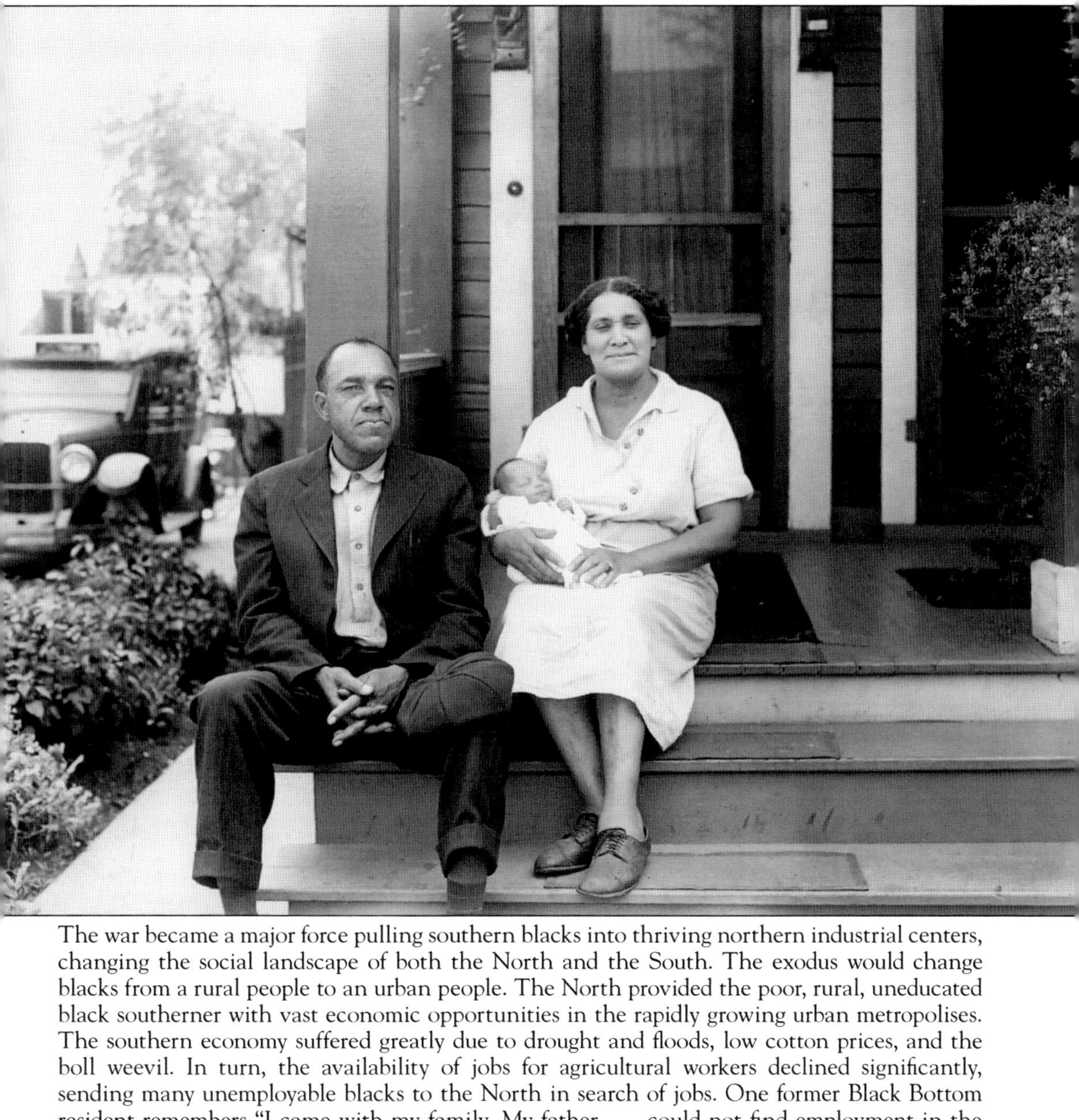

The war became a major force pulling southern blacks into thriving northern industrial centers, changing the social landscape of both the North and the South. The exodus would change blacks from a rural people to an urban people. The North provided the poor, rural, uneducated black southerner with vast economic opportunities in the rapidly growing urban metropolises. The southern economy suffered greatly due to drought and floods, low cotton prices, and the boll weevil. In turn, the availability of jobs for agricultural workers declined significantly, sending many unemployable blacks to the North in search of jobs. One former Black Bottom resident remembers "I came with my family. My father . . . could not find employment in the South . . . Detroit at the time was noted for automobiles, paints and stoves . . . The Urban League helped find a home for us on East Congress Street after the whole family was together. Later it became known as Black Bottom." This photograph was taken around the 1930s. (WRL.)

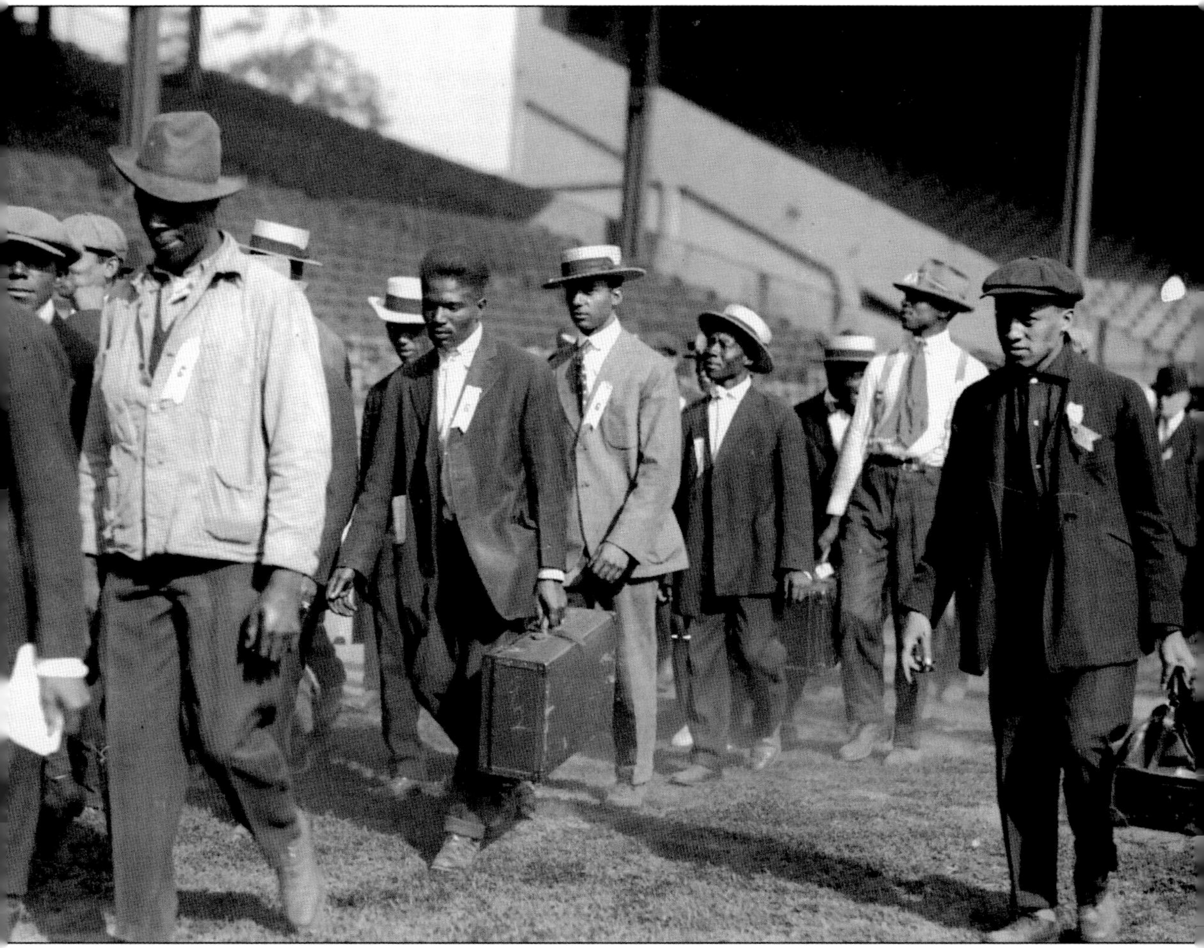

Approximately 20,000 black men volunteered for duty during World War I. Many were from Black Bottom. For these men, the war served two initiatives: the first was American democracy and the second was American freedom for blacks and an end to racial hatred and Jim Crow segregation. After serving their tour of duty, black veterans returned to Black Bottom still treated as second-class citizens and continued to struggle for decent employment, better wages, and adequate housing. In this 1920s photograph, a group of black men, some carrying suitcases or valises, leave for Camp Custer. (WRL.)

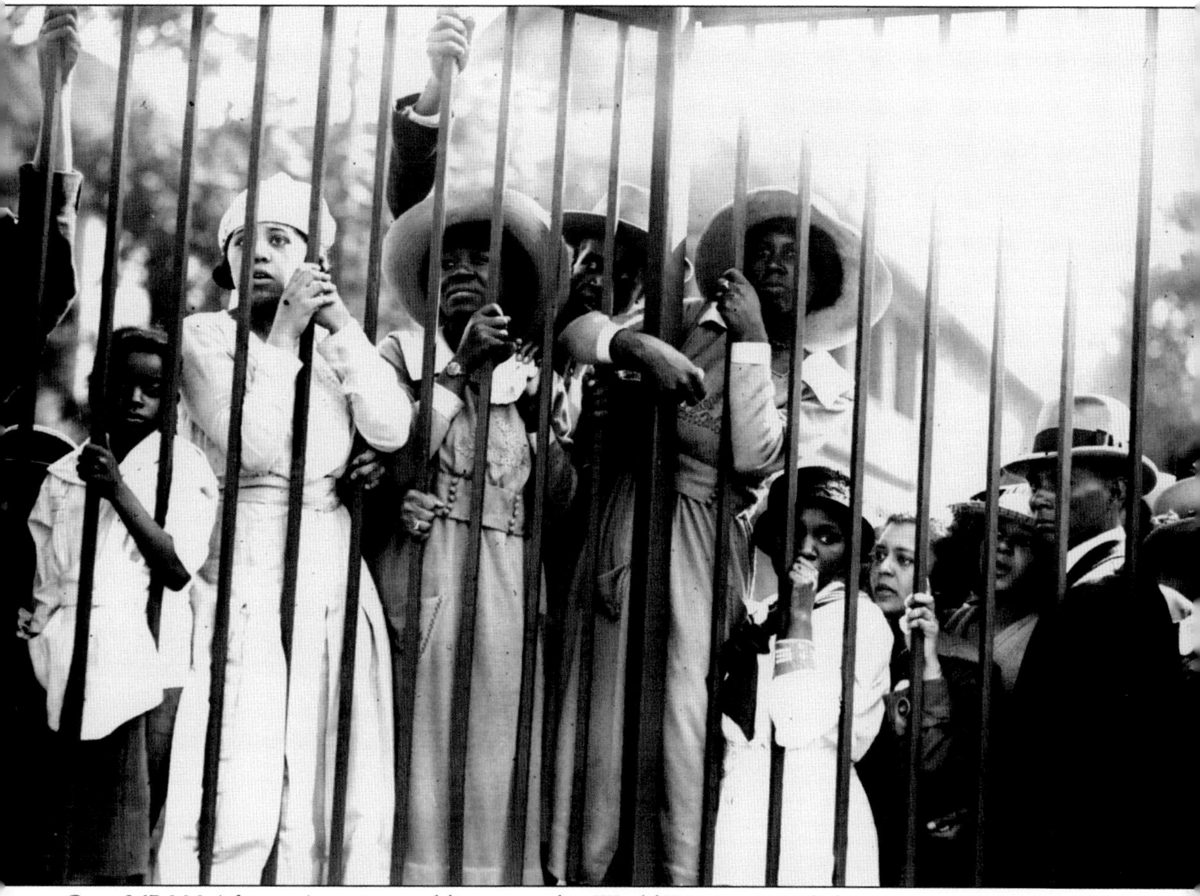

Over 367,000 African American soldiers served in World War I, 1,400 of whom were commissioned officers. During this conflict, it was the policy of the War Department to maintain segregated military units in the armed forces. The few black infantry, cavalry, and artillery units that existed at that time in the army were commanded at the top ranks by white officers, with black officers relegated to the lower ranks. In this photograph from around the second decade of the 20th century, women watch from behind a tall metal fence as their family members leave for Camp Custer in Battle Creek. (WRL.)

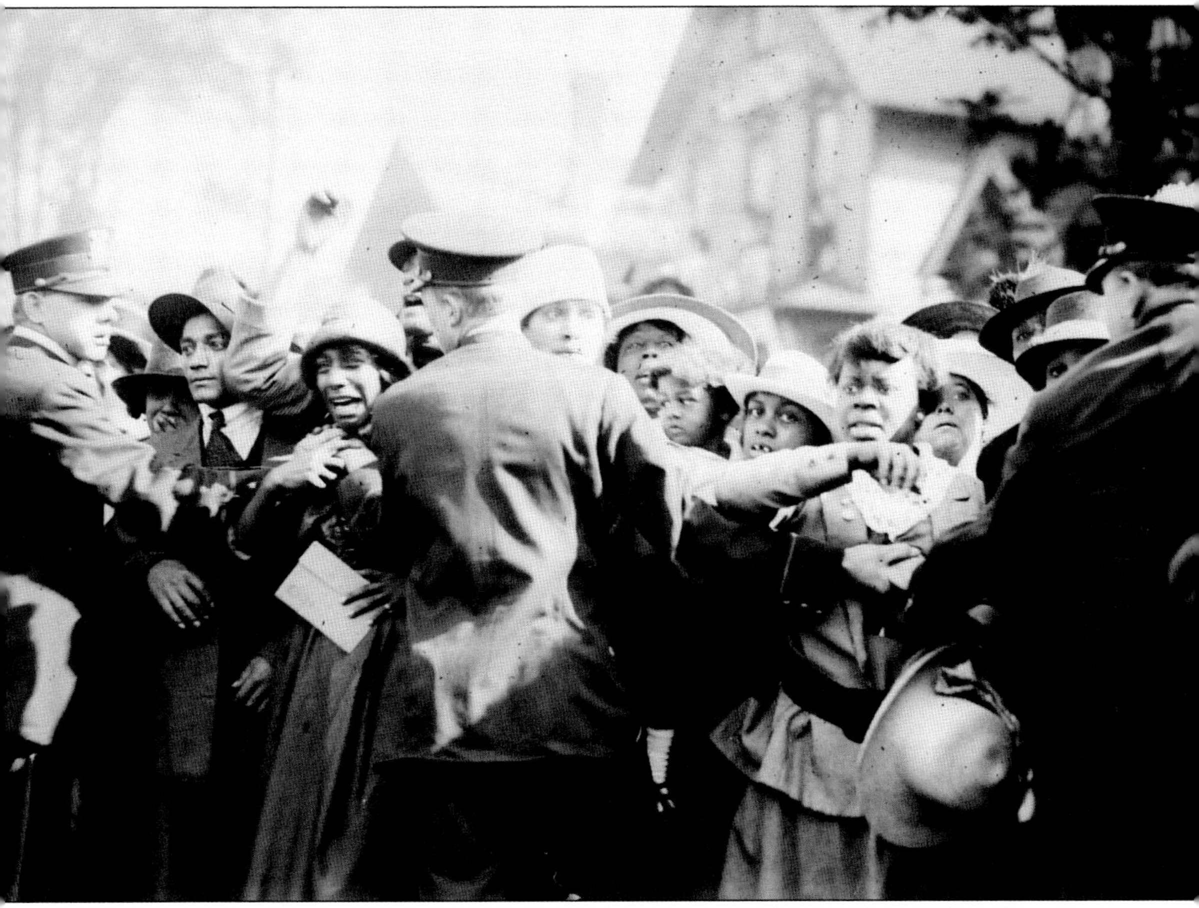

The United States entered World War I after Pres. Woodrow Wilson asked Congress to declare war on Germany. Most blacks were placed in noncombat services of supply units (labor battalions, for example). At least 100,000 blacks were sent to France during the conflict. Despite the American restriction on the use of blacks in combat units, about 40,000 blacks fought in the war. Many of them were from Black Bottom. In this photograph, taken sometime in the second decade of the 20th century, women are held back by uniformed guards, as African American recruits leave for Camp Custer. (WRL.)

Ossian Sweet, a young black doctor, practiced from an office in Black Bottom. When Sweet bought a house in a white working-class district of Detroit around 1925, angry neighbors gathered into a mob, intending to eject the Sweet family. Local police failed to act on Sweet's behalf, and shots were fired from the Sweet house. A man was killed, and the doctor and members of his family were arrested. Sweet was acquitted after a highly publicized legal battle. (WRL.)

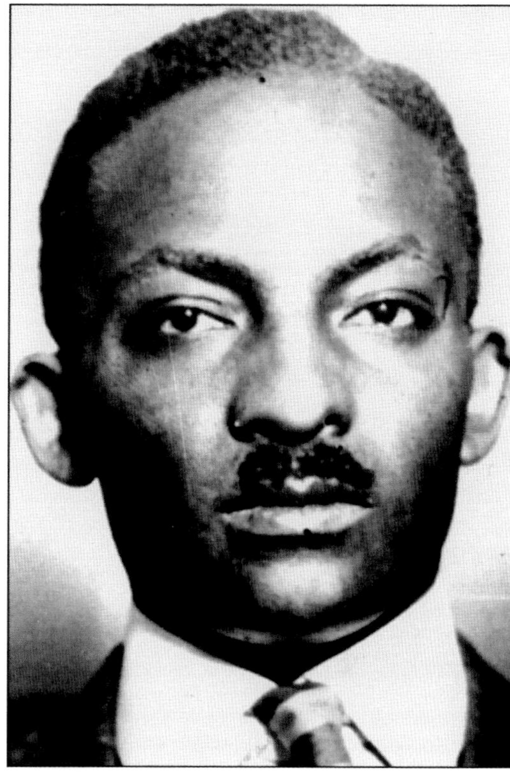

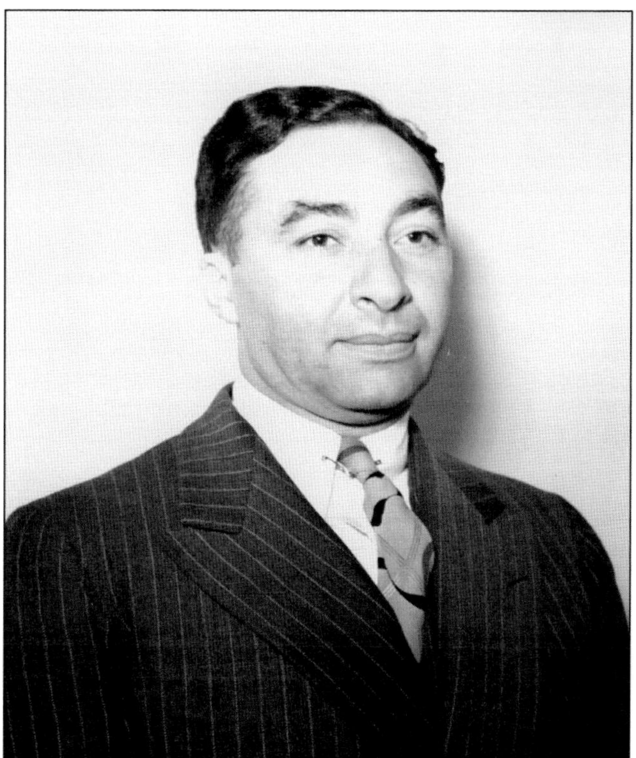

African American physician W. Harold Johnson, pictured around the 1930s, cofounded Trinity Hospital in Detroit. According to the Kellogg African American Health Care Project, "Trinity Hospital may be best known for its postgraduate surgical training and residency program for African American physicians . . . There was a need not only for the housing and treatment of the ill, but for the training and guidance of the African American medical community." (WRL.)

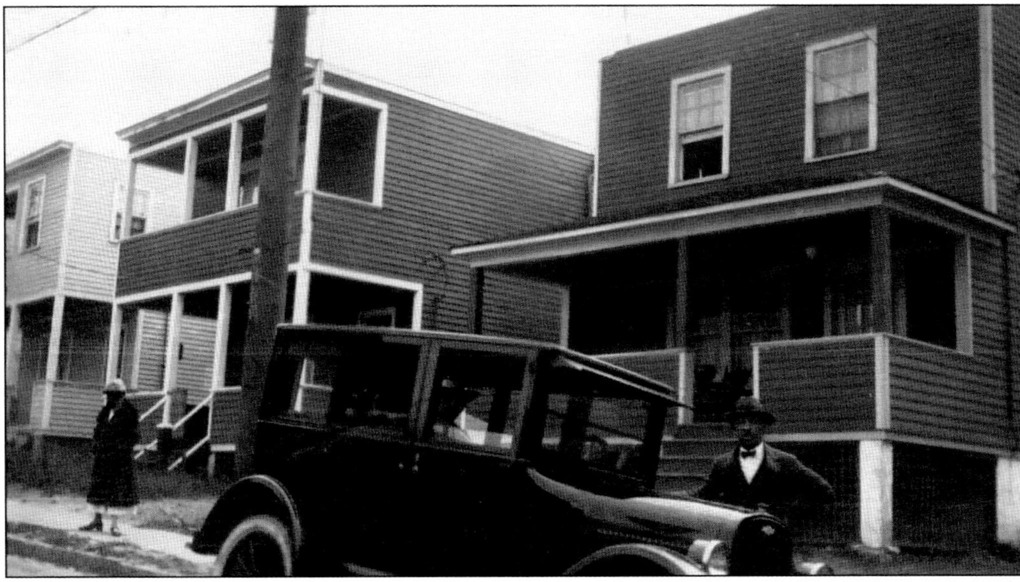

Prejudice forced home-seeking southern migrants into Black Bottom. Since the 1880s and the 1890s, the district had served as a port of entry for many of the city's foreign-born newcomers. Up through 1915, most blacks lived in Black Bottom around the St. Antoine Street district, and throughout the 1920s, black residents lived alongside Italian, Greek, and Russian Jewish newcomers. This photograph was taken sometime in the 1930s. (WRL.)

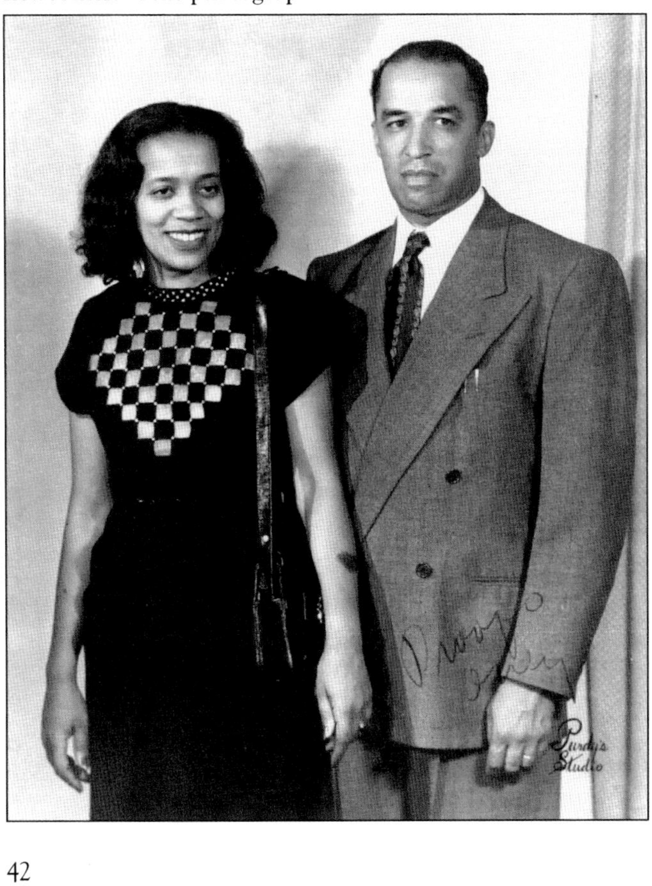

Harvey C. Jackson Jr. is pictured with his wife, Dorothea. Jackson's father was a native Michigander, and his mother was born in Ohio. Jackson opened a photography studio in Black Bottom at 474 Beaubien Street, becoming the first black proprietor of a photography studio in Detroit. The Harvey C. Jackson Photographic Collection at Burton Historical Collections is rich with views of Black Bottom life and culture, depicting schools, churches, and events in Detroit around the 1920s. (BHC.)

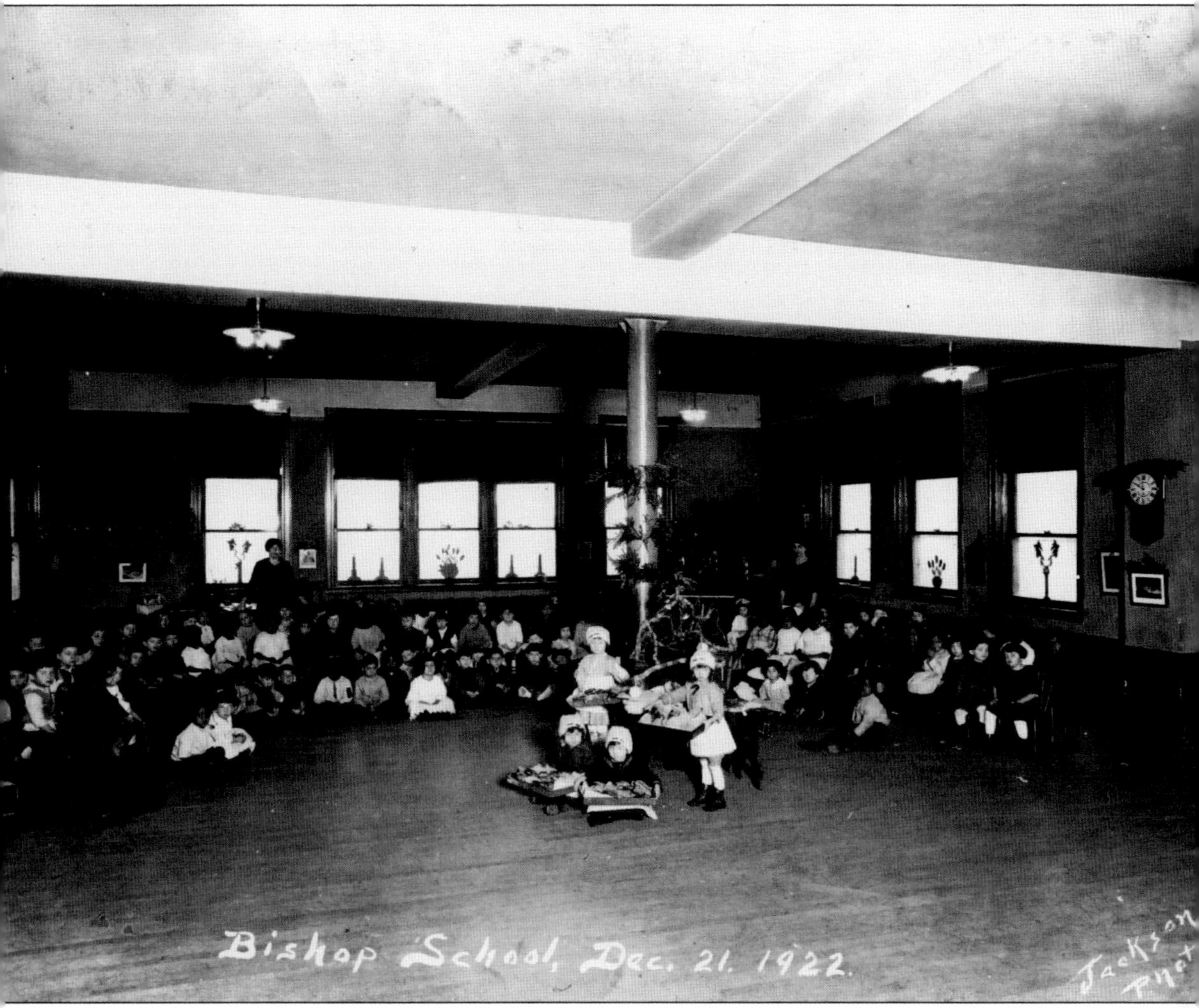

In this c. 1922 photograph, Bishop School children are sitting in a large classroom. Holiday decorations adorn the back wall, and two teachers stand in the rear of the classroom. Girls hold boxes of gifts near the small Christmas tree in the center of the room. Many Black Bottom children attended Bishop School, including several who would become members of the infamous Purple Gang. (WRL.)

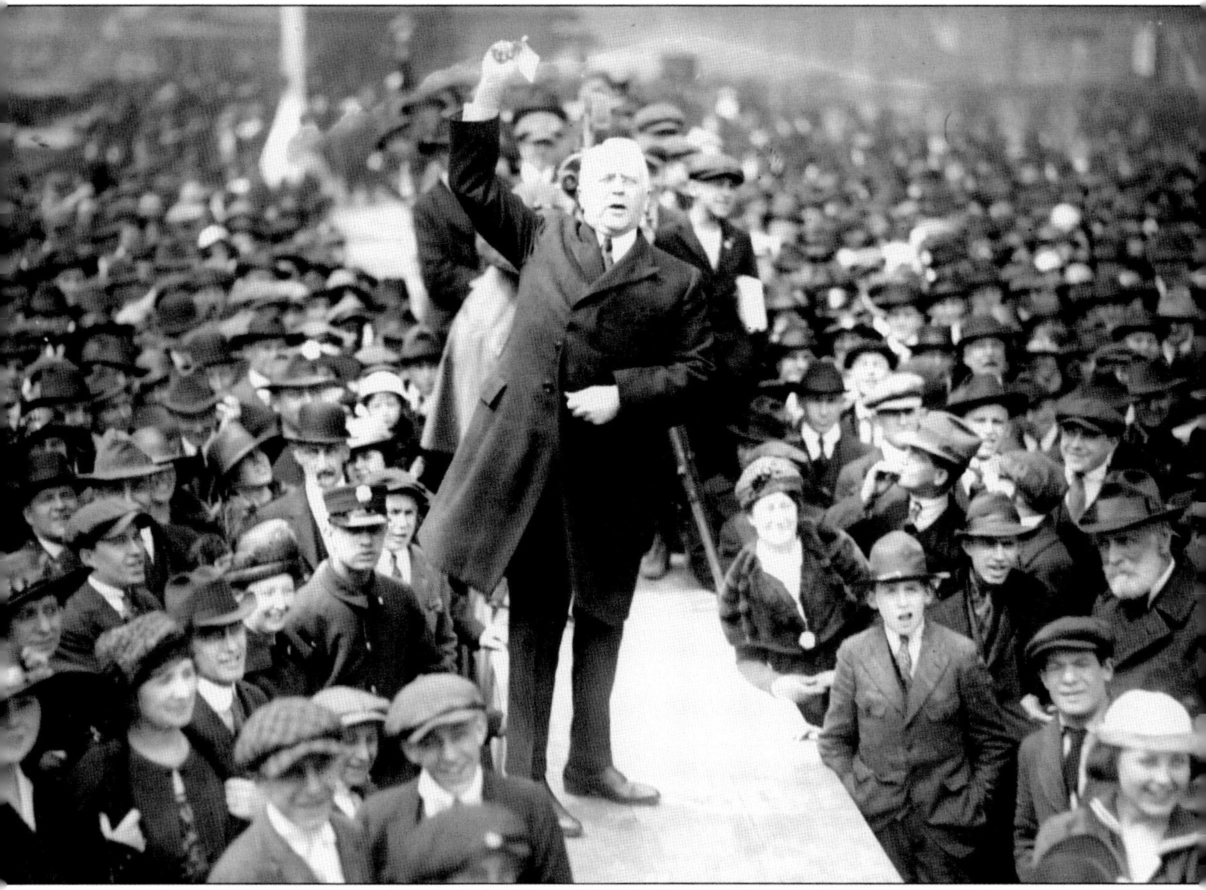

Mayor, then senator, James Couzens, pictured around the 1930s, often supported Black Bottom leaders in the struggle for better housing. Troubled by inflated rent and evictions, in the spring of 1919, he petitioned the United States Housing Corporation to establish a committee that would address the housing needs of poor inner-city residents. (WRL.)

Three

LIFE IN BLACK BOTTOM

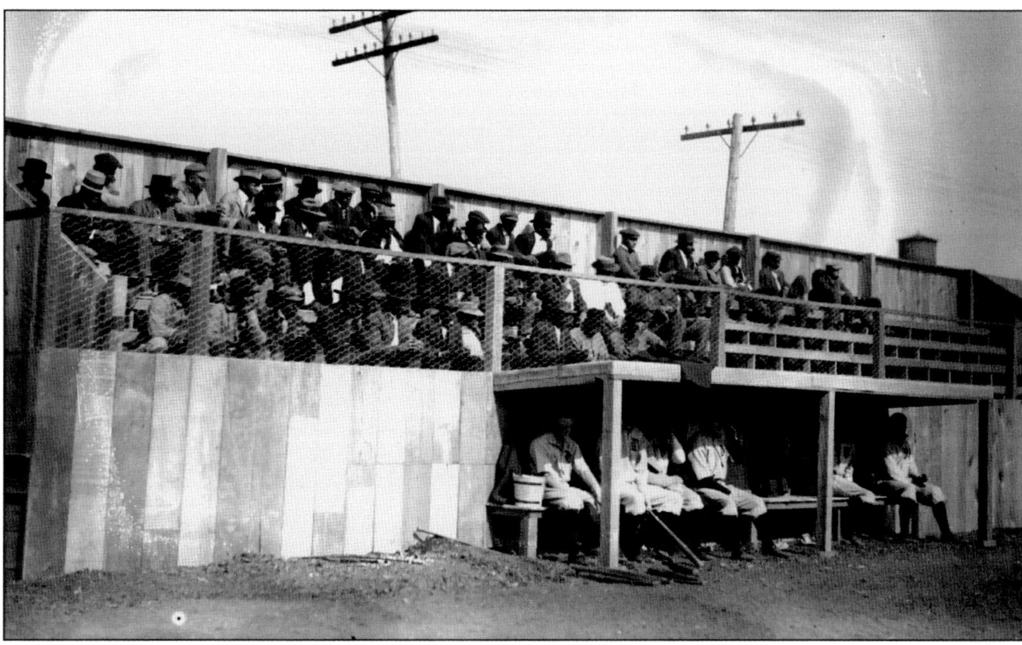

This *c.* 1911 photograph shows black men sitting in a segregated section of Navin Field (Tiger Stadium). African Americans experienced segregation on and off the bleachers. In *Turkey Stearnes and the Detroit Stars: The Negro Leagues in Detroit, 1919–1933*, Richard Bak writes, "The Detroit Stars and the rest of the Negro National League were the inevitable by-product of Jim Crow America." Sportswriter Harry Salsinger of the *Detroit News* reflected that, "the level of the game in Negro leagues is easily on a par with that being played at Navin Field." (WRL.)

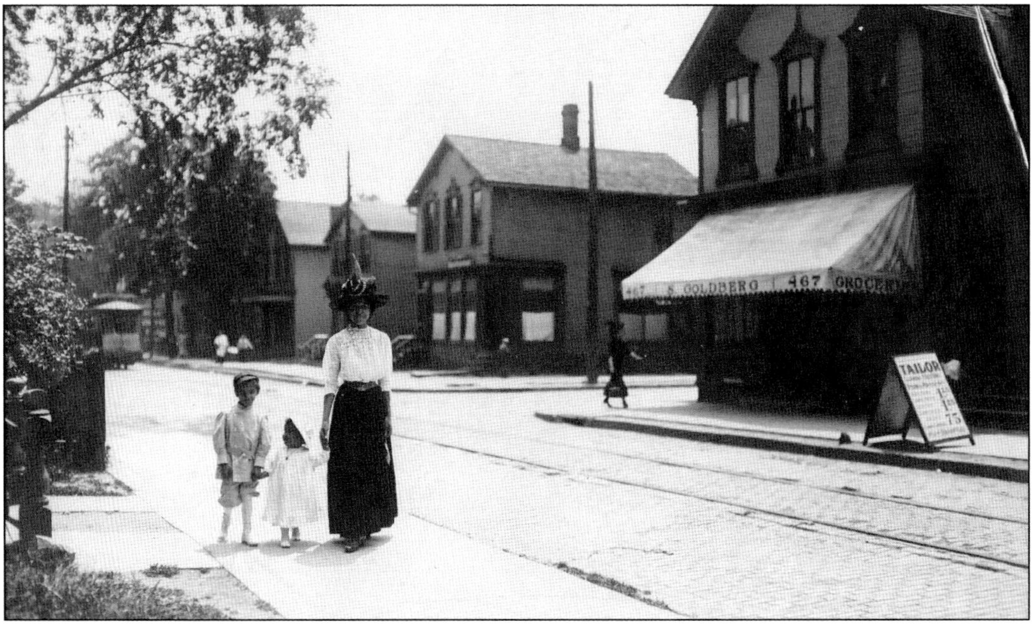

By 1920, blacks owned 350 businesses in Detroit, almost all located within the boundaries of Black Bottom. The community also had 17 physicians, 22 lawyers, 22 barbershops, 13 dentists, 12 cartage agencies, 11 tailors, 10 restaurants, 10 real estate dealers, 8 grocers, 6 drugstores, 5 undertakers, 4 employment offices, a few garages, and a candy maker. In this photograph, an African American family strolls down a quiet street in Black Bottom. The store across the street says Goldberg and is located in the St. Antoine and Hastings Streets section of Black Bottom. As Jews prospered they eventually moved toward Grand Boulevard. This photograph is from around 1930. (BHC.)

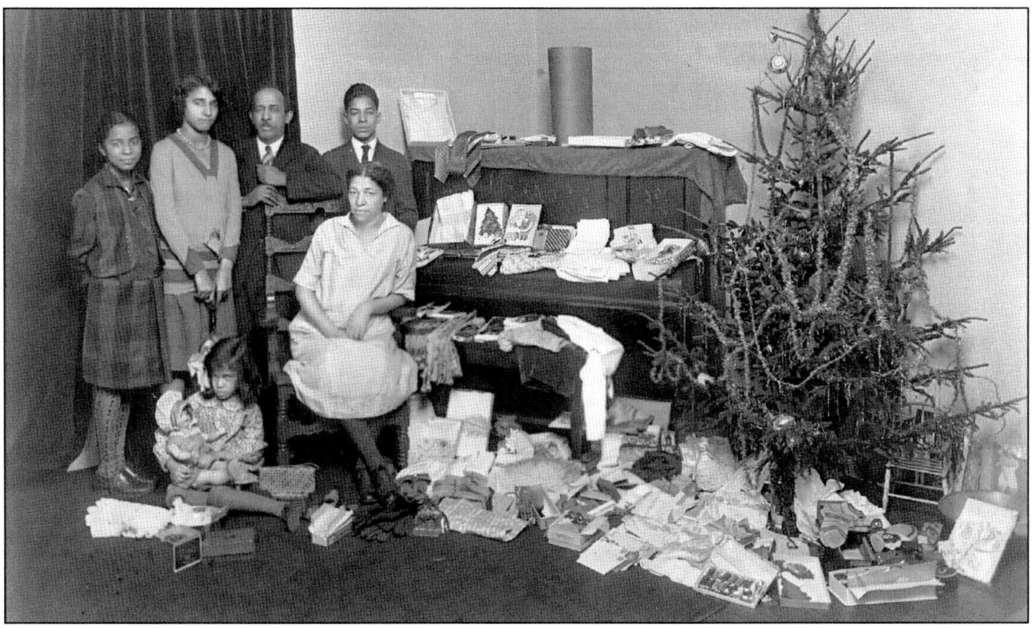

Members of the Jackson family gather together for Christmas around 1930. Housing for the African American population slowly became more available as the Black Bottom district expanded to the east and south. (BHC.)

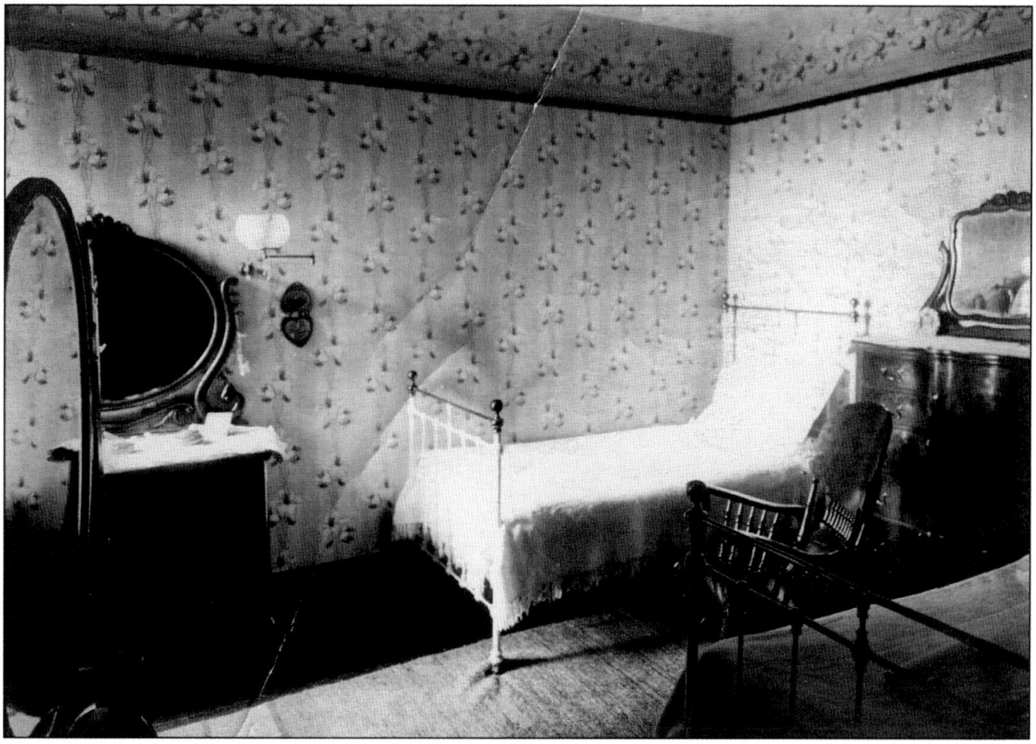

This photograph reveals the interior of a c. 1930 Beaubien Street home. "The whole sense of family and neighborhood—the legacy of sports and involvement in our community—it all comes from that time," recalled a former Black Bottom resident. (BHC.)

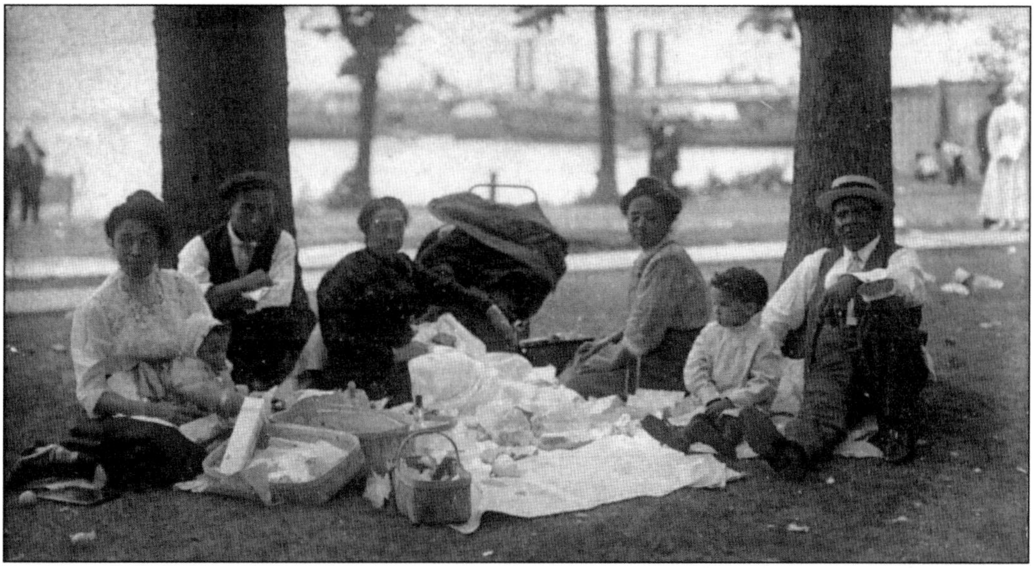

In Elaine Latzman Moon's *Untold Tales, Unsung Heroes: An Oral History of Detroit's African American Community, 1918–1967*, many former Black Bottom residents remembered joyous trips out to Belle Isle. Weekends, holidays, and birthdays were often spent on Belle Isle, riding bicycles, canoeing, horseback riding, ice-skating, and barbecuing. In this 1920s photograph, an African American family enjoys a warm and sunny day picnic on Belle Isle. (BHC.)

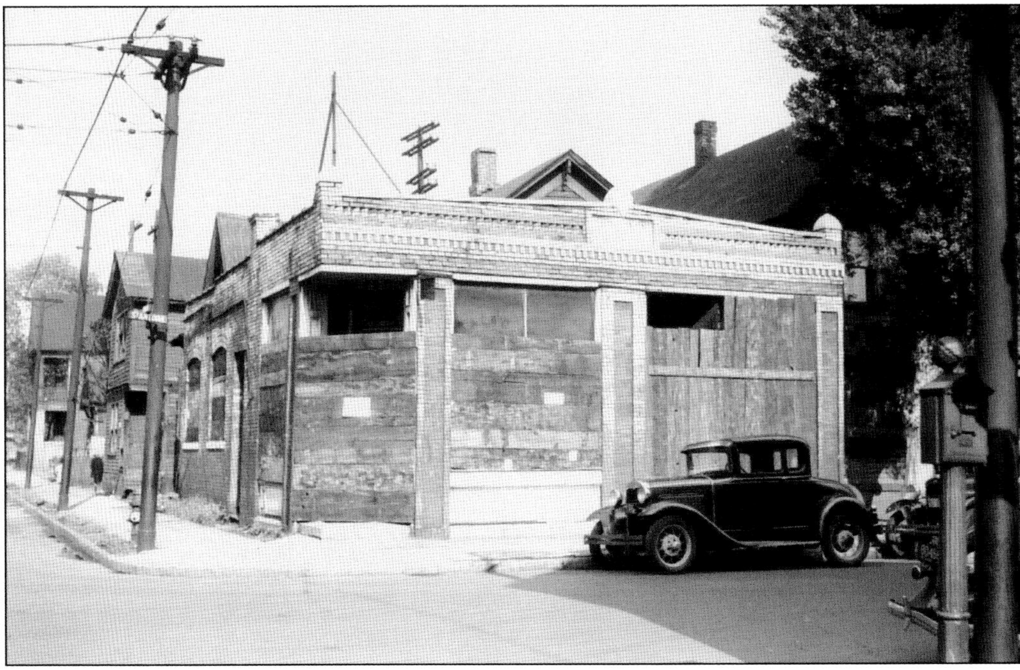

This *c*. 1935 photograph shows a boarded up store on the southeast corner of St. Antoine Street and Eliot Avenue. The store went out of business during the Depression, and the building was eventually purchased by the government for demolition. (WRL.)

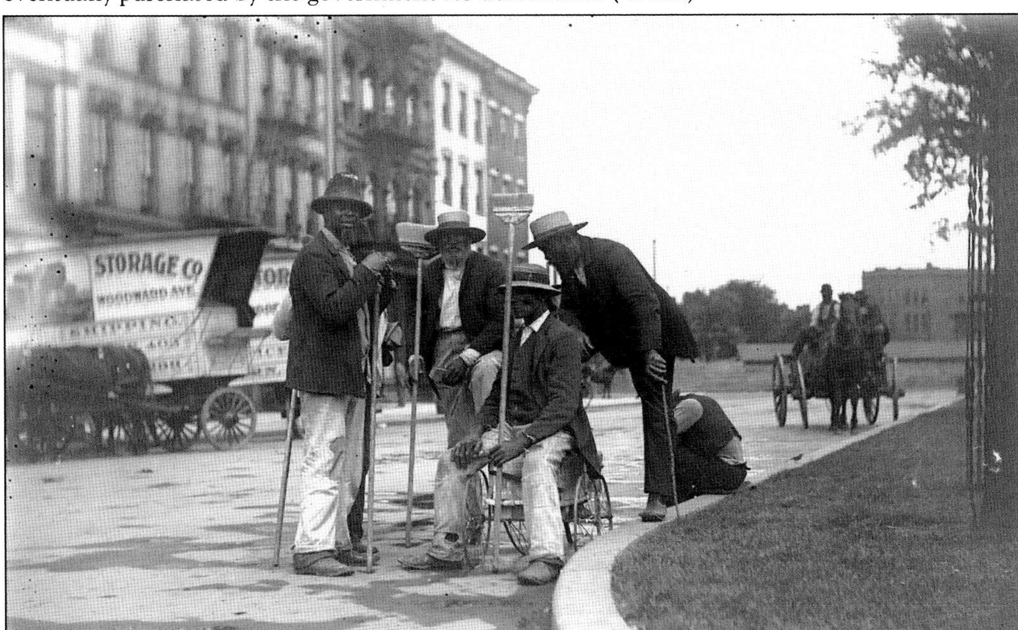

The jobs awaiting southern migrants were often the hardest, dirtiest, and most dangerous. Many white employers refused to hire black workers, and unions in Detroit in the early 1900s were predominantly white. Hate strikes were staged by white workers, both male and female, refusing to work next to blacks. In this photograph, taken sometime in the first decade of the 20th century, downtown street sweepers take a break. (BHC.)

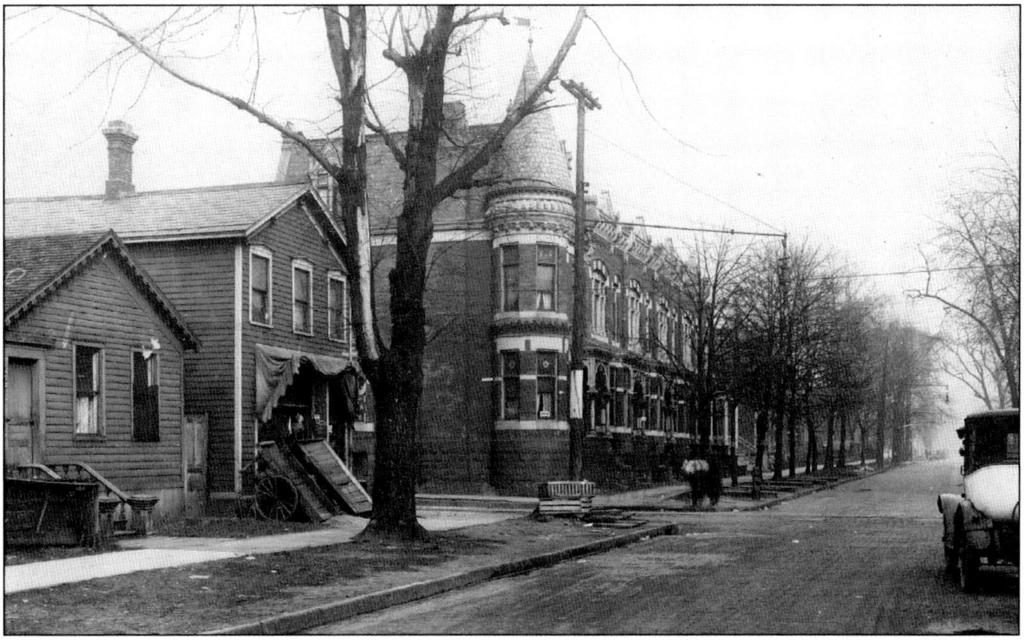

This *c.* 1920 photograph shows a boardinghouse located at the corner of Elizabeth Street in Black Bottom. As southern migrants continued to flood the Black Bottom area, the need for housing remained a primary challenge. The Detroit Urban League, along with black churches and other black aid societies, continued to assist black southerners in their quest to secure adequate room and board. (BHC.)

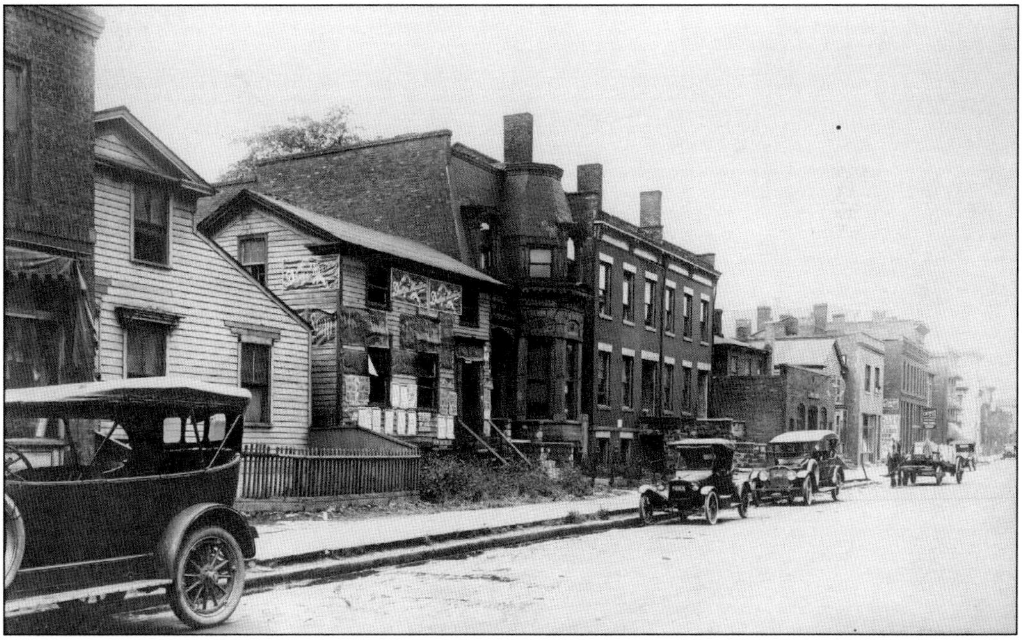

French farmers gave Black Bottom its name for its low elevation and rich black soil. The resonance of the name changed as thousands of blacks moved into the area—their racial identity became associated with the name Black Bottom in many people's minds. Black Bottom's Larned Street is pictured around 1913. (BHC.)

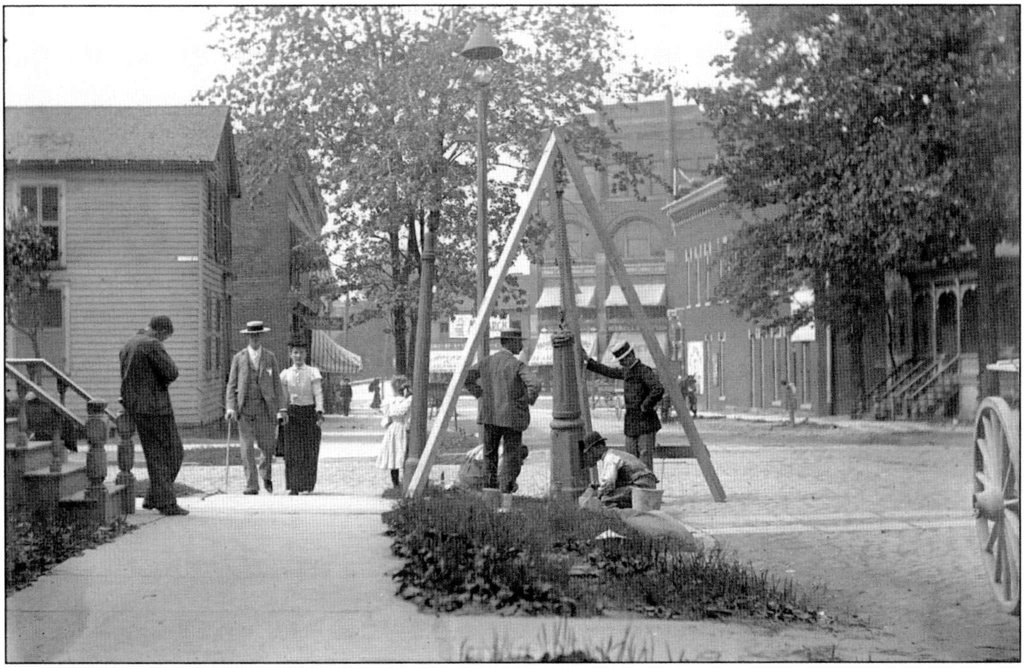

In this photograph from the 1920s, a black worker installs a streetlight while another black worker works on the bottom of the streetlight, which hangs from a tripod. The rest of the lamp is to the left. Two men, possibly city officials, observe the men working. (BHC.)

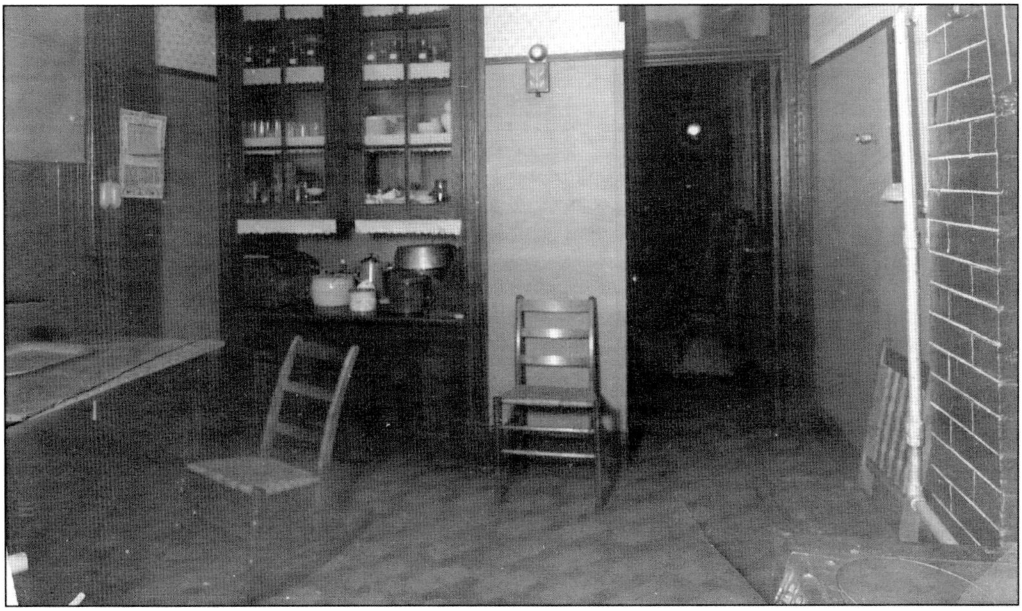

Electricity and running water were modern conveniences that few residents of Black Bottom enjoyed. In 1926, approximately 30 percent of homes in Black Bottom had no toilet. Toilets were not necessarily a luxury, however. Landlords often installed toilets because they had been pressured to install them by health officials or because they wanted an excuse to raise rents. This 1930s photograph of a home located at 2614 Beaubien Street shows a kitchen and dining room with two chairs, a table, rocking chair, flattop stove, and storage cabinet. (BHC.)

Restrictive covenants, real estate codes, and racial prejudice generally prevented blacks, especially new arrivals, from randomly finding homes as modest as this 1930s Black Bottom home. The parlor contains a desk and chair next to a fireplace, and oriental rug on the floor. (BHC.)

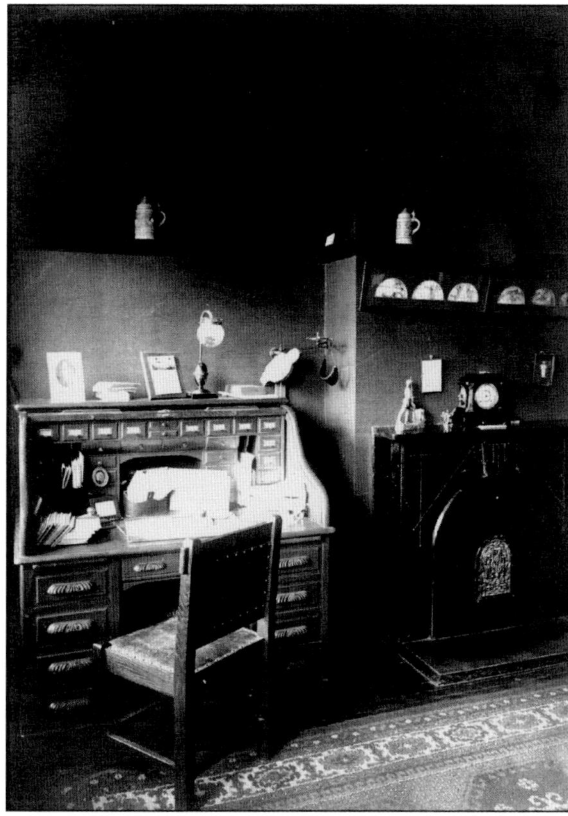

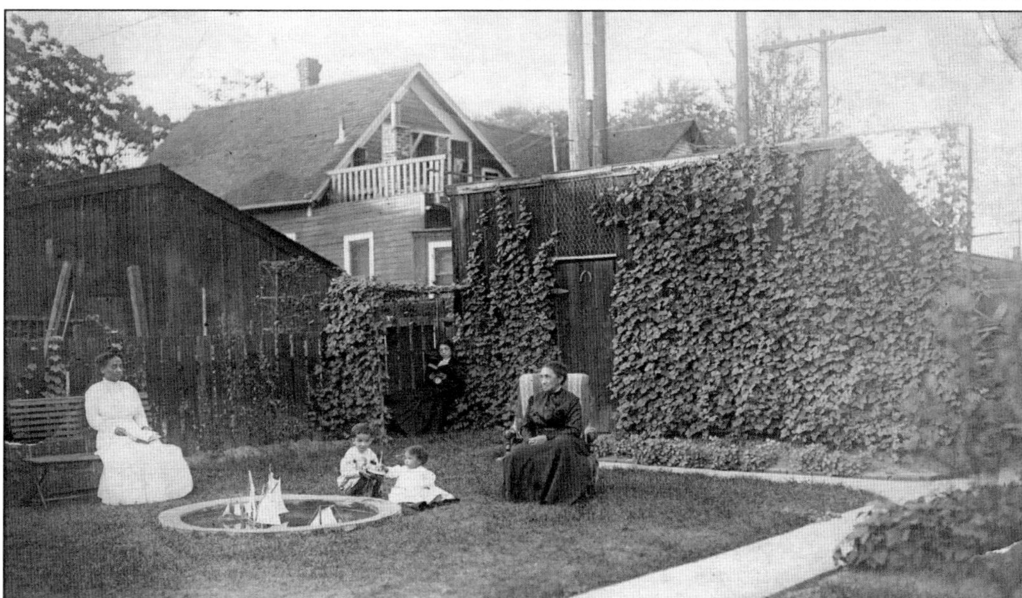

In this 1930s photograph, three black women are relaxing in a grassy backyard while two black children play with toy boats in a small pond. On the back of the photograph it states "Beaubien Home, Helen Wyngate, Mrs. Jackson II, Harvey Jackson [Jr.], Virginia Jackson, Mrs. Jackson I." (BHC.)

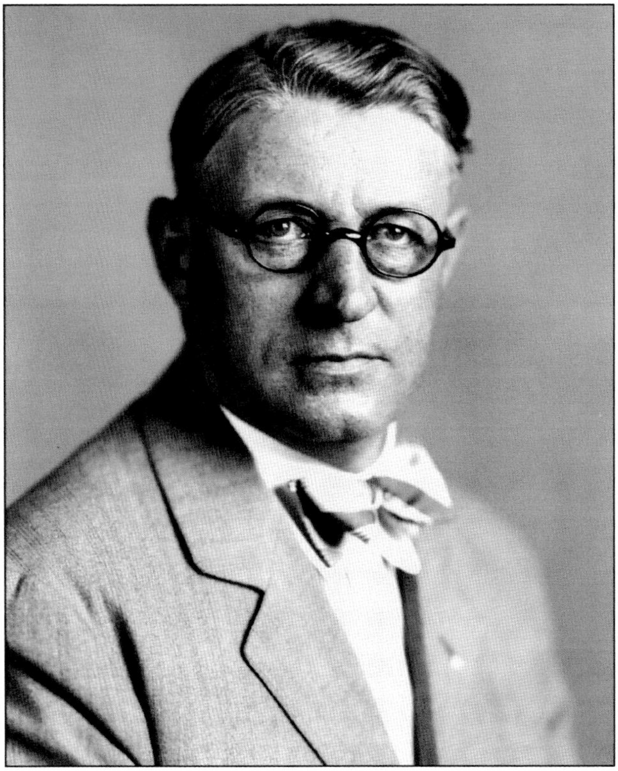

Charles E. Bowles, pictured around 1930, was the mayor of Detroit. He was recalled from office after allegations that he had tolerated or colluded with gangsters and the Ku Klux Klan. Later in his career, he unsuccessfully ran for both the Michigan State House and U.S. House. He was allegedly tied to the murder of radio commentator Gerald E. Buckley. He is buried in Evergreen Cemetery. (WRL.)

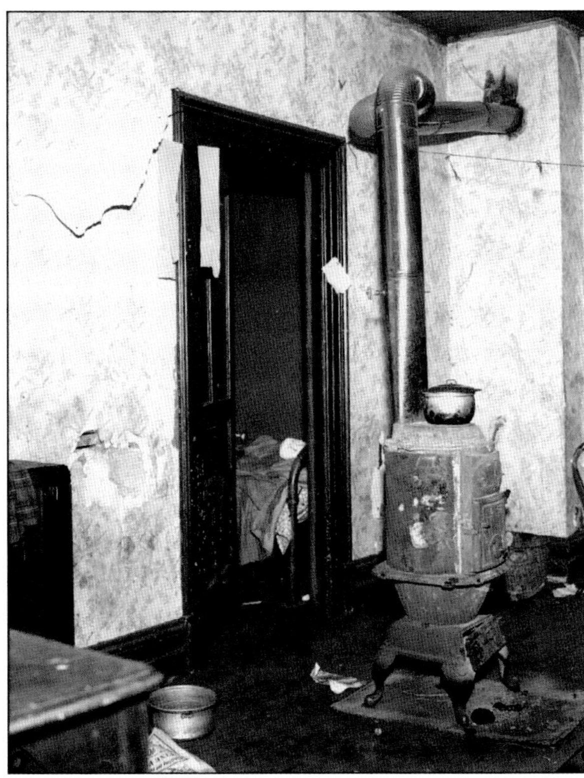

Migrants unaccustomed to northern winters suffered in the bitter cold without adequate insulation or heating in their houses. One board of health investigator reported seeing children stumbling over ice that had frozen on the floor when leaking pipes and toilets had flooded their house. Another investigator, on a stormy day, stood in each room of a four room shack in the St. Antoine Street district and saw the rain, literally, pour through the ceiling and onto the floor. The floors and walls of those dwellings were so unstable that the tenants were living in actual danger of the house tumbling down over their heads. This photograph was taken around 1938. (WRL.)

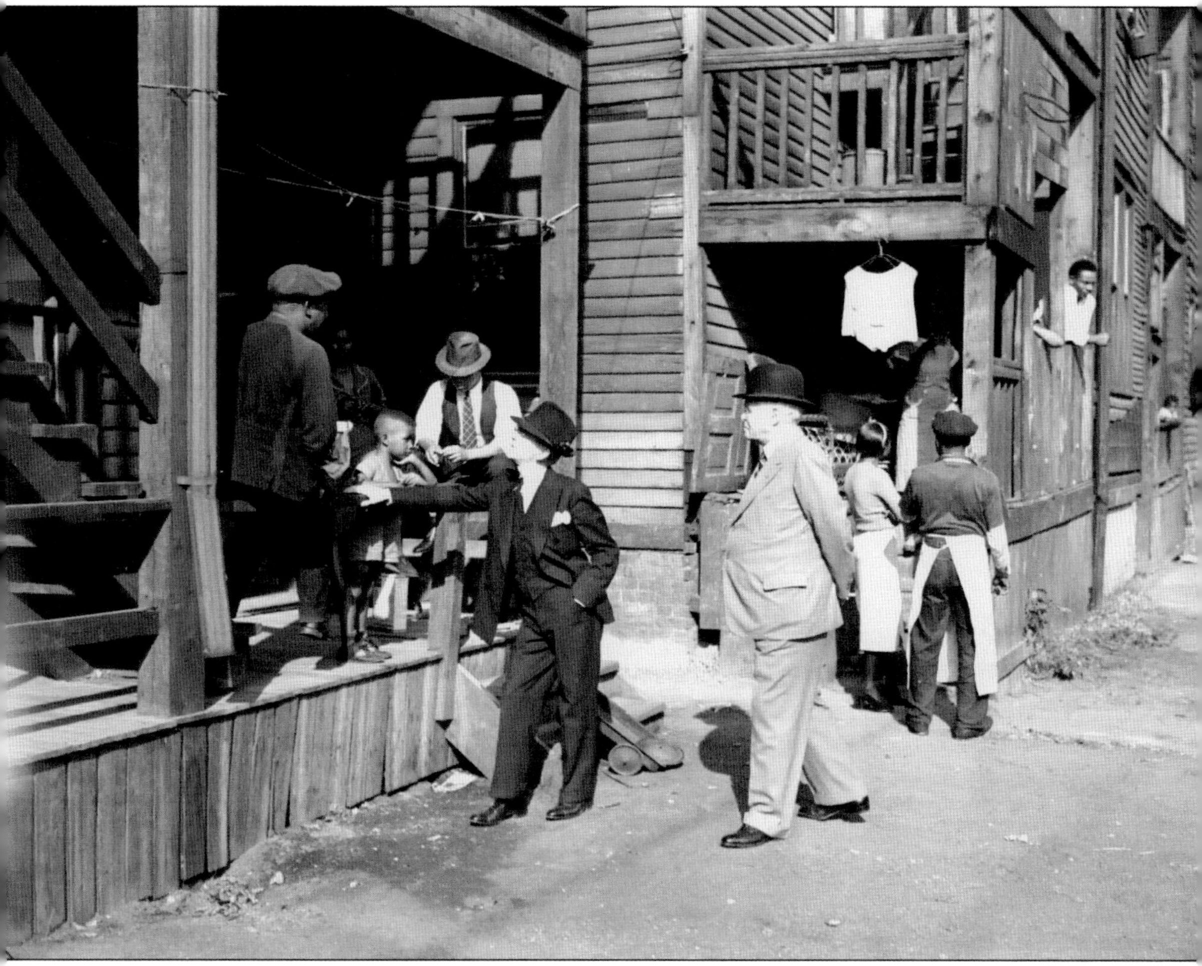

According to Elizabeth Anne Martin's study, *Detroit and the Great Migration 1916–1929*, black tenants often paid higher rents than whites who occupied the same buildings; many did not protest for fear that the landlord might order them out of their homes, leaving them with nowhere else to go. For dilapidated three- and four-bedroom homes without baths and frequently without electricity or gas, black migrants in 1916 paid more than four times the average rent paid by white renters in Detroit. From 1915 to 1920 some of the rents in the district increased by 500 percent. The rents demanded of many workers sometimes amounted to as much as two-fifths to one-half of their monthly earnings, at a time when one-sixth of a family's income was considered the appropriate amount to spend on housing. In this *c.* 1938 photograph, the board of health tours Black Bottom's inadequate housing. (WRL.)

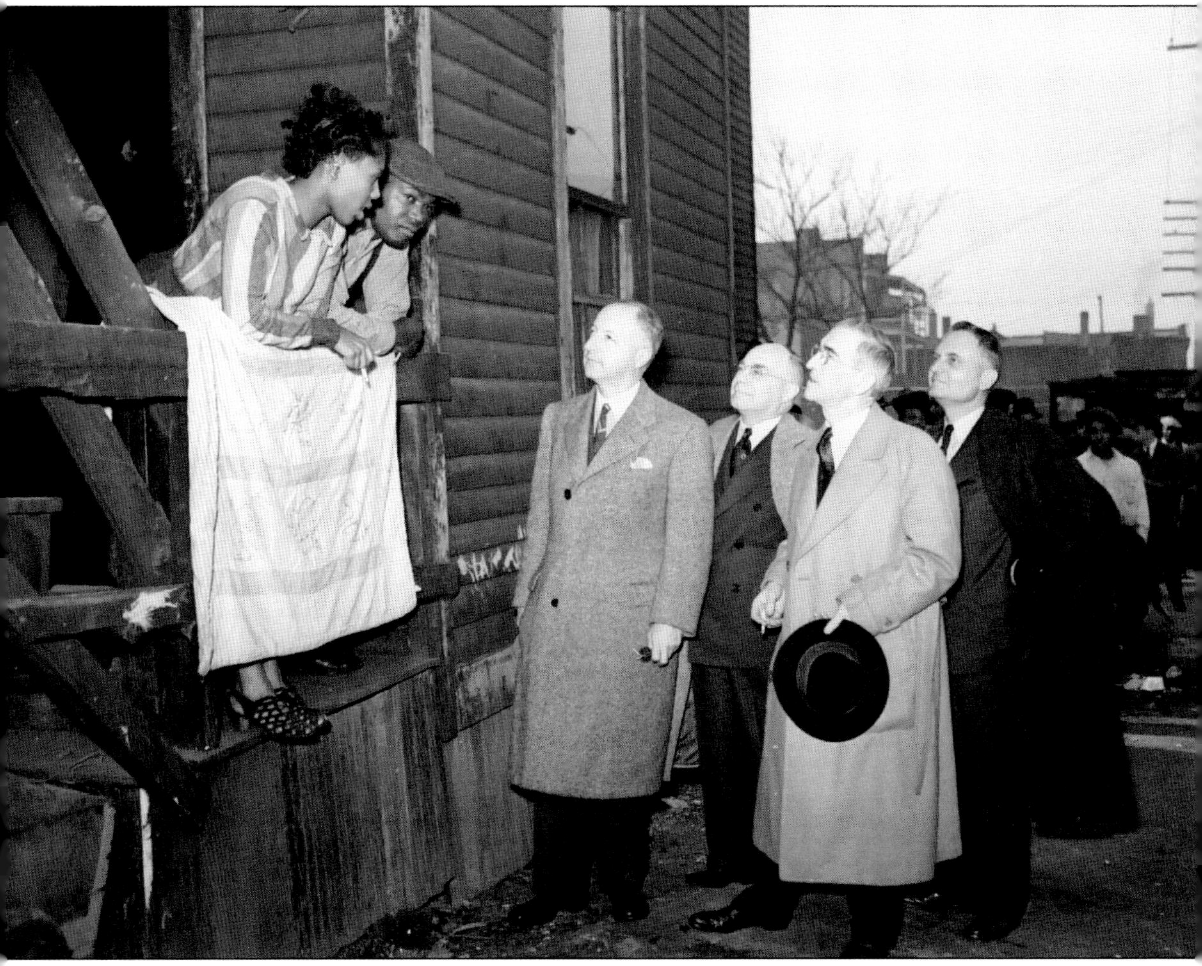

A 1926 survey indicated that over one half of the families in Black Bottom took in lodgers. Boarders exacerbated crowding, limited privacy, and led to concern among families about the propriety of having unattached males in the company of young girls and impressionable boys. Also, landlords who discovered that a family had taken in boarders generally responded by raising rents even higher. In this c. 1938 photograph, the Detroit Board of Commerce tours Black Bottom's slums to assess the need for better housing. (WRL.)

Four

THE STRUGGLE FOR DECENT HOUSING

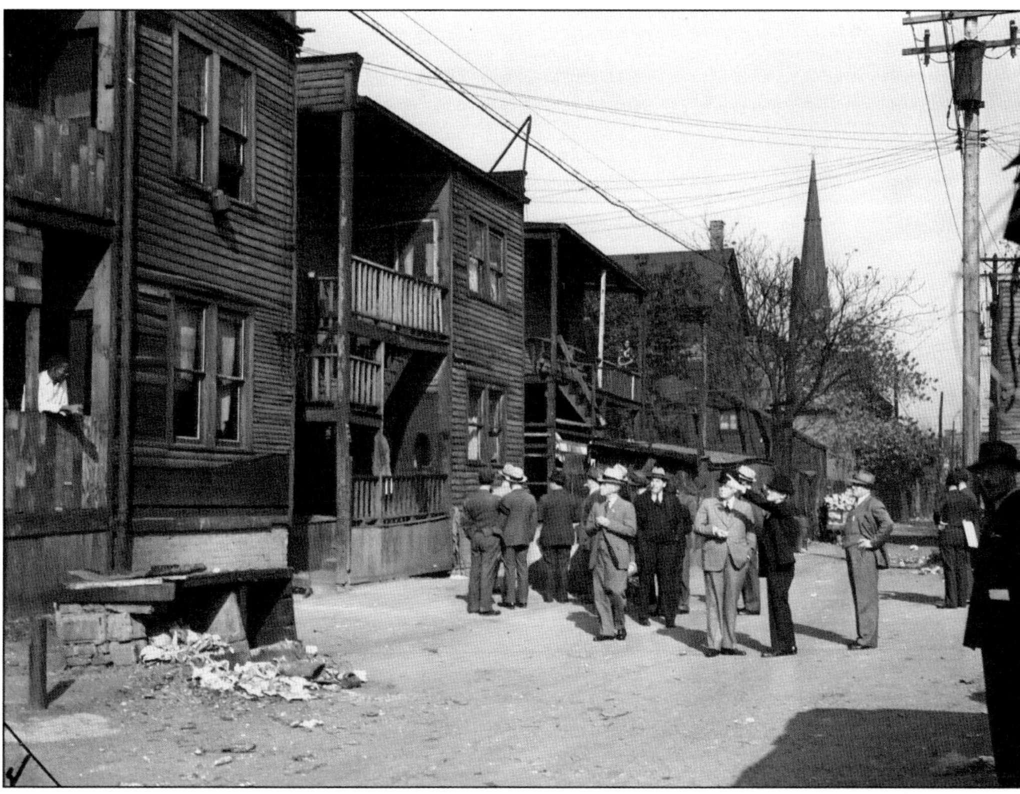

Restrictive covenants forced blacks to settle in Black Bottom areas in abominable housing conditions. The rising dilemma of inefficient housing meant that landlords could continue to charge high rent rates. In this *c.* 1938 photograph, the board of health conducts yet another tour of Black Bottom to investigate the pressing demand for better housing. (WRL.)

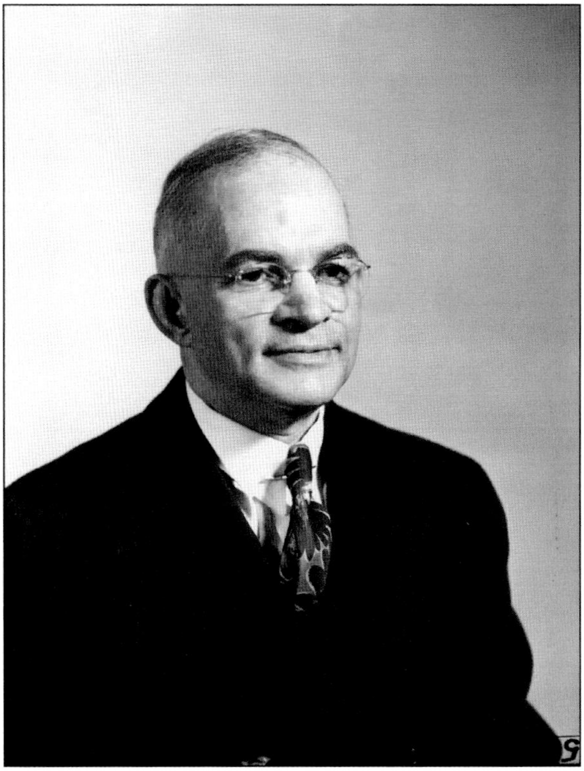

This *c.* 1947 photograph depicts Henry S. Dunbar, manager of the Brewster Homes Housing Project. (WRL.)

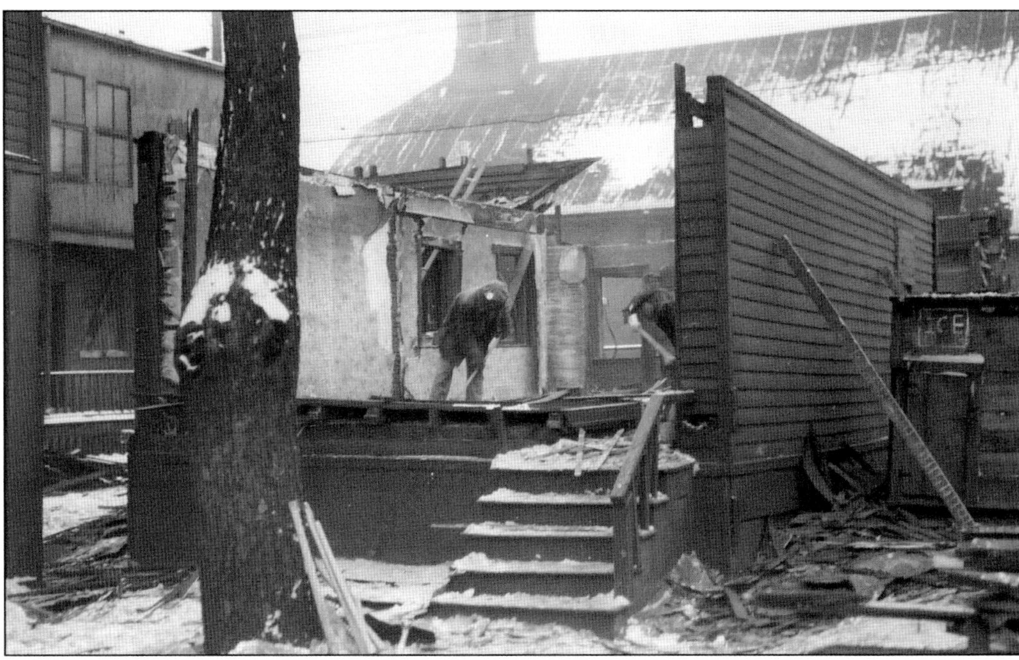

To make way for the urban renewal initiative, the board of health began condemning many houses in Black Bottom. The city proposed clearing of slum areas for newer housing projects for poor Black Bottom residents. In this *c.* 1935 photograph, two men work inside an abandoned shell of a house with no roof and three walls. (WRL.)

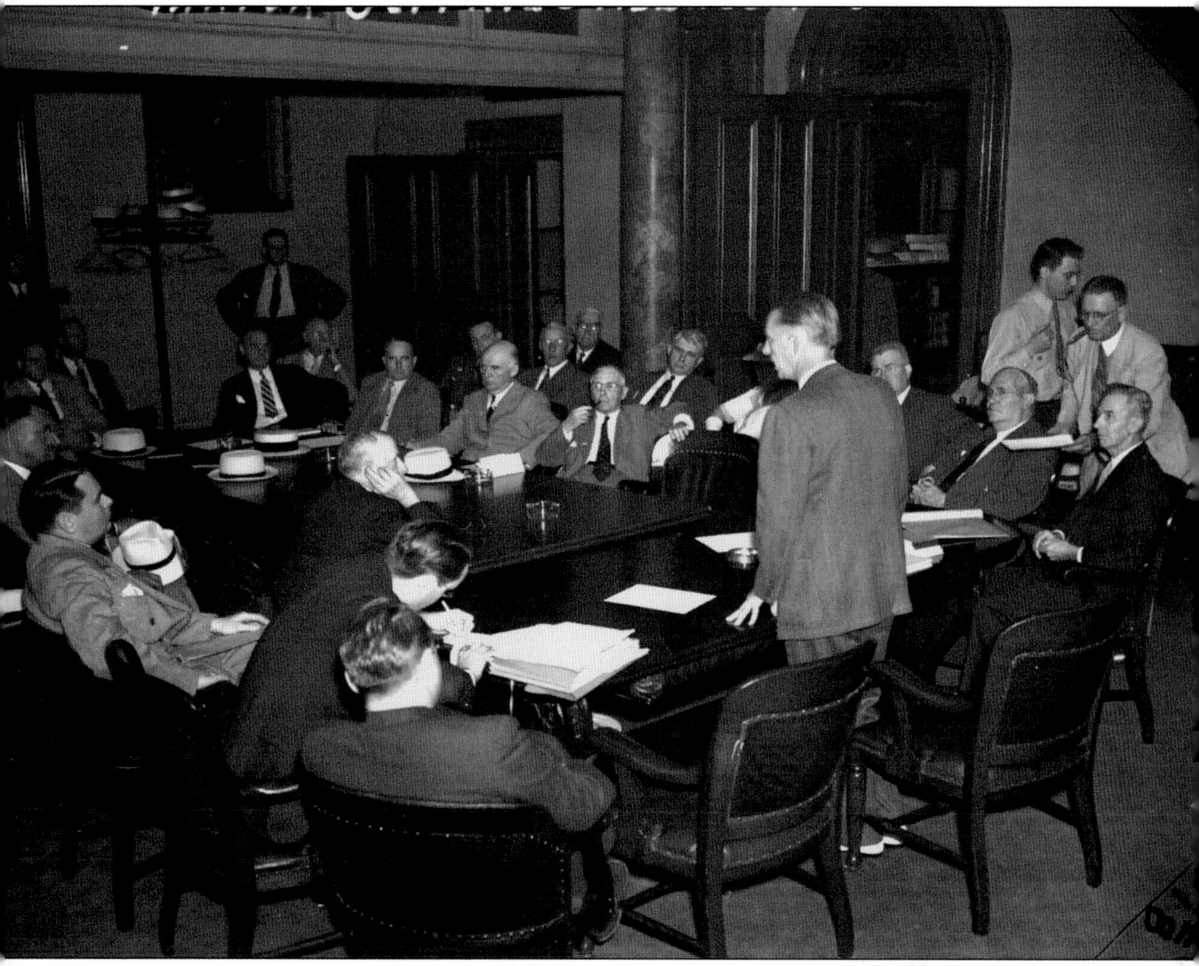

The Detroit Housing Commission offered housing aid to evicted families as city officials began plans to clear slums for urban development. This c. 1935 photograph shows, from left to right, (standing) Charles H. Awkerman, Mayor Edward Jeffries, Detective Sergeant Edward A. Wurm, Vance G. Ingalls, and George Edwards; (seated in front) Harriett D. Kelly, Edward E. Thal, Ethan W. Thompson, Horace A. White, George R. Branton, Paul W. Voorhies, Edward Graff, and chief assistant prosecutor William G. Comb. (WRL.)

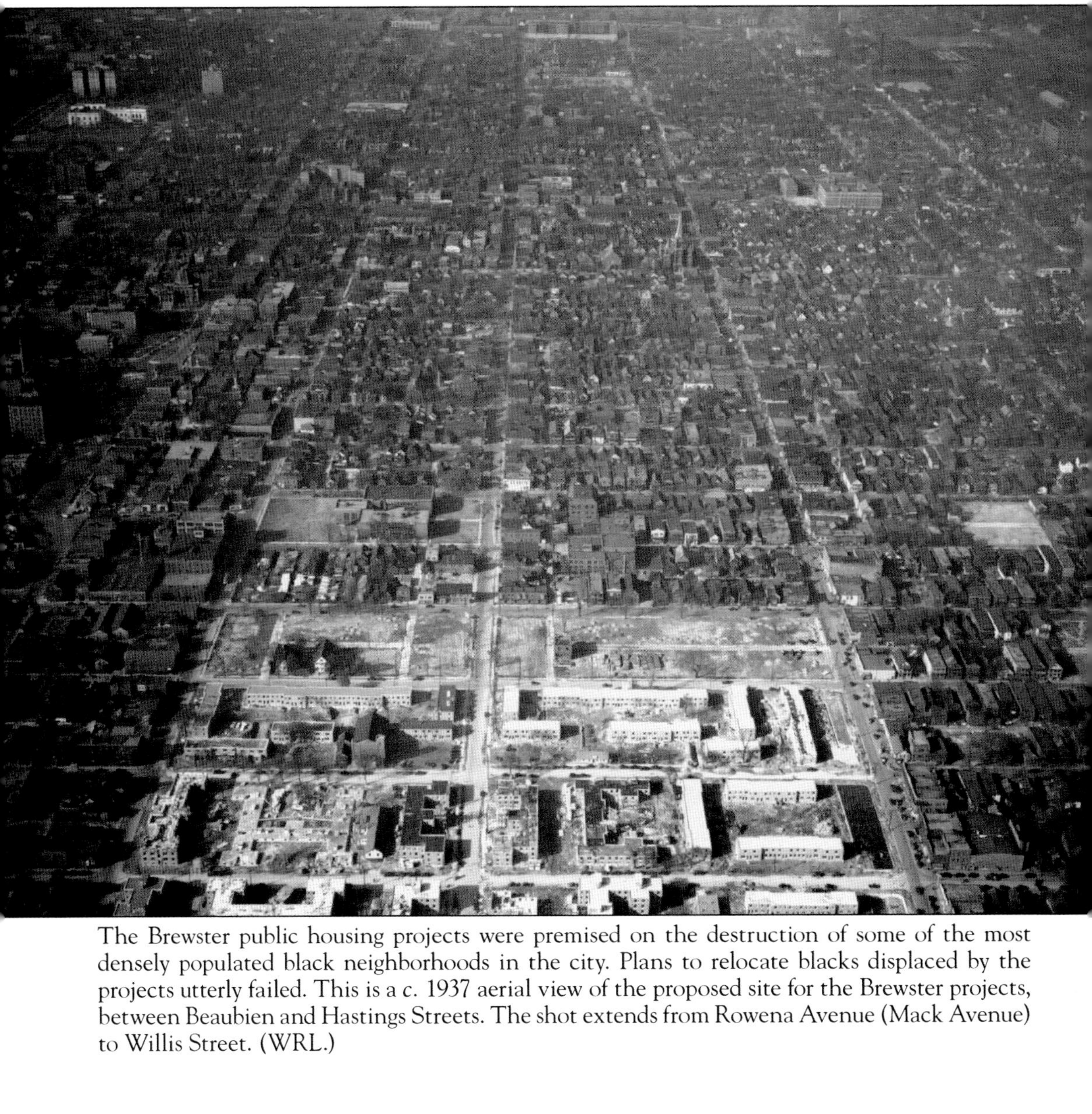

The Brewster public housing projects were premised on the destruction of some of the most densely populated black neighborhoods in the city. Plans to relocate blacks displaced by the projects utterly failed. This is a *c.* 1937 aerial view of the proposed site for the Brewster projects, between Beaubien and Hastings Streets. The shot extends from Rowena Avenue (Mack Avenue) to Willis Street. (WRL.)

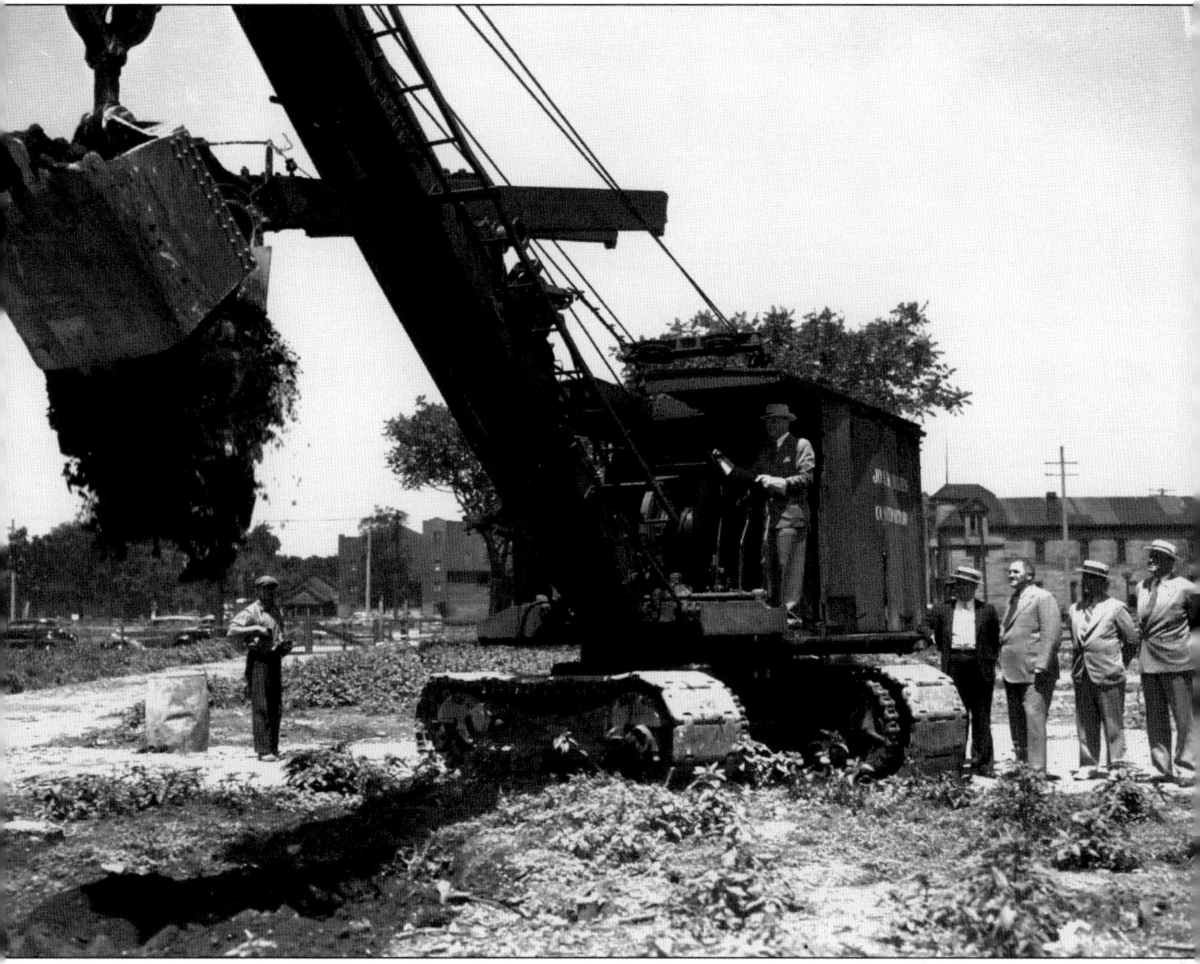

The Brewster projects were the answer to Black Bottom's housing crisis. The complex became home to Lily Tomlin, Diana Ross, Mary Wilson, Florence Ballard, and Smokey Robinson during their early years. Eddie Murphy's animated series, *The PJ's*, was based on the housing project, and it was seen in the movie *Dreamgirls*. Rap group D12's debut music video features the Brewster projects and disco superstar RuPaul mentions them in the introduction of his biggest hit, the 1992 "Supermodel (You Better Work)." This photograph was taken around 1936. (WRL.)

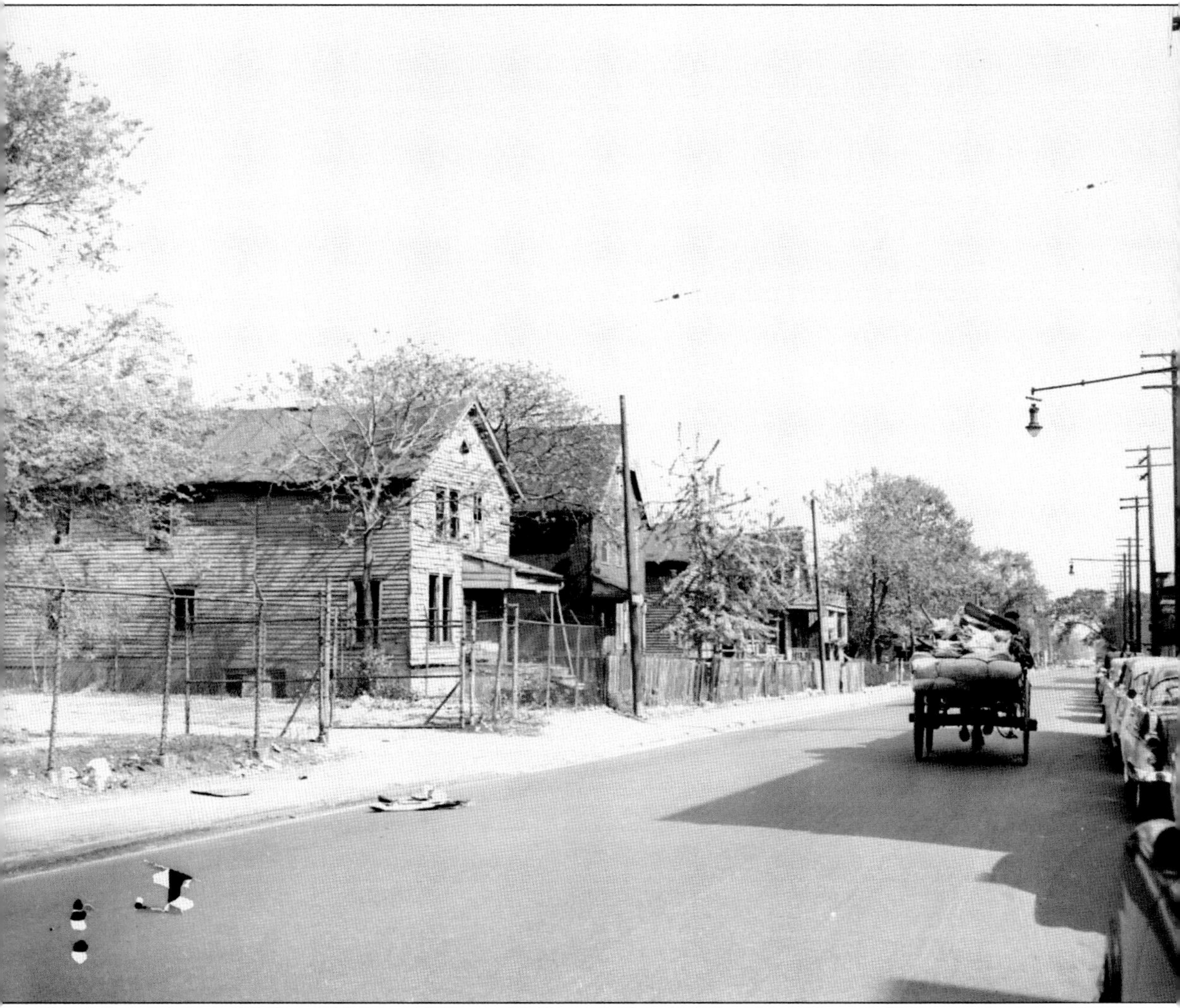

The Brewster housing project originally included over 700 low-rise structures. The combined Brewster-Douglass project was five city blocks long and three city blocks wide and housed between 8,000 and 10,000 residents at its peak capacity. To alleviate the shortage, city officials, social welfare advocates, and civil rights organizations proposed the construction of several other housing projects on open land throughout the city. This *c.* 1936 photograph shows clearance of the preexisting "slums" underway. (WRL.)

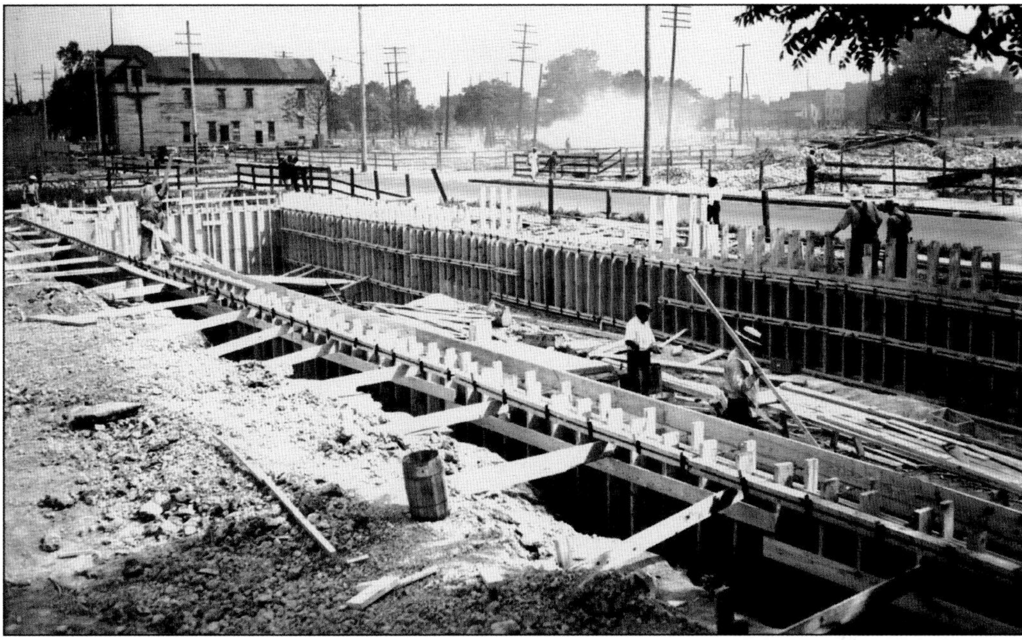

In this c. 1937 photograph, a construction site foreman discusses building plans with fellow construction workers. Pres. Franklin Roosevelt and his advisors generously spent federal dollars to create jobs and minimize the impact of the Depression. England had established a favorable and popular system of public housing, a system that served as a model for public housing in this country. (WRL.)

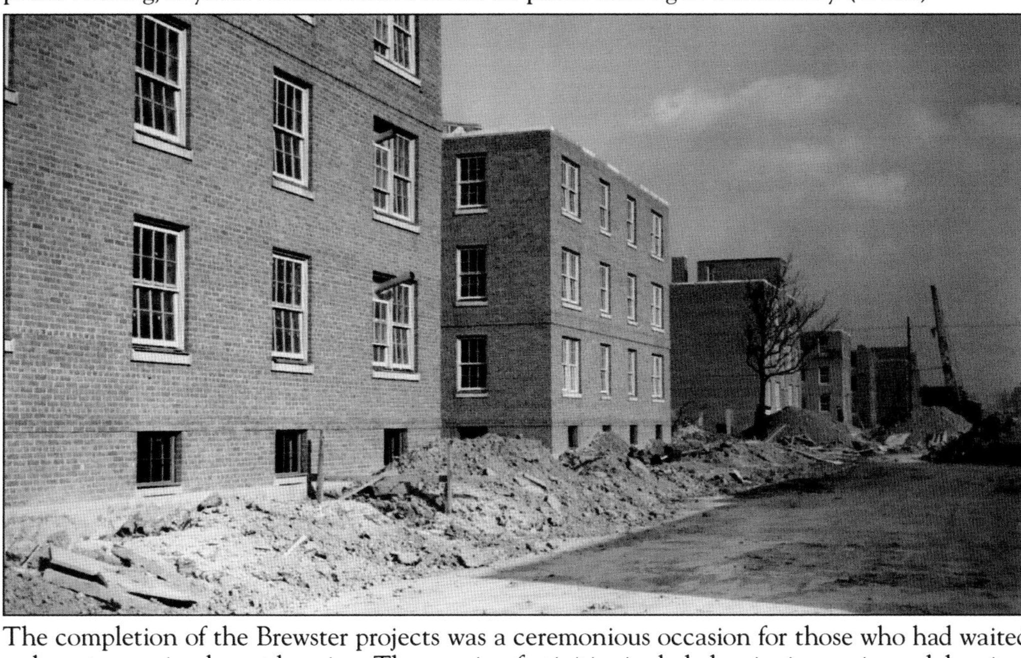

The completion of the Brewster projects was a ceremonious occasion for those who had waited so long to acquire decent housing. The ensuing festivities included a picnic, music, and dancing. The Brewster projects shortly after became home to many of Motown's hottest recording artists. Stevie Wonder and Diana Ross grew up in the "Brewsters" (as it was known), and Joe Louis began boxing at the recreation center. This c. 1937 angle shot shows the newly developed Brewster projects on Watson Street. (WRL.)

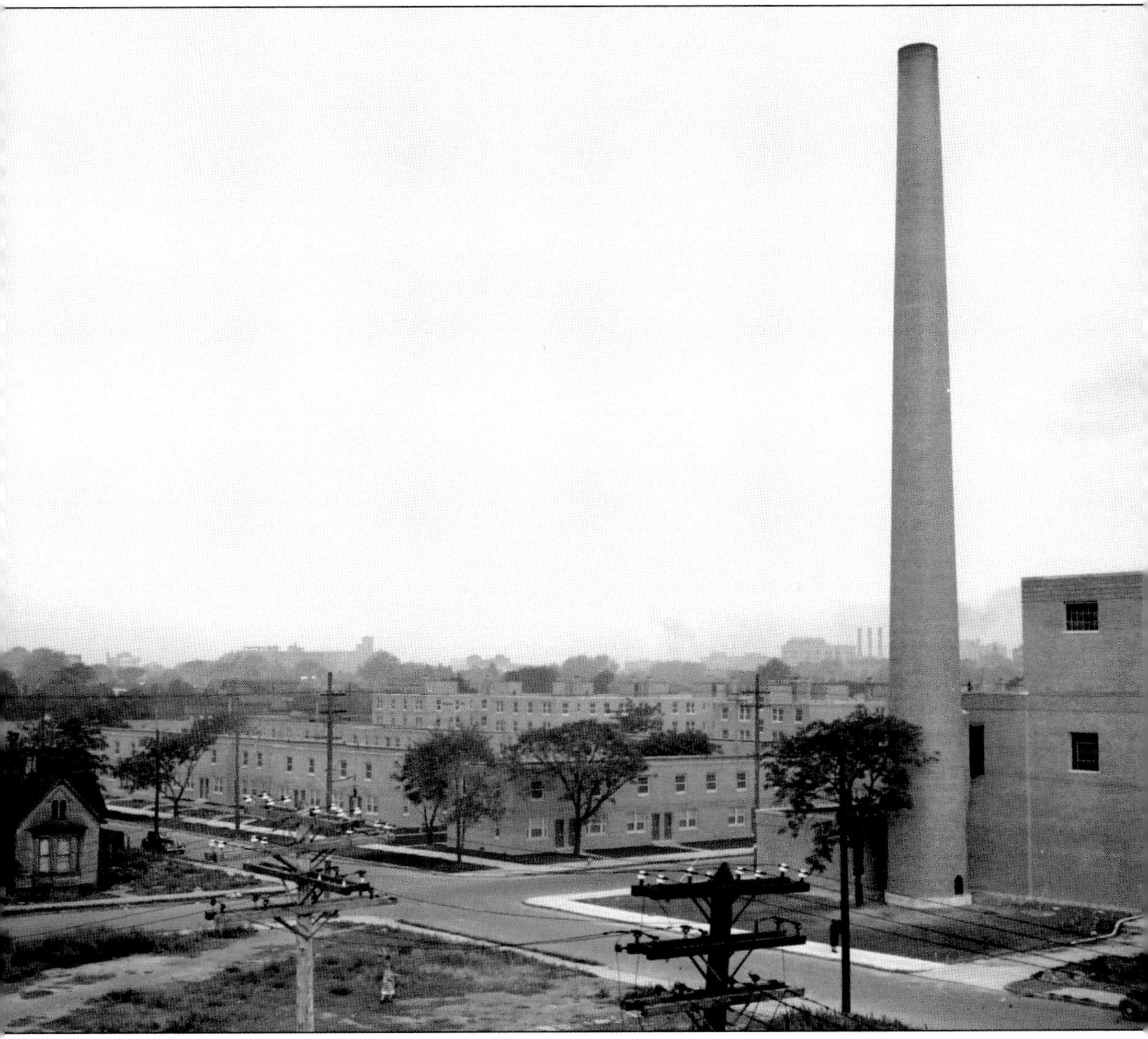

Several problems confronted the planners who wanted to build public housing for blacks. Whites were not willing to integrate housing facilities, and they secured alliances with their political leaders to block construction of nearby housing projects designated for blacks. That meant the only locations to build such homes were in black neighborhoods. Thus, the area near the intersection of Brewster and St. Antoine Streets was selected for the nation's first public housing for blacks. Mayors, contractors, builders, architects, and unemployed construction workers greatly appreciated in flow of federal dollars during the Depression since there was virtually no new private construction. This photograph was taken around 1937. (WRL.)

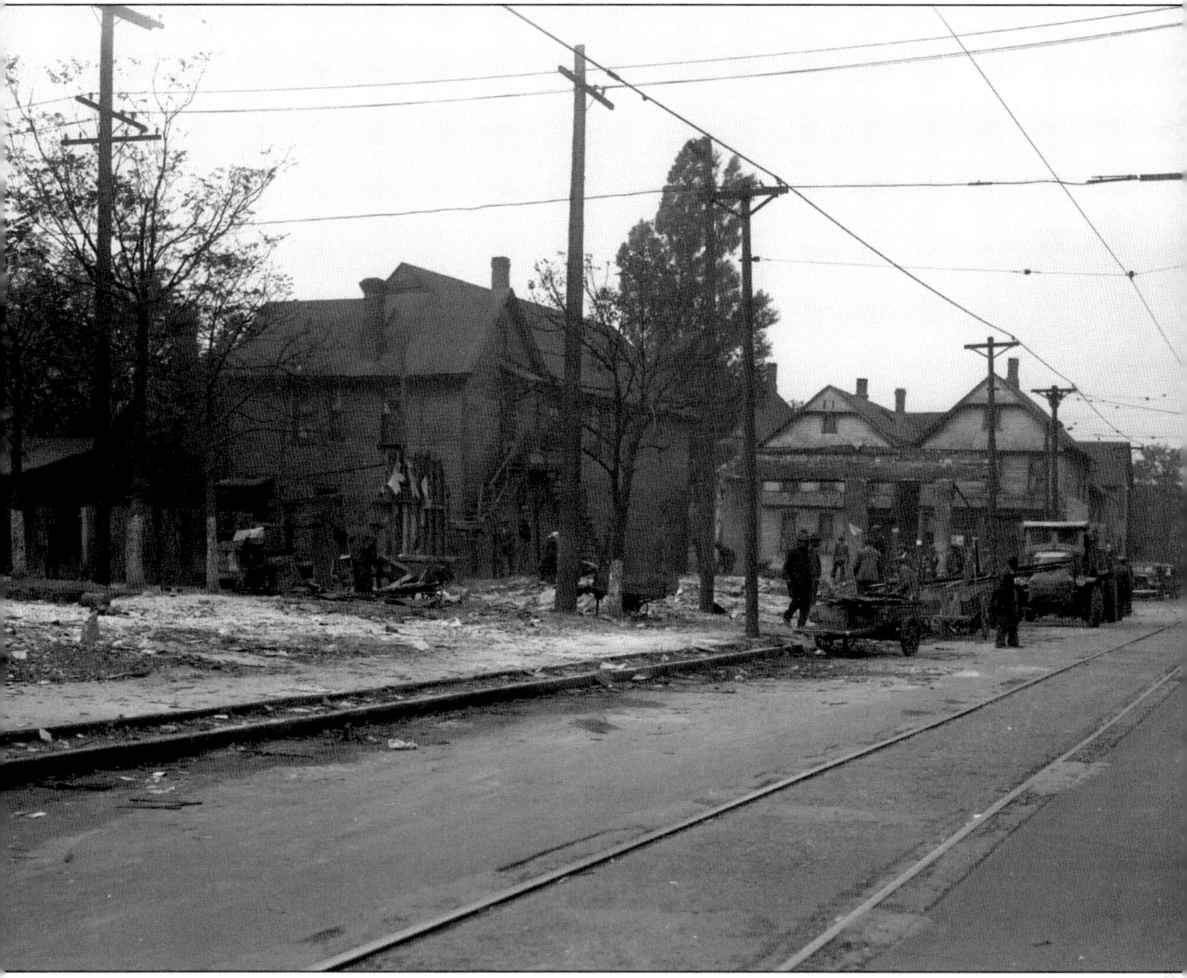

Nearby Hastings Street was demolished to make way for the Chrysler Freeway. As the slum clearance efforts progressed, Black Bottom sank into dismal and desolate conditions. Some blighted areas remained for 10 years before developers began demolition. This *c.* 1935 photograph shows the southeast corner of Eliot and St. Antoine Streets. (WRL.)

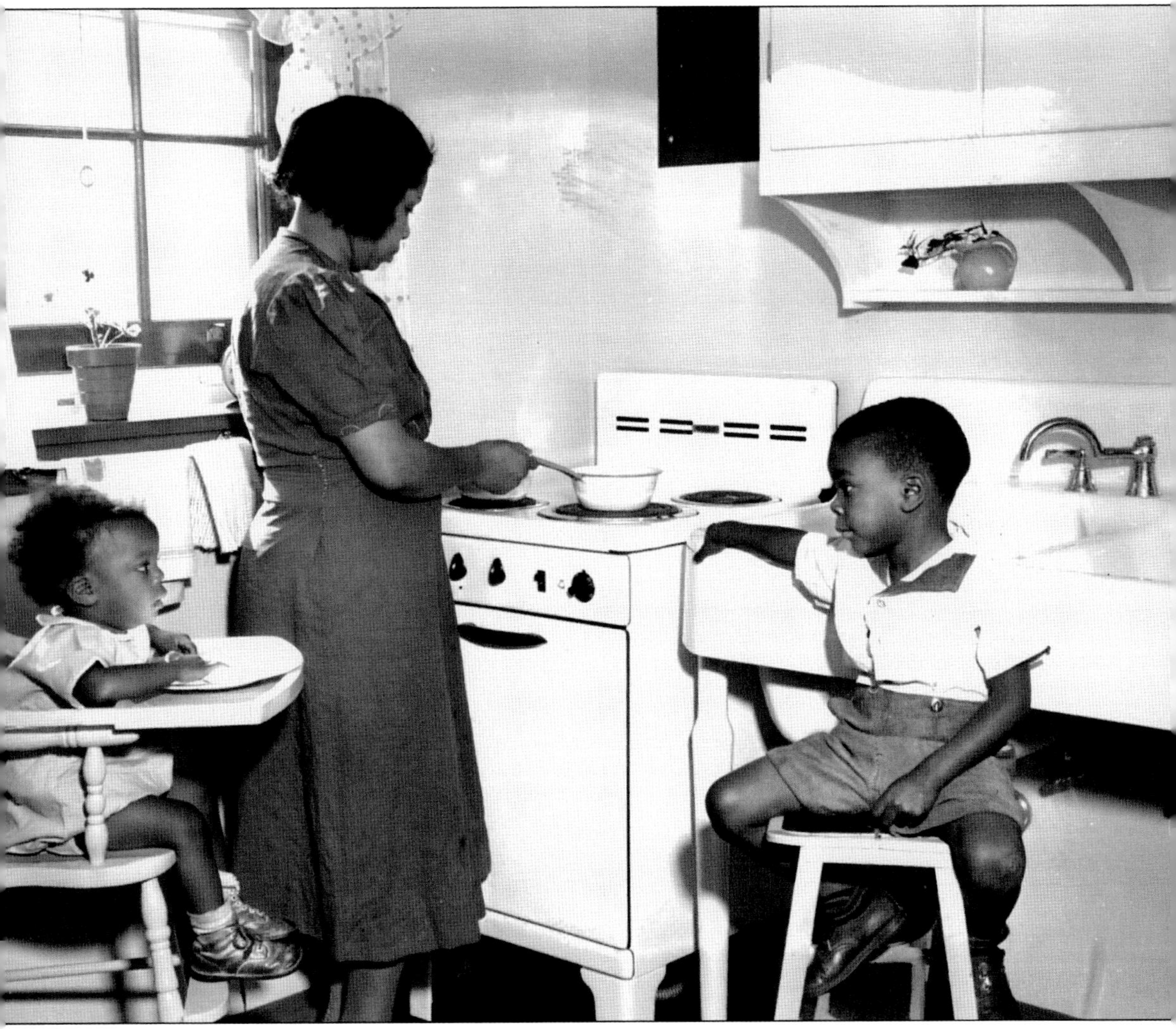

The redbrick minicity west of the Chrysler Freeway and just north of downtown became a great place for people to raise families. The criteria for residency mandated that at least one parent be employed, and unannounced housing inspections were the rule. Crime was rare, remembers Verna Slaughter. "You could leave your doors open, night and day, no problem." Another former Brewster resident recalled how "people looked out for each other. Everybody looked out for everybody else's children, and they were respected for that." Life in the Brewster projects was pretty good. Children were safe and the community thrived and prospered. Resident Allen Hughes remembered, "We pitched horseshoes, we went swimming, shot pool, we danced and we sang." This photograph was taken around 1938. (WRL.)

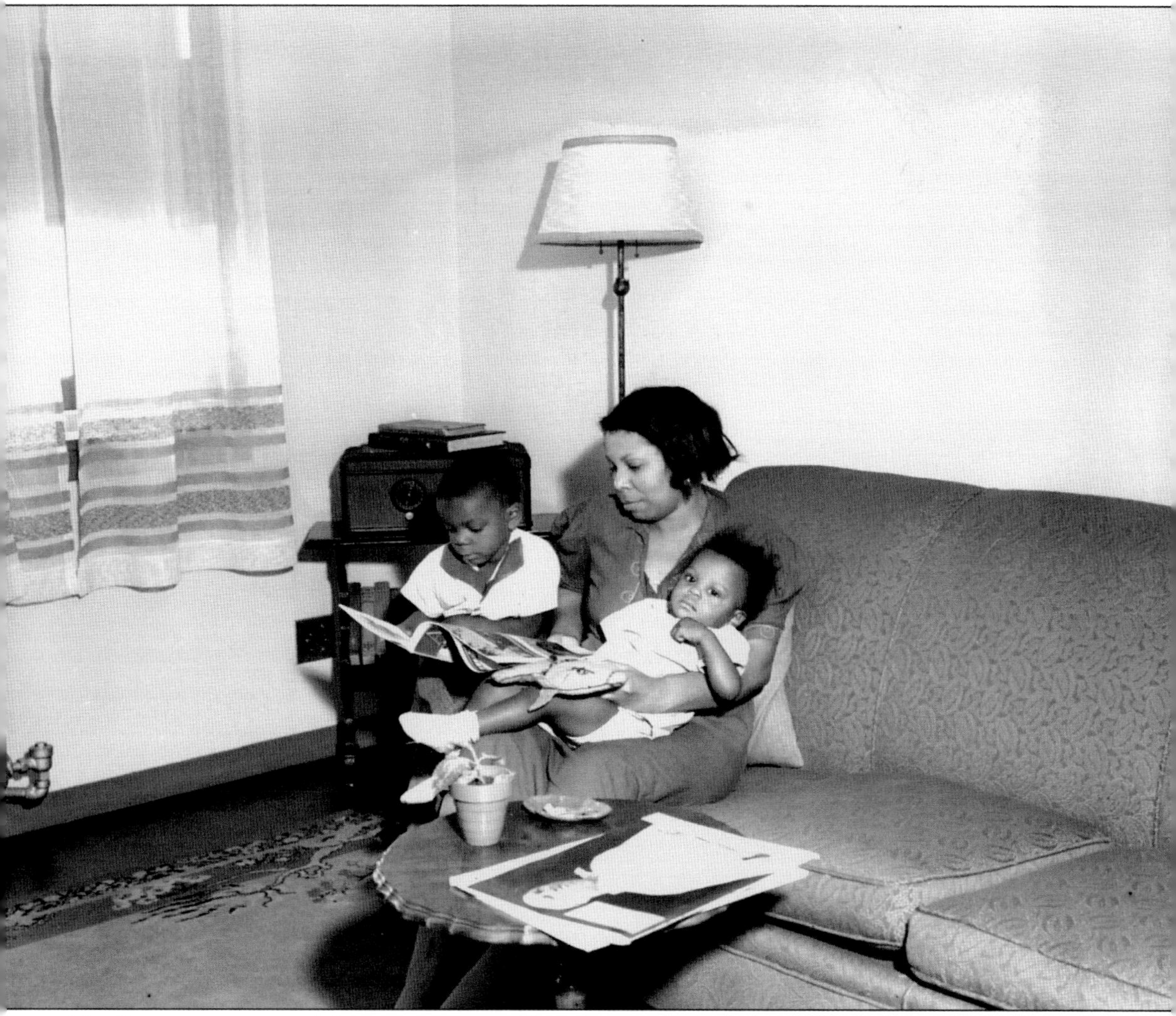

The Brewster projects did not compare to the more expensive, desirable neighborhoods where some whites lived, but it was certainly more adequate than the slums that many blacks had become accustomed to. Allen Hughes, now 53, explained, "What I'm saying is that when you're poor, you don't realize you're poor till you see how the other person is living." This *c.* 1938 photograph shows Brewster projects resident Maggie Holmes and her children. (WRL.)

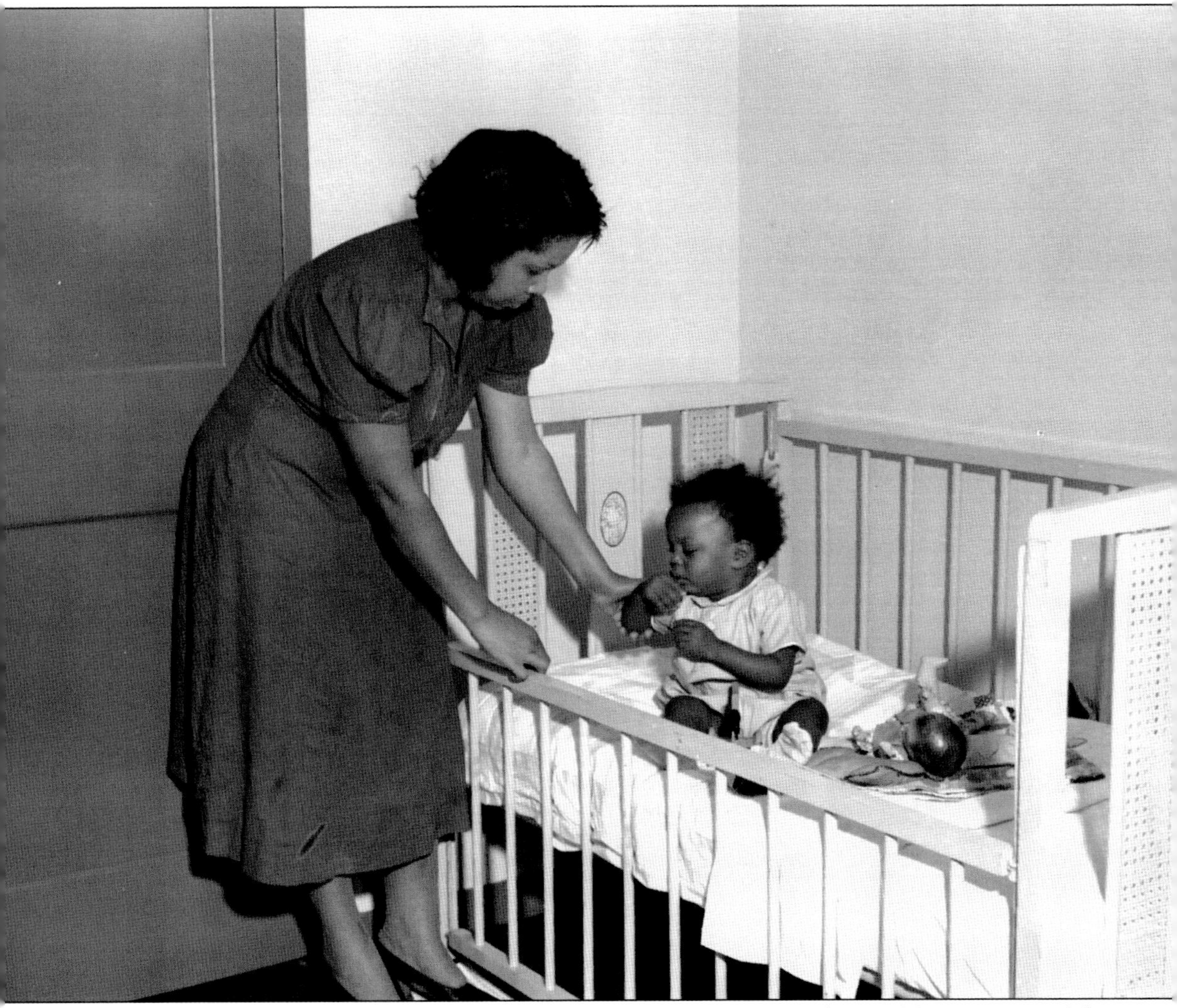

The Brewster projects were dedicated by First Lady Eleanor Roosevelt in 1935. It was one of the nation's first experiments in public housing. In this *c.* 1938 photograph, Maggie Holmes proudly tends to her toddler. Early residents were largely working-class; nevertheless, many were able to see their children grow up to attend college. The original Brewster Homes were demolished in 1991 and the development was replaced by 250 townhouses. (WRL.)

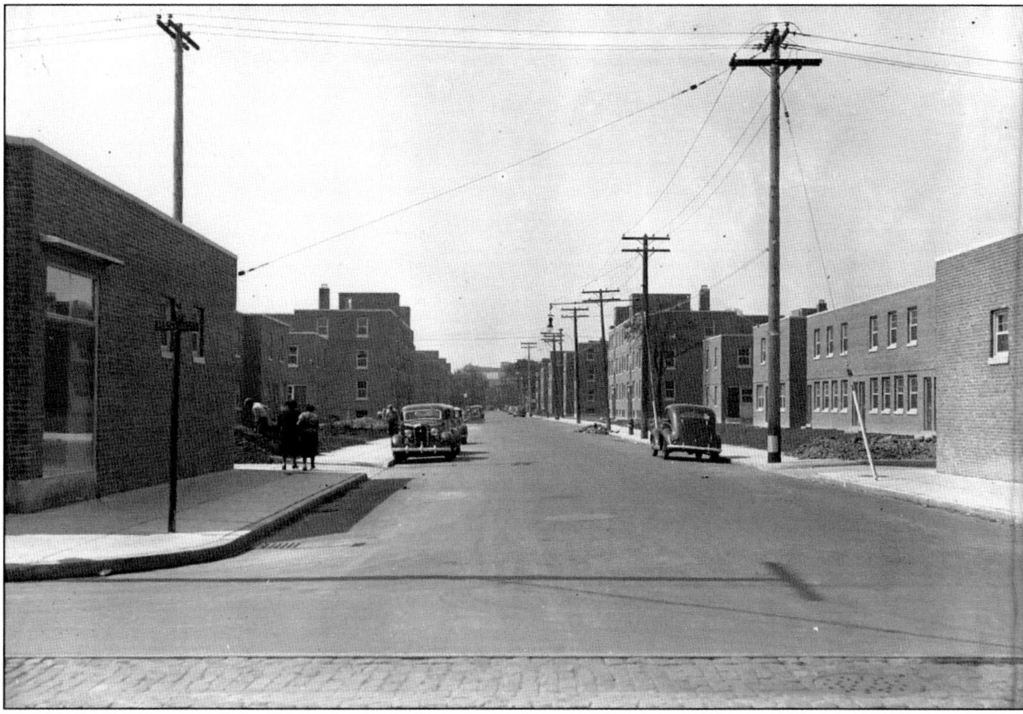

The original Brewster projects comprised two-story row houses and three-story apartment buildings. When the Douglass projects were built adjacent in 1952, 14-story high-rises had been added to the mix. In this c. 1938 photograph, two women walk past the construction site of the Brewster housing project near the corner of Hastings Street. (WRL.)

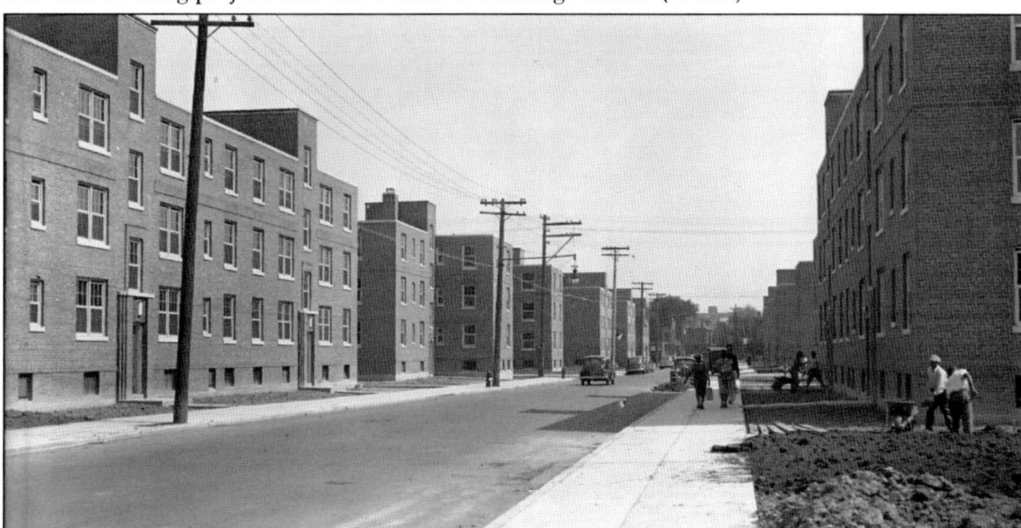

When construction crews completed the Brewster projects in 1941, there were 941 units bounded by Beaubien, Hastings, and Wilkins Streets and Mack Avenue. Residents were required to be employed, and there were limits on what they could earn. Former residents described Brewster as a "community filled with families that displayed love, respect, and concern for everyone in a beautiful, clean, and secure neighborhood." This c. 1939 photograph shows women walking near the Brewster housing project construction site. (BHC.)

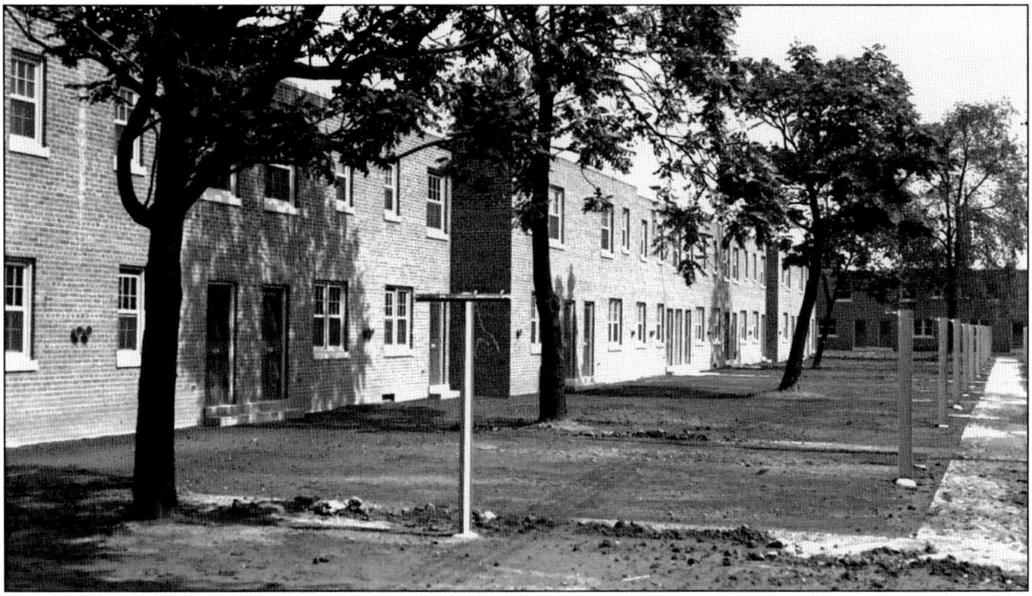

A former Detroit police lieutenant who grew up in the Brewster projects said, "I can tell you this from my own experience: That when I moved to the projects [at age 13 in 1950], I felt it was like dying and going to heaven." Residents enjoyed green lawns, flowers, and intact families, as well as a sense of pride and honor. "The people of the surrounding areas thought we were the elites," said Barbara Battle Hunt, a 73-year-old former resident. "They say, 'Here come one of those snooty project girls.'" This *c.* 1939 photograph shows a backyard area. (BHC.)

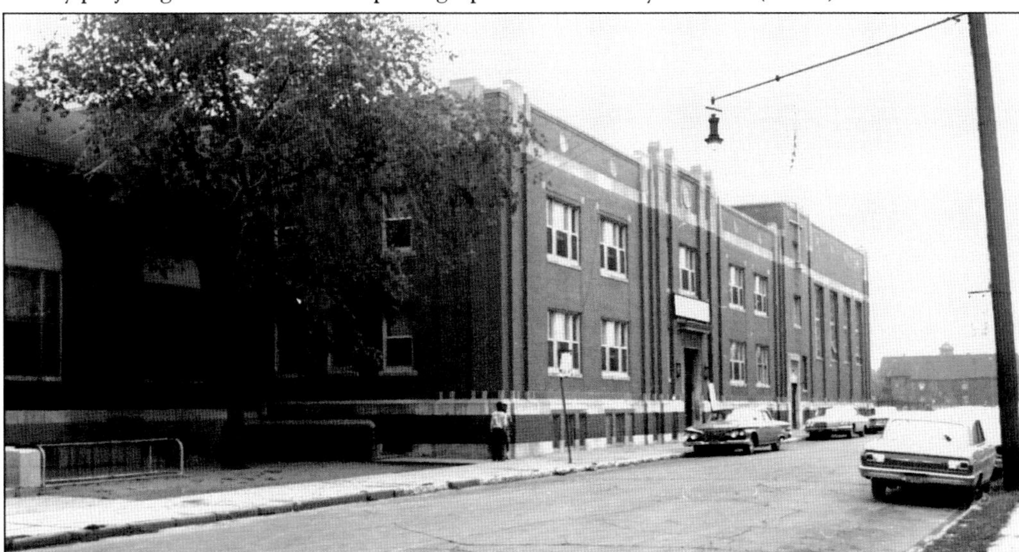

This 1965 photograph shows the Brewster-Douglass Homes Recreation Center, located at 2700 St. Antoine Street and 527 West Street. After the riots of 1943 and 1967, the Brewster projects underwent change. By 1950, many of the "elite" families were on the move—moving into more affluent areas. Former resident, 73-year-old Frances Hodge, recalled "They started moving in welfare people that really didn't have the interest in keeping up the apartments." Marilyn Richardson Jackson, age 50, said, "'Poor' has taken on a whole new connotation: low morale, on the welfare, broken homes, dirty, children born out of wedlock." (WRL.)

Five

ELEANOR ROOSEVELT VISITS BLACK BOTTOM

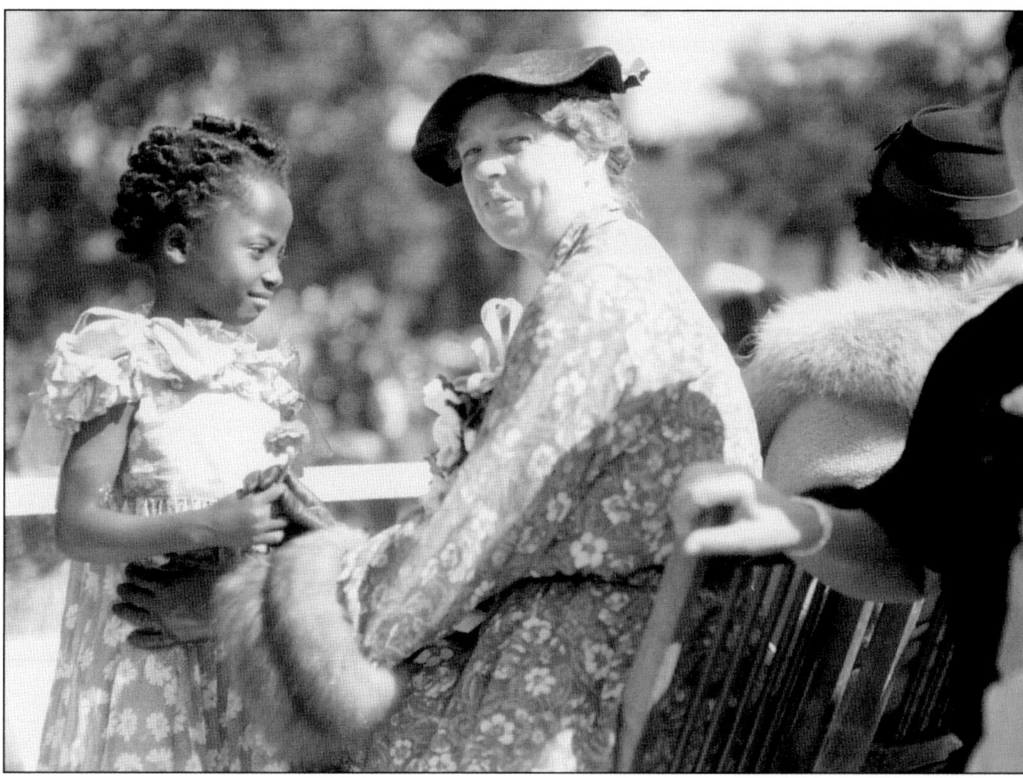

On September 9, 1935, the Black Bottom community gathered at 651 Benton Street for a the Black Bottom street pageant festival to initiate the building of the Brewster Homes, the first federally funded housing project designed for blacks. Here Eleanor Roosevelt poses with Black Bottom resident Geraldine Walker. Roosevelt visited Black Bottom for the opening of the slum clearance project at 651 Benton Street. (WRL.)

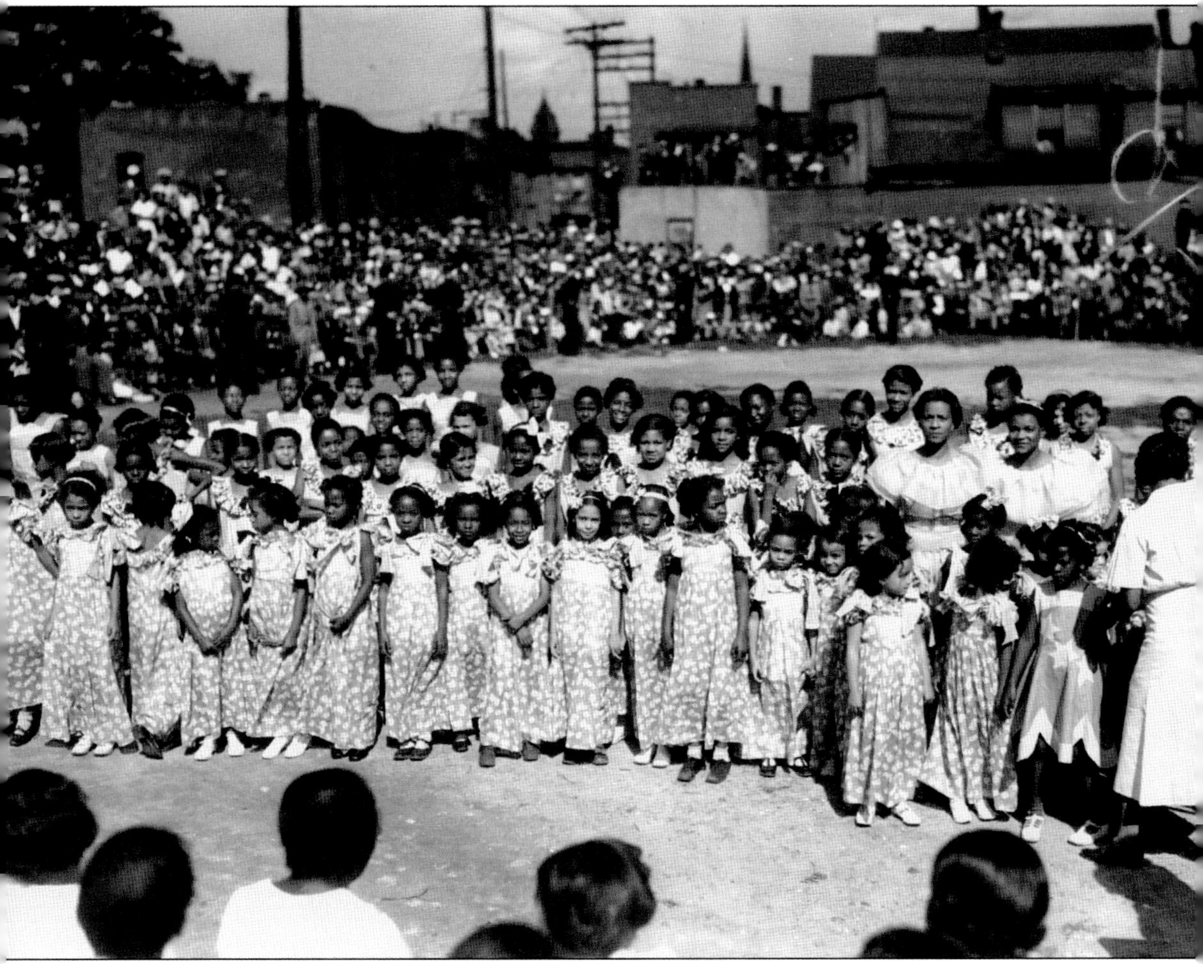

The historical marker describing the Brewster projects reads "Between 1910 and 1940 Detroit, Michigan's black population increased dramatically. Faced with restrictions on where they could live, many African Americans were forced into substandard housing. In 1935 First Lady Eleanor Roosevelt broke ground for the Brewster Homes, the nation's first federally funded public housing development for blacks. The homes opened in 1938 with 701 units." Here a group of children perform for First Lady Eleanor Roosevelt and city housing officials. African Americans responded favorably to Eleanor Roosevelt because she actively fought against racism and embraced a civil rights agenda. She believed in equal rights and quality education for everyone regardless of race, and the struggle for human rights became her top public priority. (WRL.)

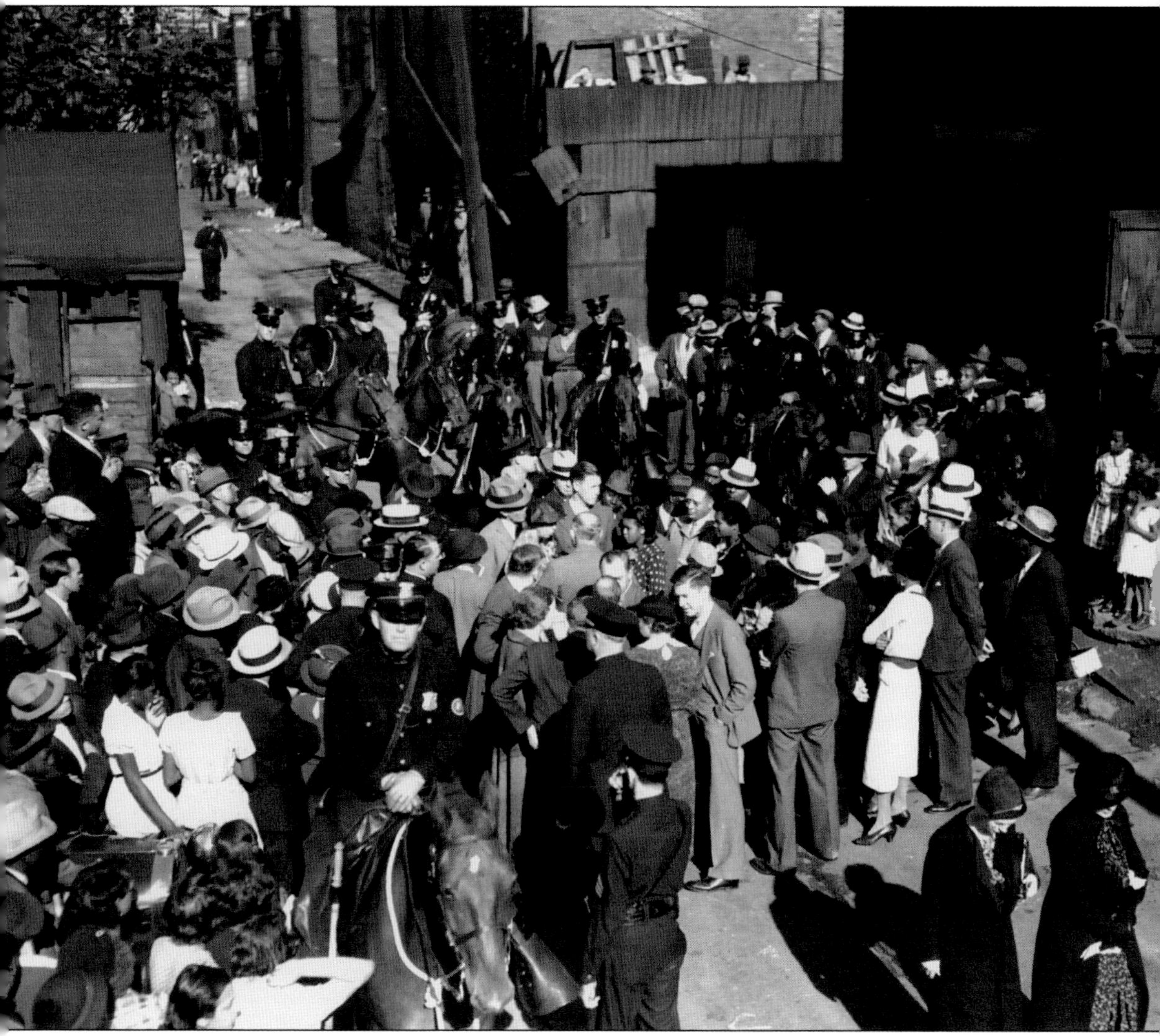

White Detroiters visited the Black Bottom festival for a chance to see Roosevelt, around 1935. Whites rarely ventured into the Black Bottom community, although Paradise Valley was a popular destination for its jazz and blues joints, soul food, and scandalous-at-the-time interracial sexual encounters. By 1938, 701 Brewster projects units were ready for occupancy, and when construction was completed three years later, there were 941 homes. (WRL.)

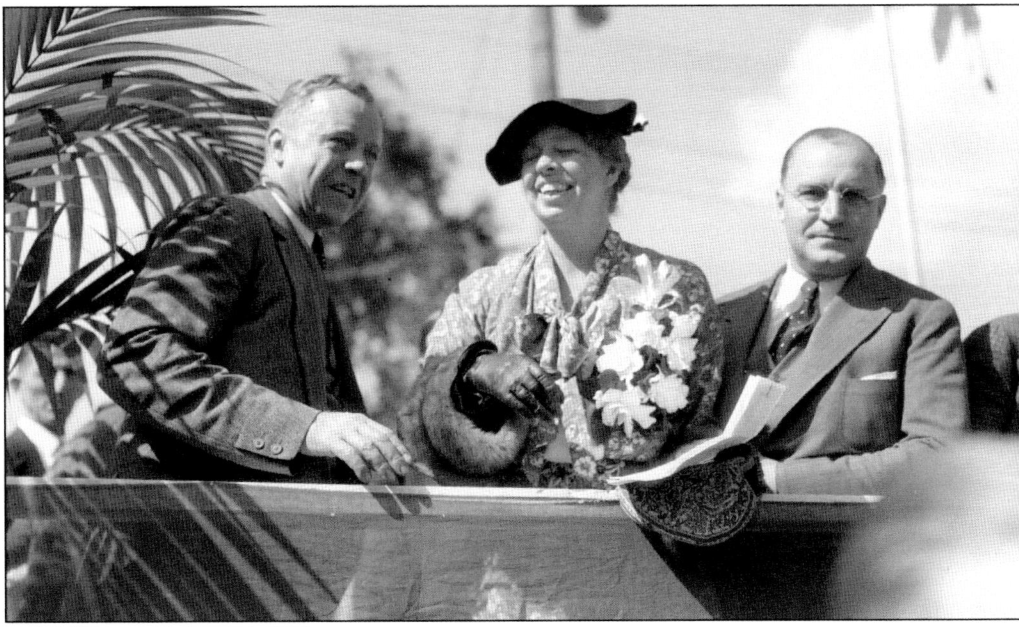

"Wherever the standard of education is low, the standard of living is low," Eleanor Roosevelt once said, urging states to address the inequities in public school funding. The black newspapers praised her efforts and deeds to better the lives of black people. In this c. 1935 photograph, First Lady Roosevelt attends the slum clearance project at 651 Benton Street with Detroit superintendent Fred Frahm (left) and her younger brother G. Hall Roosevelt. (WRL.)

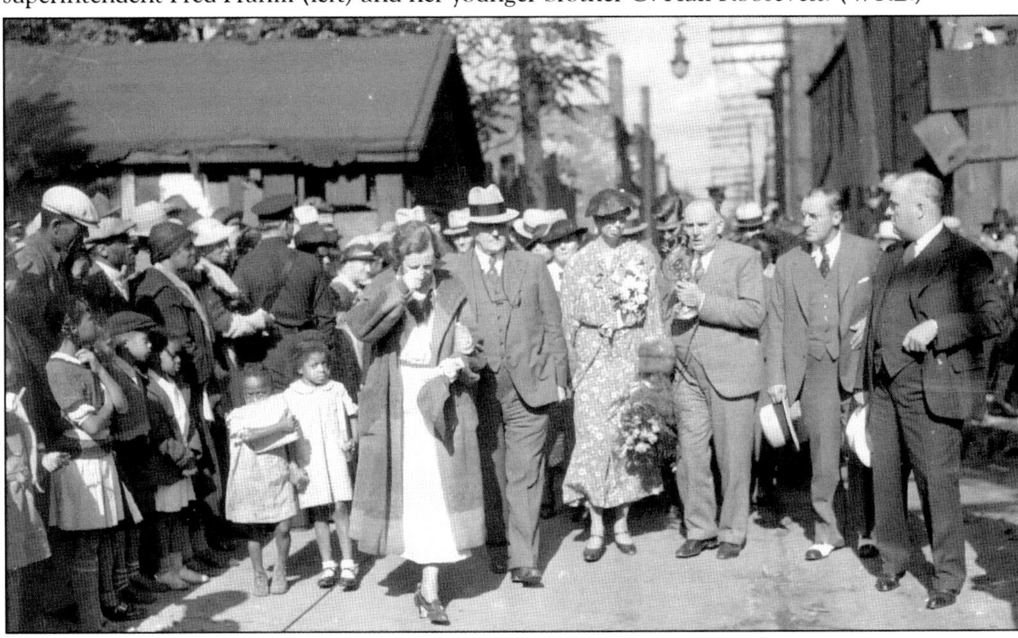

Mary McLeod Bethune helped to shape Roosevelt's understanding of the problems facing blacks. She brought lists of requests for the First Lady's intervention when the two met and often sent reports, novels, and other reading material to Roosevelt's attention. The two remained friends and Roosevelt called Bethune her closest friend. In this c. 1935 photograph, First Lady Roosevelt joins other city officials on a tour of Black Bottom. (WRL.)

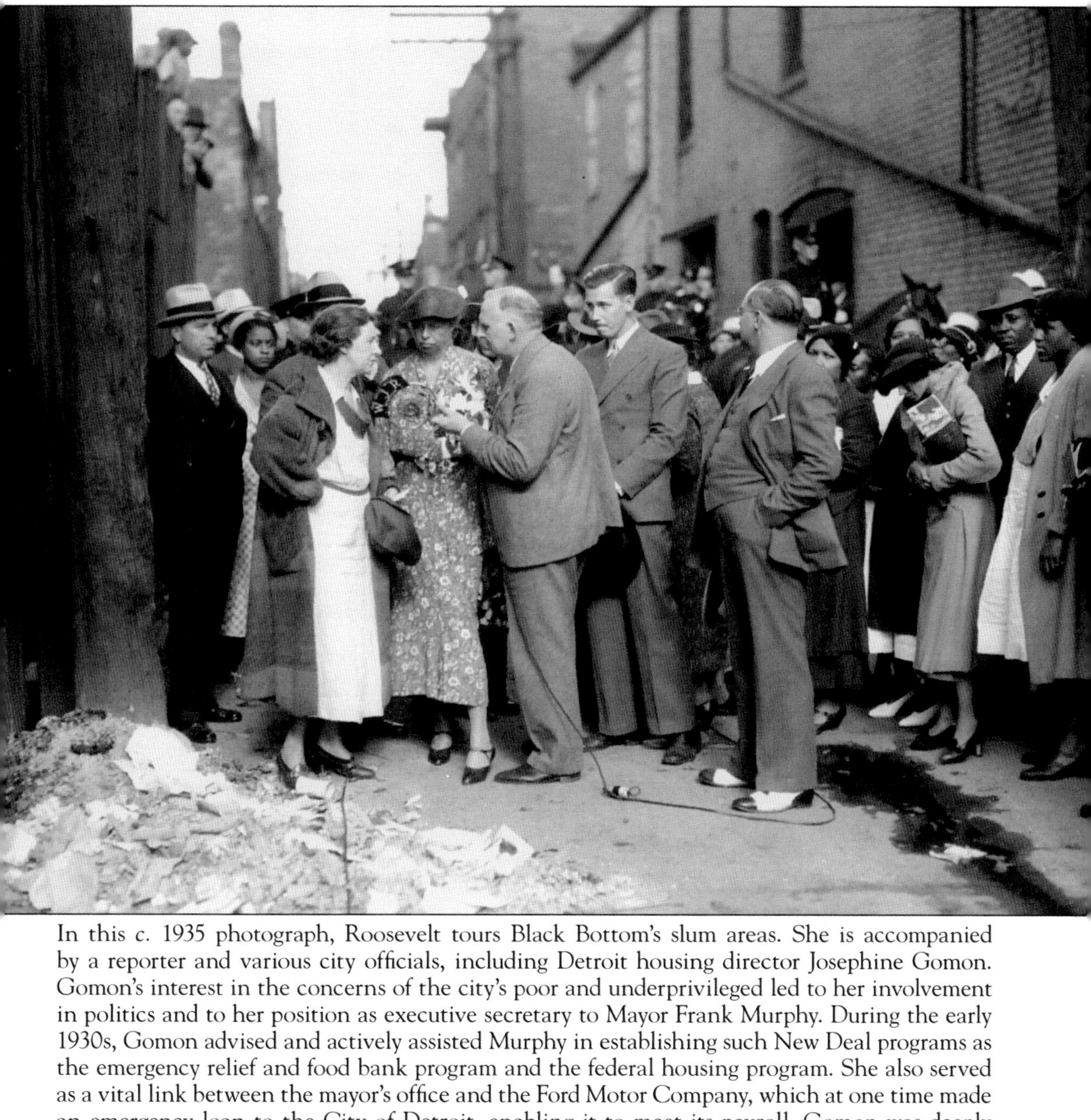

In this c. 1935 photograph, Roosevelt tours Black Bottom's slum areas. She is accompanied by a reporter and various city officials, including Detroit housing director Josephine Gomon. Gomon's interest in the concerns of the city's poor and underprivileged led to her involvement in politics and to her position as executive secretary to Mayor Frank Murphy. During the early 1930s, Gomon advised and actively assisted Murphy in establishing such New Deal programs as the emergency relief and food bank program and the federal housing program. She also served as a vital link between the mayor's office and the Ford Motor Company, which at one time made an emergency loan to the City of Detroit, enabling it to meet its payroll. Gomon was deeply involved in serving the cause of social justice within the community in other ways as well; she was a founding member of the American Civil Liberties Union in Michigan and worked closely with Clarence Darrow on several Detroit-based civil liberties cases. She also became an advisor to Franklin Roosevelt. (WRL.)

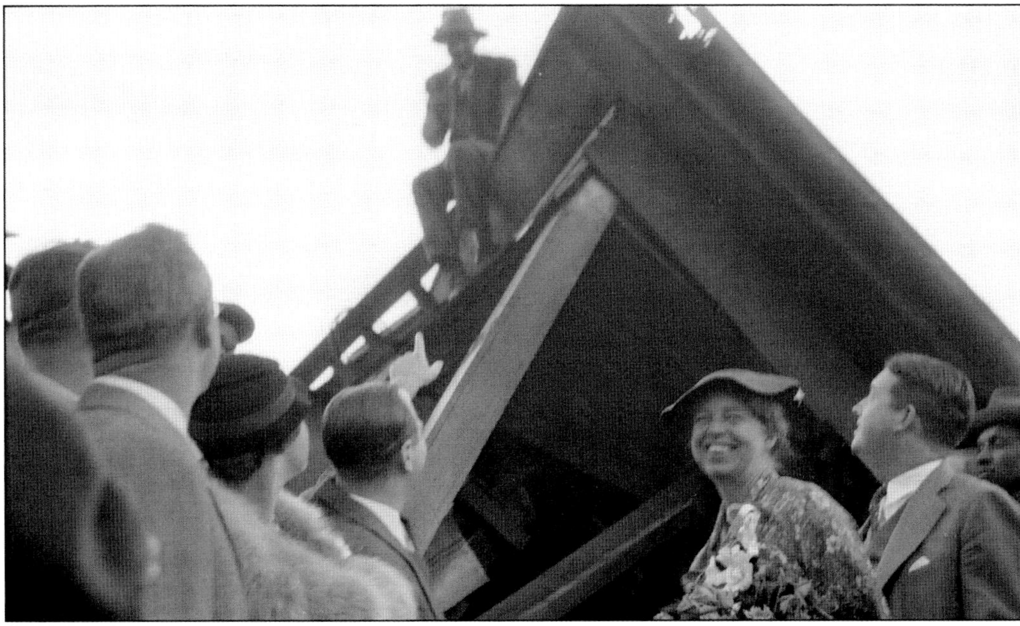

In *The Moral Basis of Democracy*, Eleanor Roosevelt asserted that people of all races have inviolate rights to "some property." She insisted that education, housing, and employment were basic human rights that society had a moral and political obligation to provide. "This means achieving an economic level below which no one is permitted to fall, and keeping a fairly stable balance between that level and the standard of living." This photograph was taken on September 9, 1935. (WRL.)

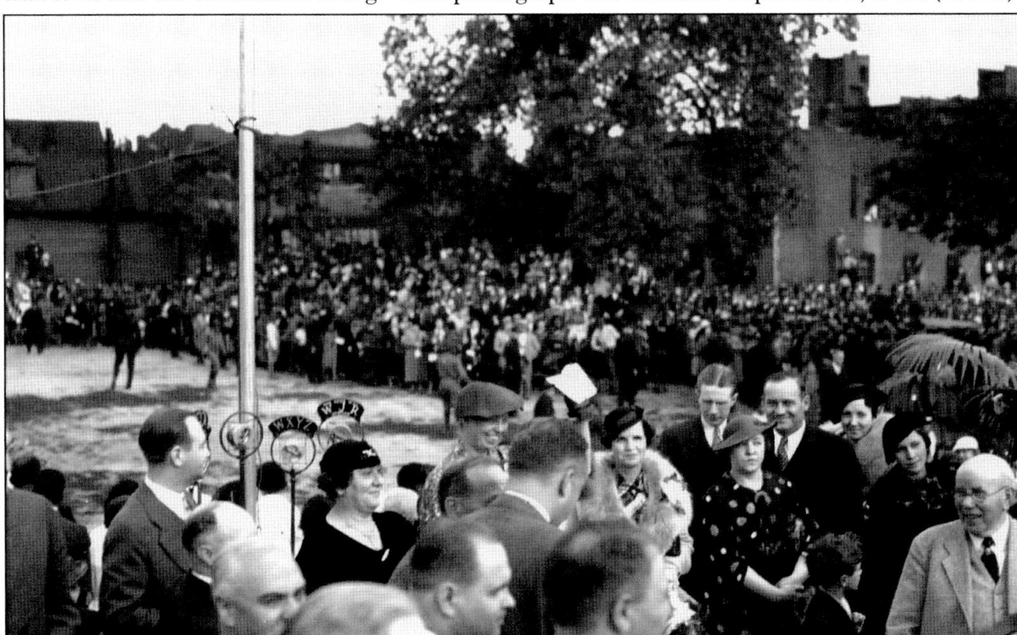

In a 1942 article in the *New Republic*, Roosevelt noted, "One of the main destroyers of freedom is our attitude toward the colored race." What Rudyard Kipling called the "White Man's Burden," she said in the *American Magazine*, is "one of the things we cannot have any longer." In this c. 1935 photograph, Roosevelt stands among a crowd of people, smiling and waving. (WRL.)

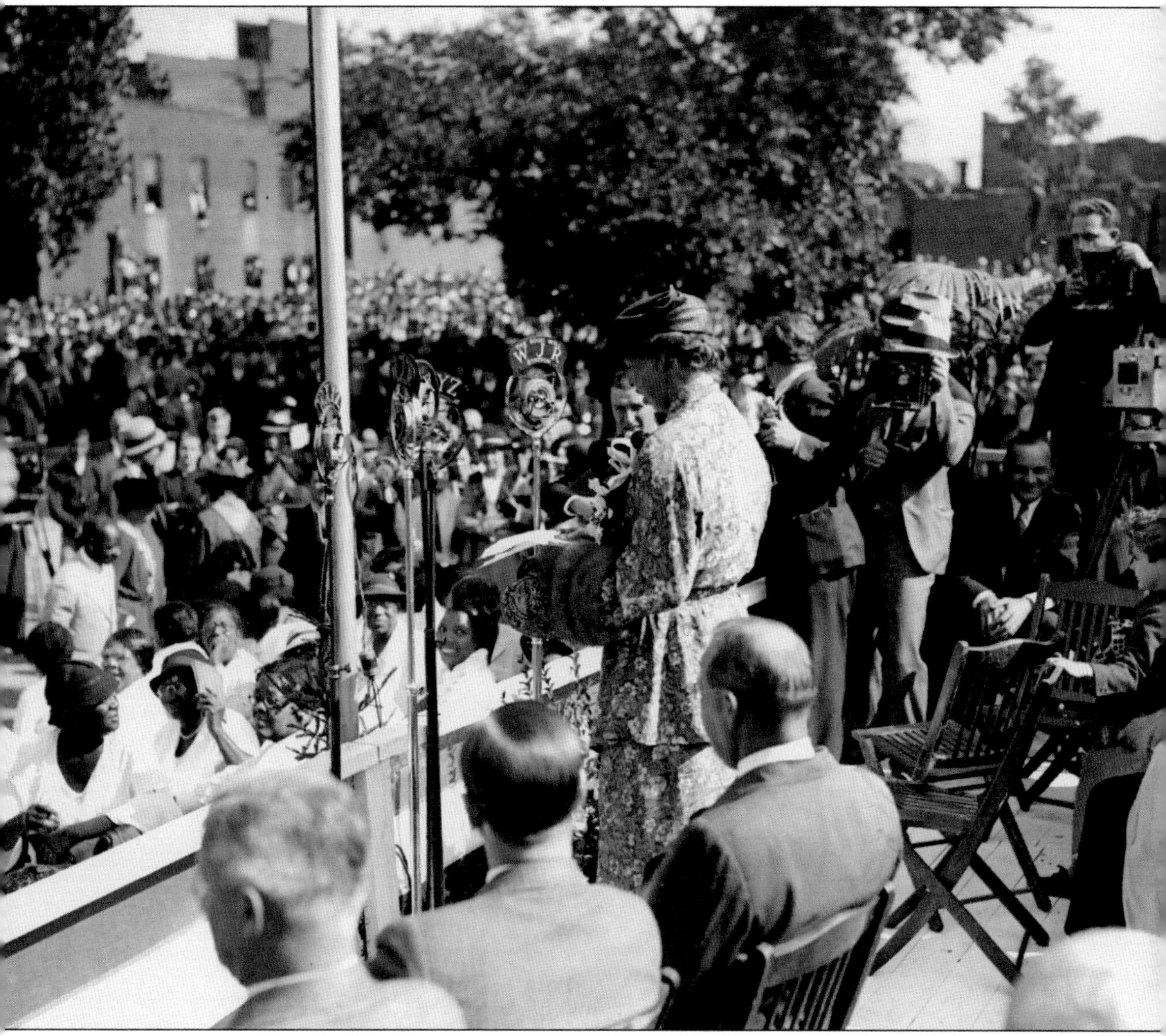

When white America refused to see how segregation mocked American values, Roosevelt addressed this issue sternly and directly: "We have never been willing to face this problem, to line it up with the basic, underlying beliefs in Democracy." Oftentimes, Roosevelt's outspoken attitude toward civil rights created tensions within the wartime White House. When Detroit erupted in flames after black families moved into the projects, many in the White House blamed Roosevelt for the riot, agreeing with the southern press that "it is blood on your hands, Mrs. Roosevelt." While touring the Pacific, Eleanor did not let the Detroit riot affect her efforts. She was photographed visiting wounded black soldiers. She returned home and continued to support various integration efforts. The *Alabama Sun* devoted an entire issue to "Eleanor and Some Niggers." In this *c.* 1935 photograph, Roosevelt speaks to a crowd of people at the Black Bottom street pageant festival at 651 Benton Street. (WRL.)

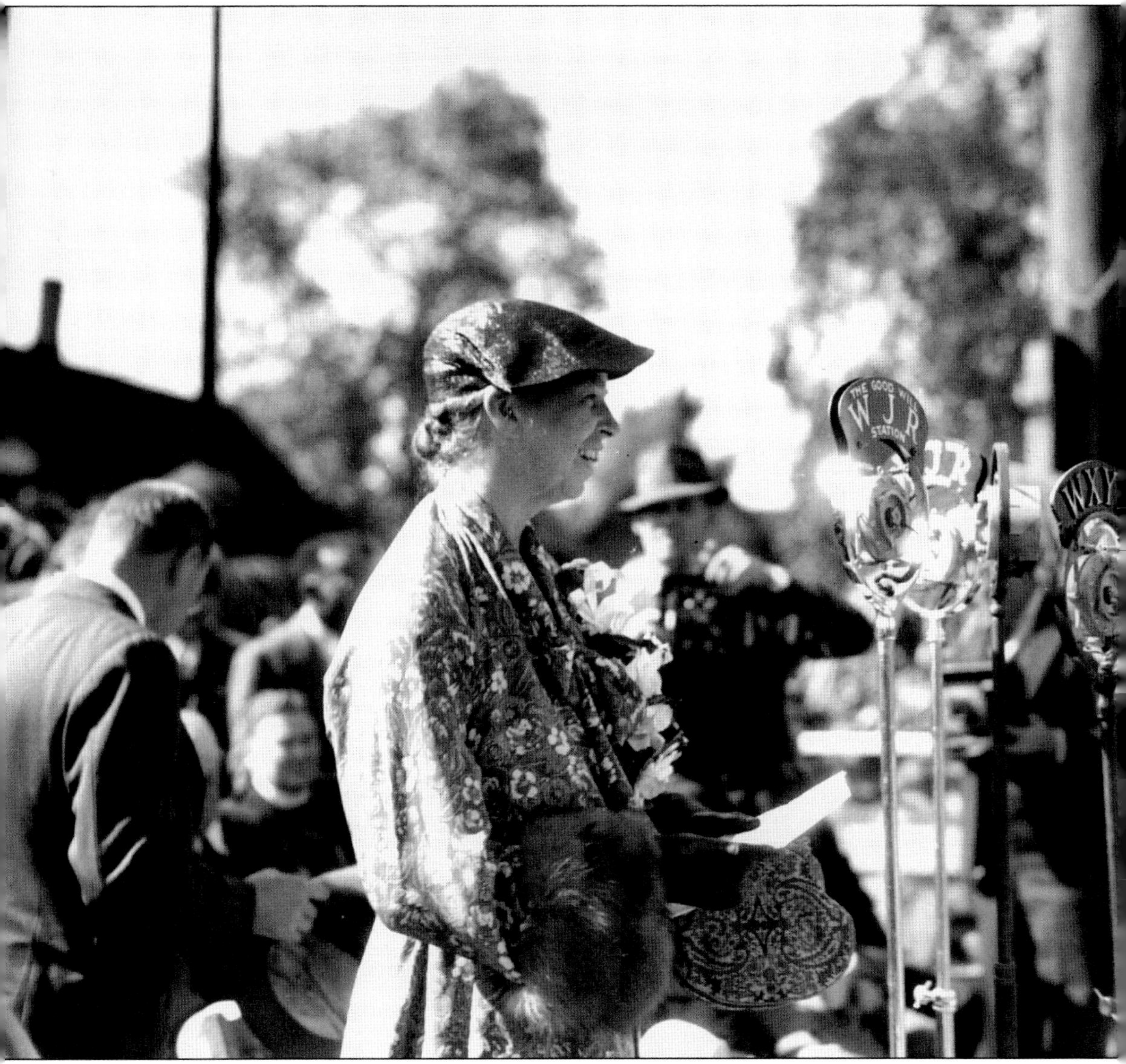

Eleanor Roosevelt made many enemies by supporting civil rights initiatives. In an interview on Roosevelt's legacy, Vernon Jarrett said, "I presume that the worst attacks on Eleanor Roosevelt came in the wake of the Detroit riots, beginning in 1942 and culminating in that awful scene in 1943. Eleanor Roosevelt had urged the introduction of blacks into the Sojourner Truth Housing Project in Detroit. Now incidentally, the housing project was named after an African American heroine, Sojourner Truth." In this photograph, First Lady Roosevelt speaks into a group of microphones at the groundbreaking ceremony for the Brewster projects. It is from around 1935. (WRL.)

Six

SCHOOLS, CHURCHES, AND ORGANIZATIONS

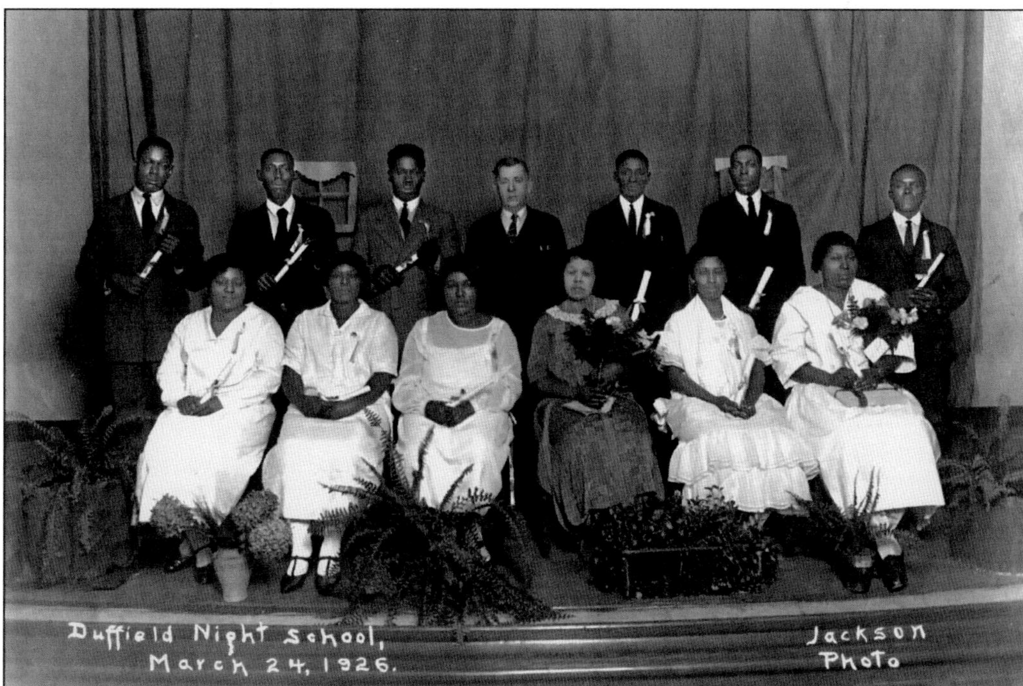

Persistent social inequity made it difficult for black citizens to obtain education toward societal advancement. Many classrooms, some holding more than 100 children, had no desks or blackboards. Some black teachers received one-tenth the pay rate of white teachers. Few black communities could raise enough money to keep schools open or to improve those already in operation. Some adults entered night classes in efforts to gain job opportunities. This c. 1926 photograph depicts night school students holding diplomas; the teacher stands at the center. (BHC.)

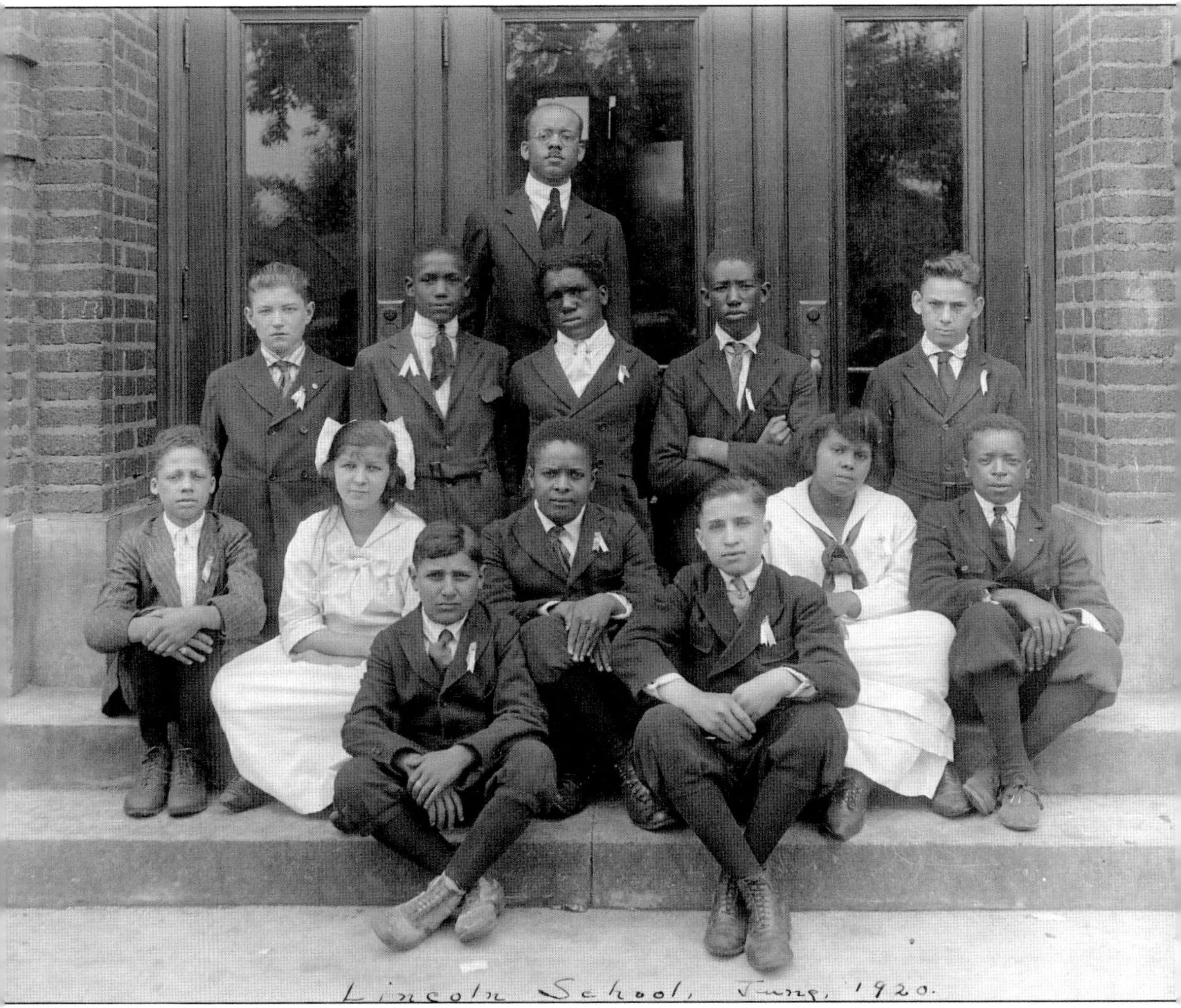

By 1940, teenagers were much more likely to go to high school than adolescents in earlier decades. Many teenagers from working-class families used to go to work after eighth grade, but during the Depression of the 1930s, things happened to make all American teenagers more likely to attend high school for at least a few years. Since jobs were scarce during the 1930s, adults took many jobs that teens used to get. Also attendance in high school was made mandatory by law for 14 and 15 year olds. As educational opportunities opened for Black Bottom residents, many entered surrounding schools like Duffield, Lincoln, and Miller. In this c. 1920 photograph, 12 students, 2 girls, the rest boys, and a black male teacher pose on the front steps of Lincoln School building. Students have ribbons pinned on their left shoulders. (BHC.)

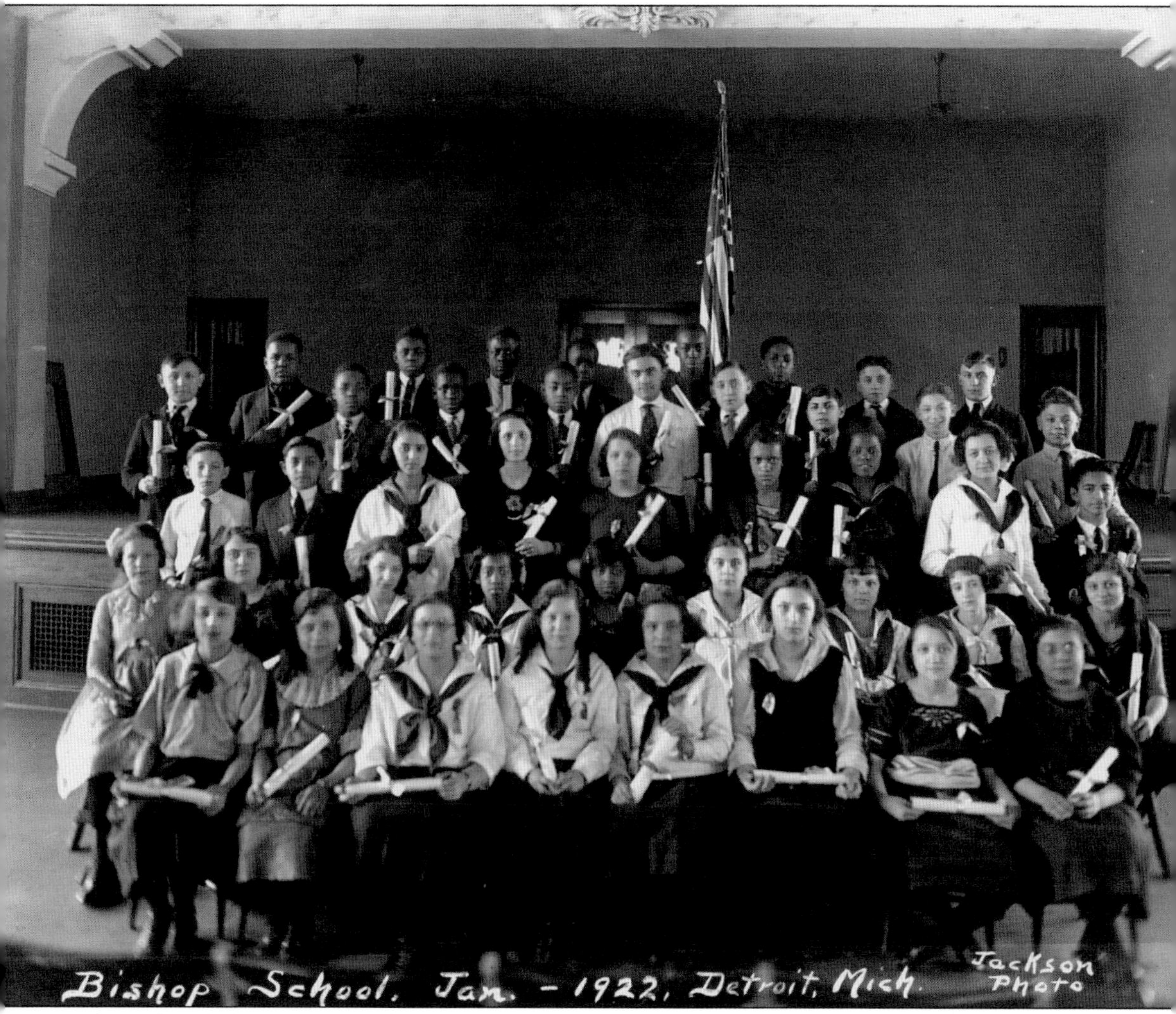

Kids in the Black Bottom neighborhood went to Miller, Eastern, Bishop, and Duffield schools. All the kids, white and black, were from the same economic background on the east side. Miller High School was on Dubois Street, and it had 1,997 students in 1940. Notice this c. 1922 class photograph has both white and black students assembled in front of the stage, students in the front are seated, students in the back are standing, and all are holding rolled up diplomas tied with a ribbon. An American flag stands in the background. (BHC.)

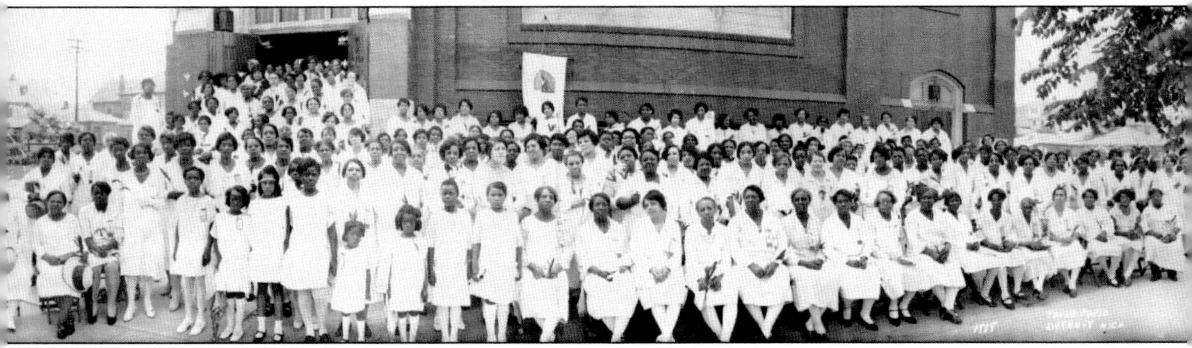

With Black Bottom's population growing rapidly as a result of the burgeoning war industries, black leadership faced the challenge of facilitating the transformation of the rural uneducated southern agricultural worker into the expanding urban industrial metropolis. The black church served as a vital resource center for Detroit and Black Bottom's black community. Detroit's black migration dilemma encouraged some black ministers to start churches. Therefore any examination of black social, political, and cultural strivings must begin with the black church. By 1941, Detroit's Bethel African Methodist Episcopal (AME) Church, Second Baptist Church, and the Detroit Urban League would prove to be major resource centers for the Black Bottom community. (BHC.)

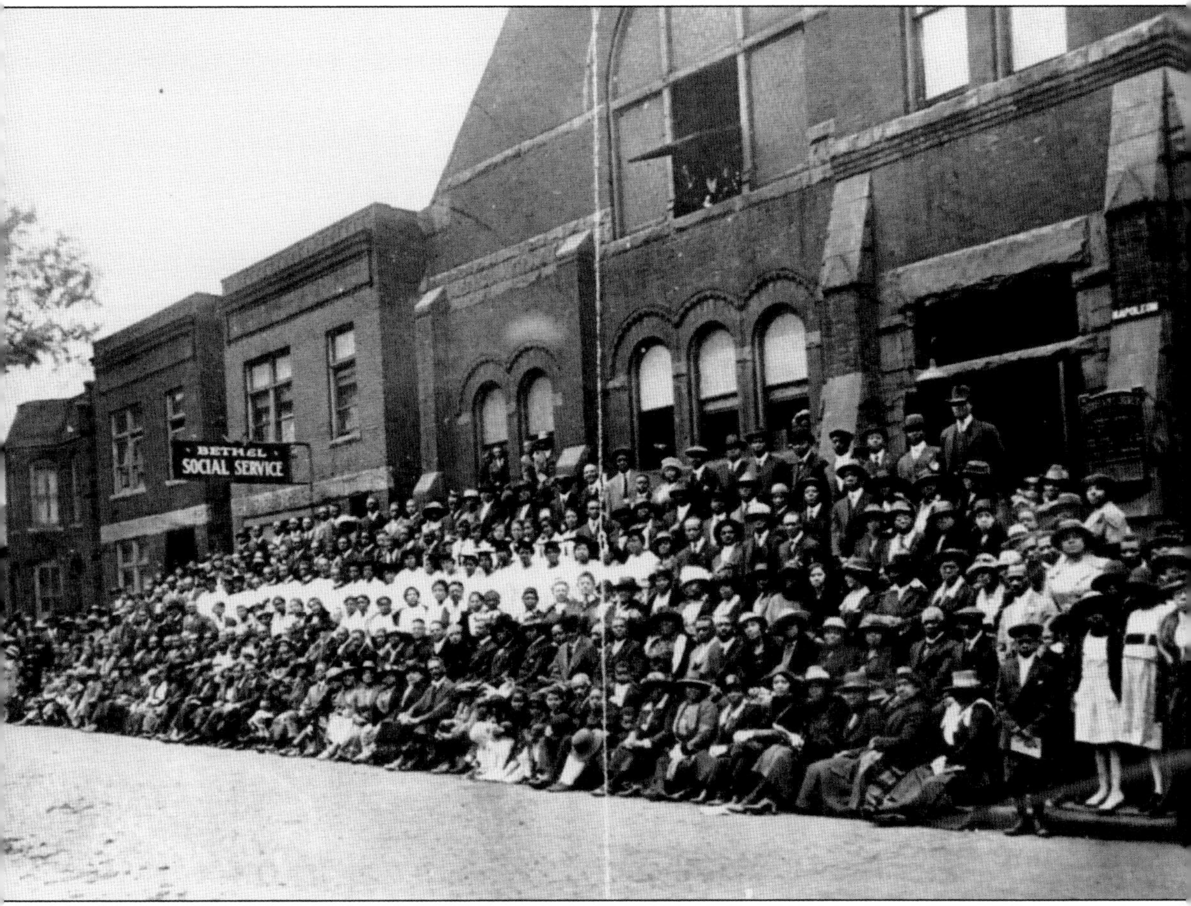

In 1839, black citizens founded the Bethel AME Church. The church held meetings in a hall donated by the Detroit Common Council, building a hall of their own in the 1840s. In 1841, the church assumed its present name and organization. The church served needy residents in numerous ways, such as providing a school, an agency to assist southern migrants, and a bureau for labor and housing. The church worked with other groups to help new residents find housing, jobs, and food. By 1941, Bethel AME Church had become a vital part of the Black Bottom community. This photograph was taken in the 1920s. (BHC.)

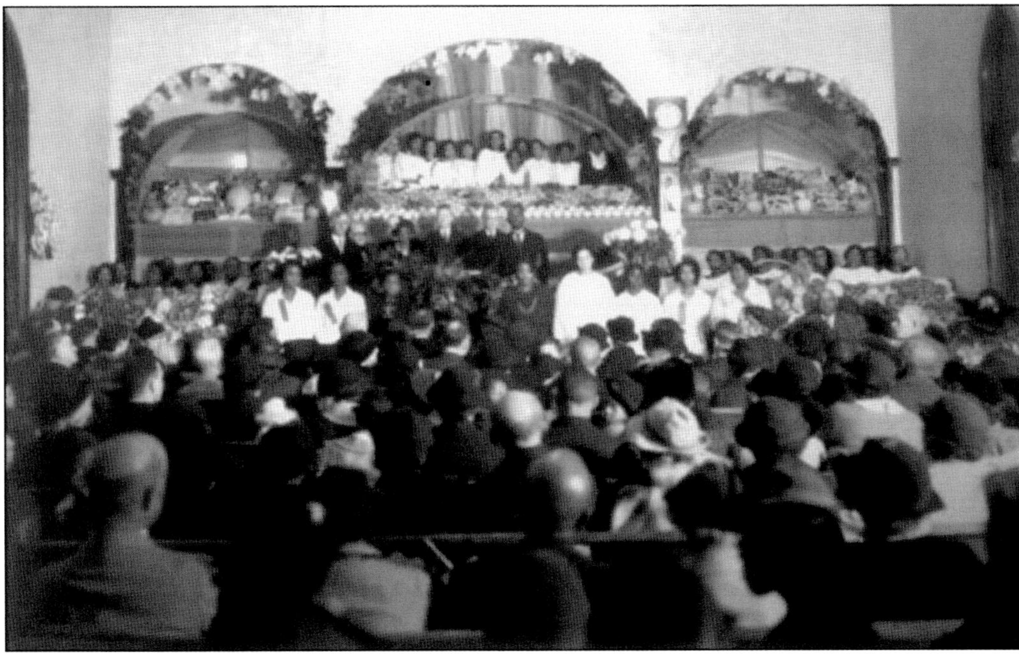

Second Baptist Church is the oldest black congregation in Black Bottom and eventually settled at 441 Monroe Avenue near Hastings and Lafayette Streets. From its beginnings, the church has occupied a prominent place in Detroit's black community, serving as a meeting place for early abolitionists including Frederick Douglass, John Brown, and Sojourner Truth. Before the Detroit Urban League became active, Second Baptist Church helped to settle black migrants. This photograph was taken in the 1940s. (BHL.)

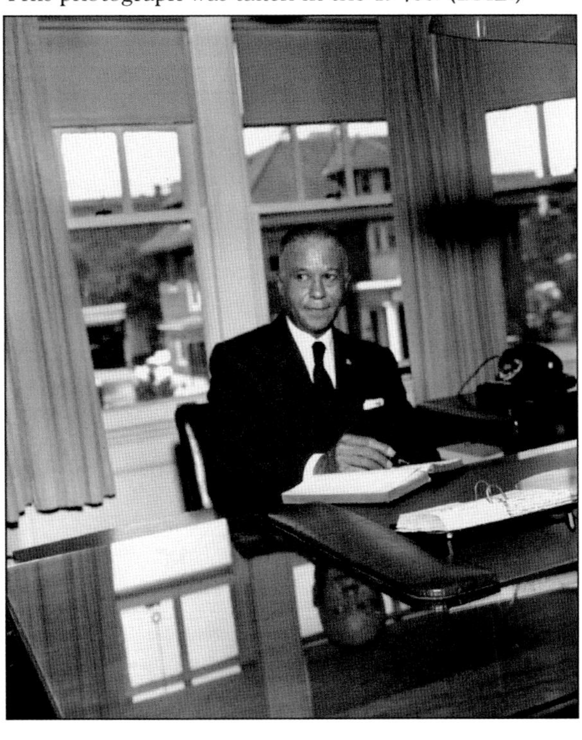

John C. Dancy succeeded Forester Washington as director of the Detroit Urban League. He began gathering information illuminating black life in Black Bottom, understanding that the neighborhood was home to the highest concentration of black citizens in Detroit. Dancy concentrated his efforts on securing better housing and employment for Black Bottom residents. This photograph was taken around 1958. (WRL.)

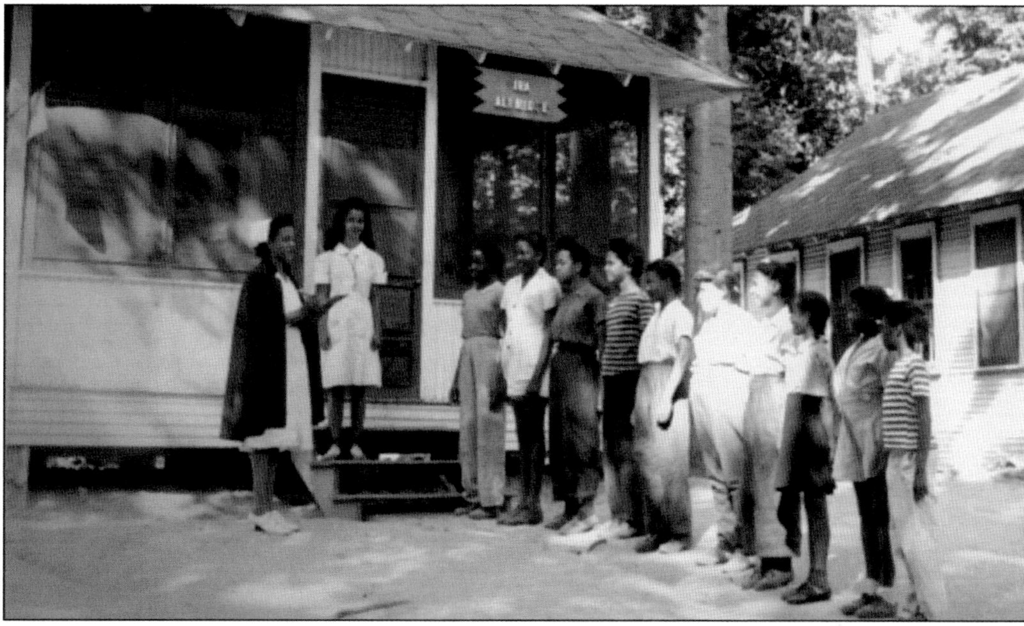

Because of discrimination in public areas, Black Bottom residents were forced to create their own social and recreational outlets. Paradise Valley emerged out of the social, political, and cultural isolation of blacks. Dancy's great Greener Pastures Camp for underprivileged black youth was also created to counteract the prejudice suffered. In this photograph, a nurse gives instruction to young girls at Green Pastures Camp around 1932. (BHL.)

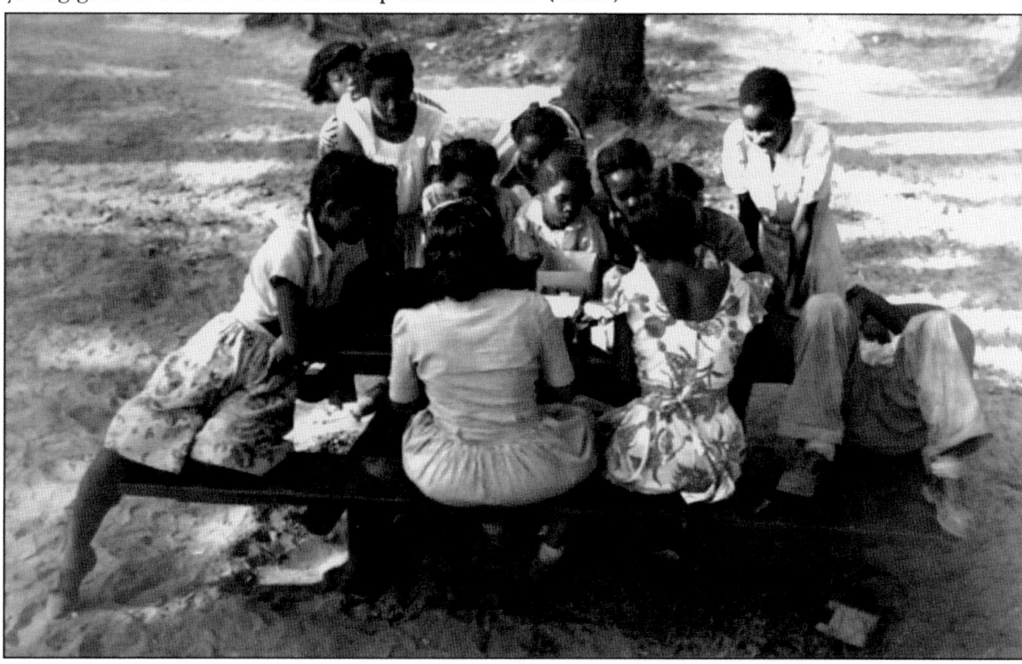

The only program that seemed to bloom during the dry and dark days of the Depression was the Greener Pastures project. A variety of programs benefited Black Bottom residents and helped to raise the quality of life for black children in Black Bottom. In this *c.* 1932 photograph, a group of girls and a boy enjoy arts and crafts on a picnic table at Green Pastures Camp. (BHL.)

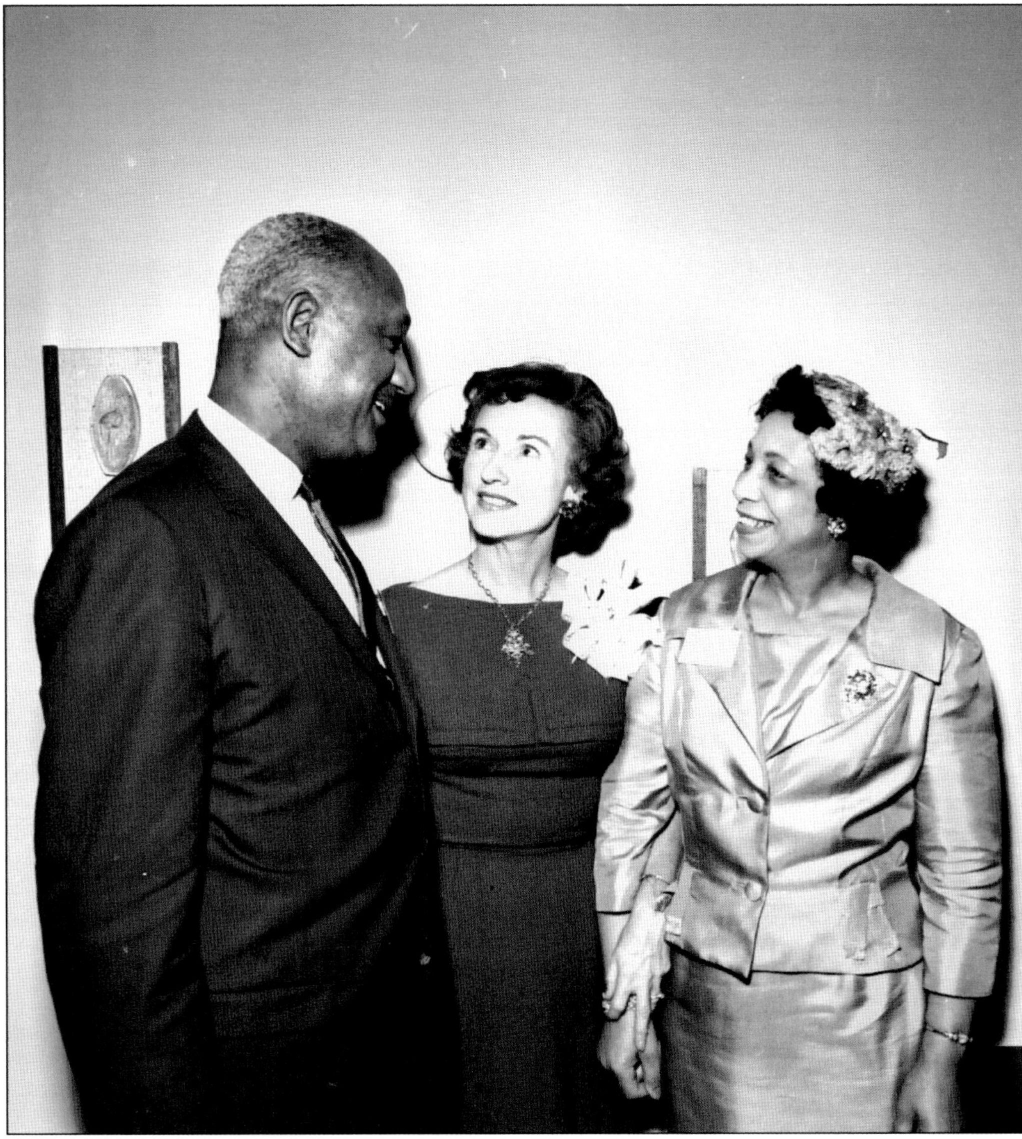

In 1944, Dr. Francis A. Kornegay became the Detroit Urban League's vocational services secretary. In 1945, Kornegay's department serviced 2,339 people, placing many in jobs, and giving the rest vocational and educational guidance, housing assistance, veteran advice, and vocational testing. Here Dr. Kornegay converses with Mrs. Karl Radden and Mrs. George Romney. This photograph was taken around 1958. (WRL.)

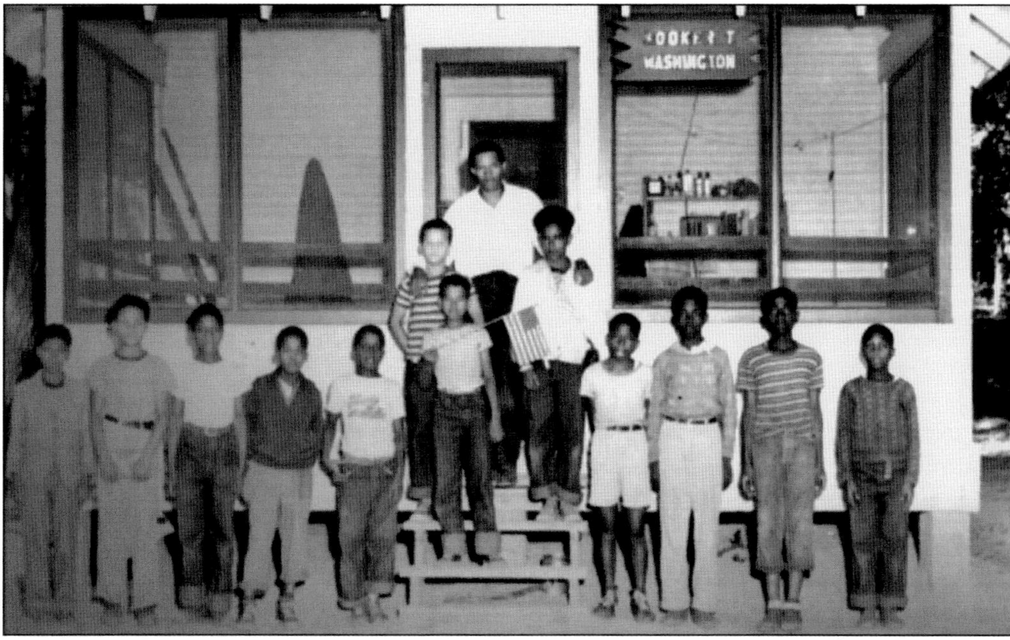

One Detroit Urban League official noted that "even the Christian Association Camps of Detroit do not take Negroes to camp along with white children but offer them a couple of weeks at the beginning or end of the season when it is almost too cool for real pleasure; nor has the largest summer camp for children in Michigan which is maintained by one of Detroit's daily newspapers ever admitted Negro children." In this c. 1932 photograph, campers pose in front of a cottage at Green Pastures Camp. (BHL.)

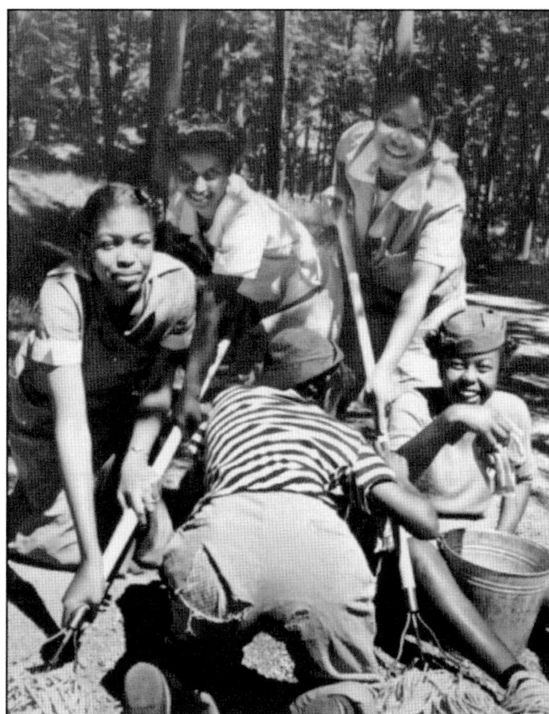

Many black institutions assisted in "the protection of young black girls coming from the South for domestic training." The Detroit Urban League along with black churches worked to ensure that young black girls coming to Detroit were provided with safe shelter and decent employment. In this c. 1931 photograph, girls learn housekeeping at Green Pastures Camp. (BHL.)

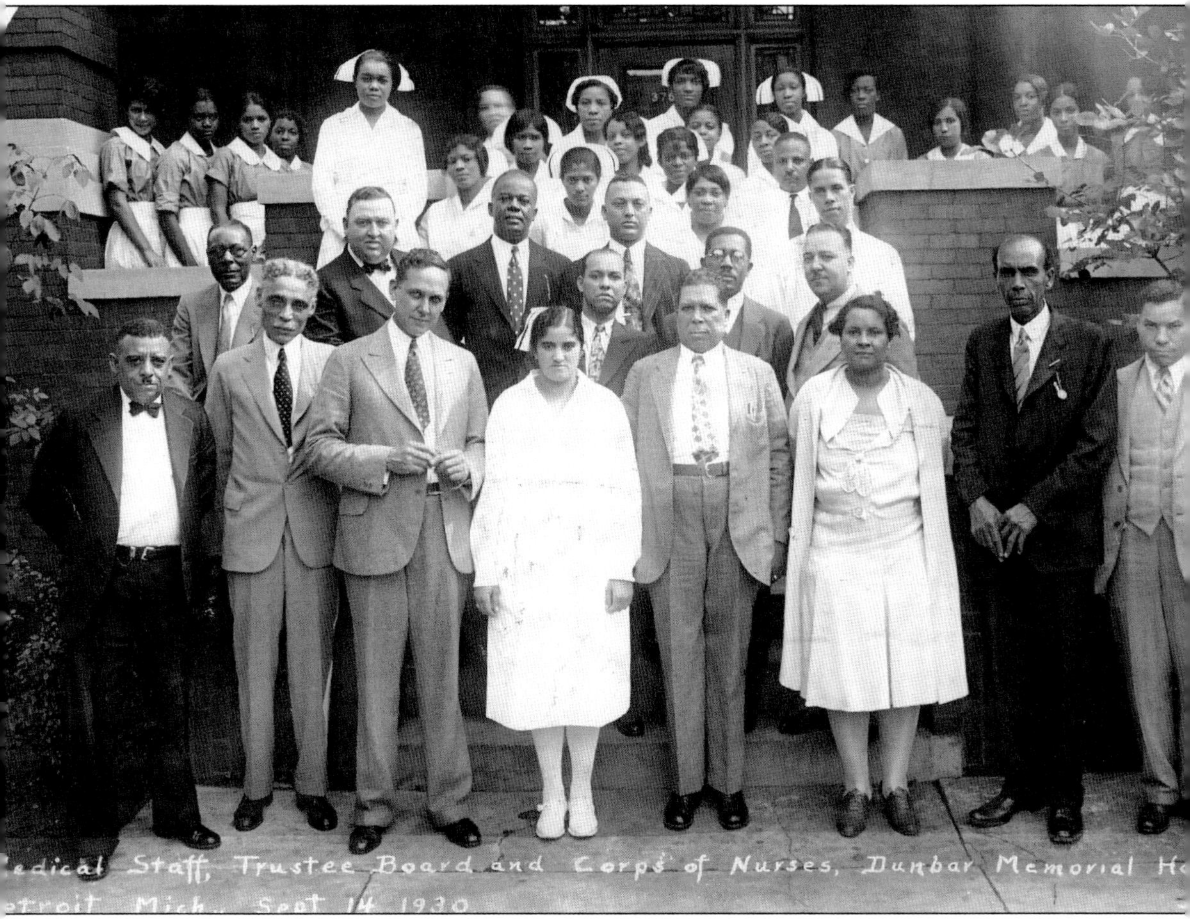

In this c. 1930 photograph, Dunbar Memorial Hospital's medical staff, trustee board, and corps of nurses pose for a shot on the steps of Dunbar Memorial Hospital. Dunbar Memorial Hospital emerged in the wake of the black self-help movement. Pictured are Henderson, Dr. John Thomas, Cleage O., Greene, Henry Owen, Greenridge, Burton, and Osby. (BHC.)

Responding to the needs of the expanding Black Bottom community, black hospitals such as Dunbar provided an institutional base for black medical professionals who could not find employment with white hospitals. Equally important, these hospitals provided jobs within the black community. This photograph was taken around 1980. (WRL.)

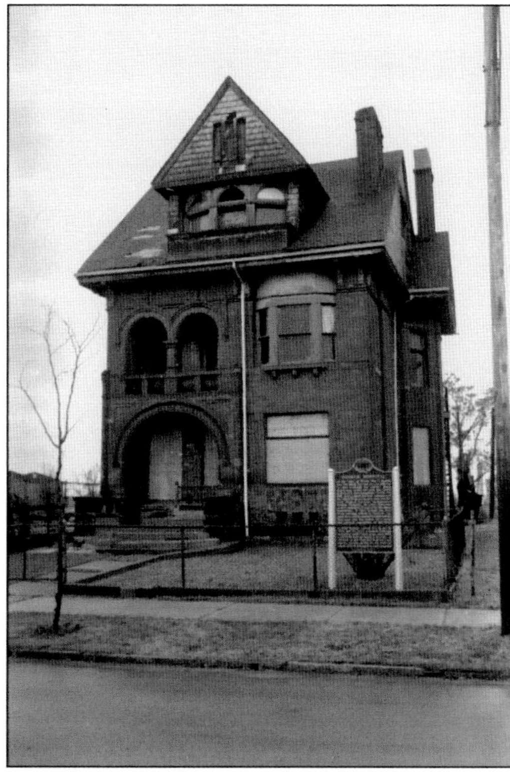

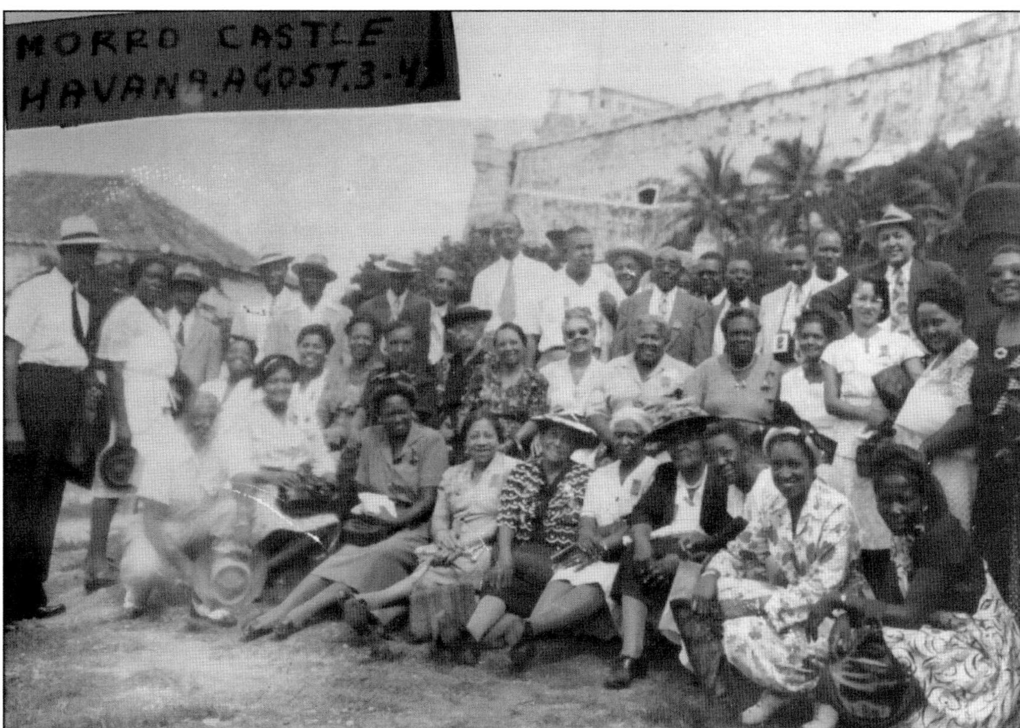

The Housewives League of Detroit is seen in Havana, Cuba, in 1947. (BHC.)

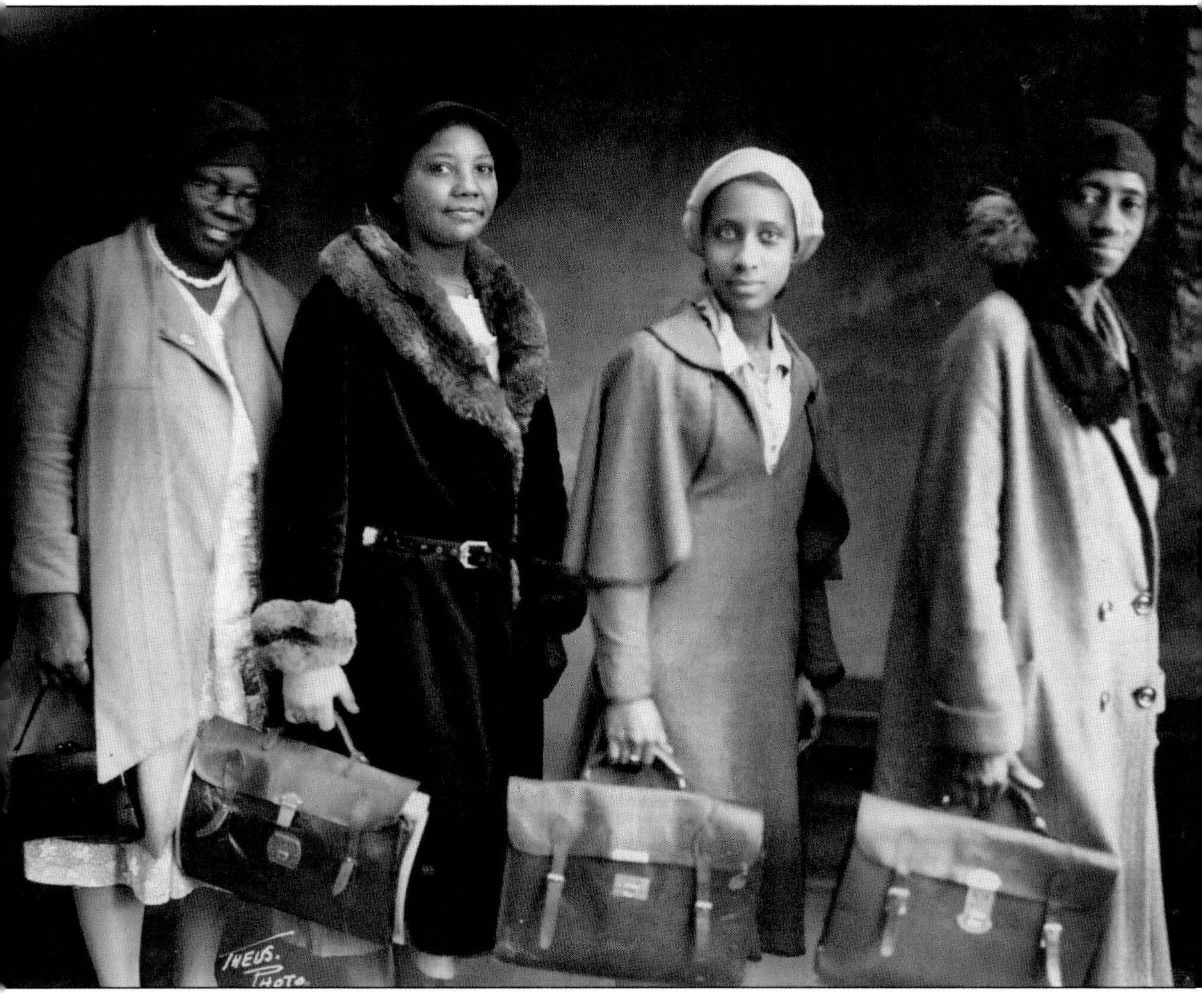

In his memoirs, *Talk of the Town*, former Black Bottom resident and entrepreneur Sunnie Wilson remembers the positive impact the Booker T. Washington Trade Association and Housewives League of Detroit had on Black Bottom's black business community: "By the time I settled in Detroit, I was pleased to see black businessmen coming together to build a strong community. Various entrepreneurs joined together in black business association. The Booker T. Washington Trade Association, founded by Reverend William Peck of the A.M.E. Church, and another that held Thursday luncheons were especially effective in the community. Eventually, I became a member of both those organizations. The Thursday meetings assisted black professionals finding work. For example, if a real-estate man needed work, the organization would help him find the proper business connections." This photograph shows the Housewives League of Detroit around 1930. (BHC.)

Second Baptist Church leader Rev. William H. Peck and his wife, Fannie Peck, founded the Booker T. Washington Trade Association and the Housewives League of Detroit. The Booker T. Washington Trade Association understood the economic power that black housewives possessed and aided Black Bottom's economic growth, stressing the importance of patronizing black-owned businesses and other efforts to support black economic welfare. This is a photograph of Fannie B. Peck from around 1939. (BHC.)

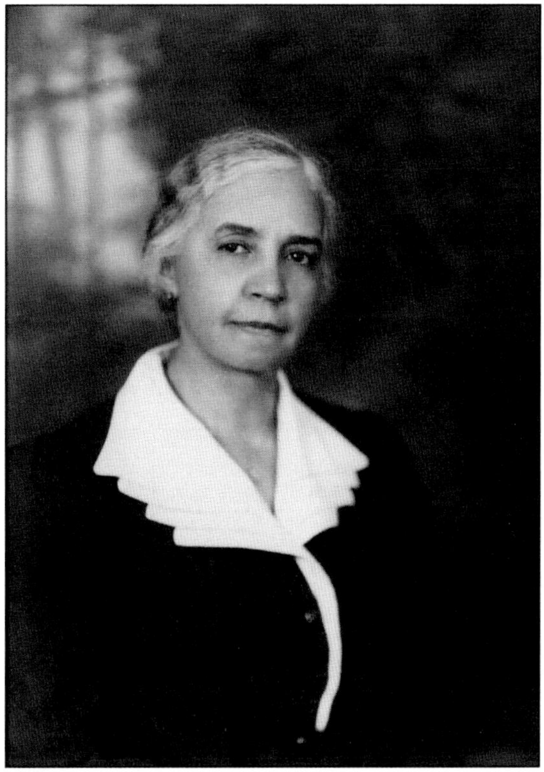

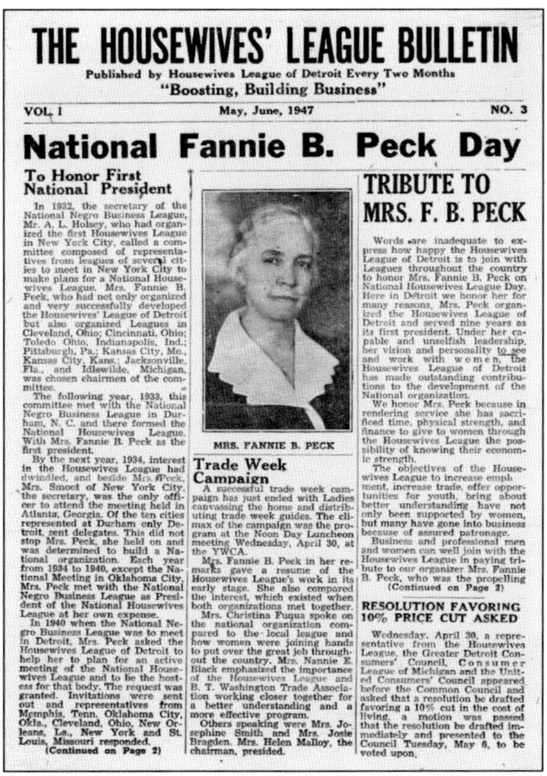

THE HOUSEWIVES' LEAGUE BULLETIN

Published by Housewives League of Detroit Every Two Months
"Boosting, Building Business"

VOL. I — May, June, 1947 — NO. 3

National Fannie B. Peck Day

To Honor First National President

In 1932, the secretary of the National Negro Business League, Mr. A. L. Holsey, who had organized the first Housewives League in New York City, called a committee composed of representatives from leagues of several cities to meet in New York City to make plans for a National Housewives League. Mrs. Fannie B. Peck, who had not only organized and very successfully developed the Housewives' League of Detroit but also organized Leagues in Cleveland, Ohio; Cincinnati, Ohio; Toledo Ohio, Indianapolis, Ind.; Pittsburgh, Pa.; Kansas City, Mo., Kansas City, Kans.; Jacksonville, Fla., and Idlewilde, Michigan, was chosen chairmen of the committee.

The following year, 1933, this committee met with the National Negro Business League in Durham, N. C. and there formed the National Housewives League. With Mrs. Fannie B. Peck as the first president.

By the next year, 1934, interest in the Housewives League had dwindled, and beside Mrs. Peck, Mrs. Smoot of New York City, the secretary, was the only officer to attend the meeting held in Atlanta, Georgia. Of the ten cities represented at Durham only Detroit, sent delegates. This did not stop Mrs. Peck, she held on and was determined to build a National organization. Each year from 1934 to 1940, except the National Meeting in Oklahoma City, Mrs. Peck met with the National Negro Business League as President of the National Housewives League at her own expense.

In 1940 when the National Negro Business League was to meet in Detroit, Mrs. Peck asked the Housewives League of Detroit to help her to plan for an active meeting of the National Housewives League and to be the hostess for that body. The request was granted. Invitations were sent out and representatives from Memphis, Tenn. Oklahoma City, Okla., Cleveland, Ohio, New Orleans, La., New York and St. Louis, Missouri responded.

(Continued on Page 2)

MRS. FANNIE B. PECK

Trade Week Campaign

A successful trade week campaign has just ended with Ladies canvassing the home and distributing trade week guides. The climax of the campaign was the program at the Noon Day Luncheon meeting Wednesday, April 30, at the YWCA.

Mrs. Fannie B. Peck in her remarks gave a resume of the Housewives League's work in its early stage. She also compared the interest, which existed when both organizations met together.

Mrs. Christina Fuqua spoke on the national organization compared to the local league and how women were joining hands to put over the great job throughout the country. Mrs. Nannie E. Black emphasized the importance of the Housewives League and B. T. Washington Trade Association working closer together for a better understanding and a more effective program.

Others speaking were Mrs. Josephine Smith and Mrs. Josie Bragden. Mrs. Helen Malloy, the chairman, presided.

TRIBUTE TO MRS. F. B. PECK

Words are inadequate to express how happy the Housewives League of Detroit is to join with Leagues throughout the country to honor Mrs. Fannie B. Peck on National Housewives League Day. Here in Detroit we honor her for many reasons, Mrs. Peck organized the Housewives League of Detroit and served nine years as its first president. Under her capable and unselfish leadership, her vision and personality to see and work with women, the Housewives League of Detroit has made outstanding contributions to the development of the National organization.

We honor Mrs. Peck because in rendering service she has sacrificed time, physical strength, and finance to give to women through the Housewives League the possibility of knowing their economic strength.

The objectives of the Housewives League to increase empl[illegible] ment, increase trade, offer opportunities for youth, bring about better understanding have not only been supported by women, but many have gone into business because of assured patronage.

Business and professional men and women can well join with the Housewives League in paying tribute to our organizer Mrs. Fannie B. Peck, who was the propelling

(Continued on Page 2)

RESOLUTION FAVORING 10% PRICE CUT ASKED

Wednesday, April 30, a representative from the Housewives League, the Greater Detroit Consumers' Council, Consumer League of Michigan and the United Consumers' Council appeared before the Common Council and asked that a resolution be drafted favoring a 10% cut in the cost of living, a motion was passed that the resolution be drafted immediately and presented to the Council Tuesday, May 6, to be voted upon.

Dr. Austin Curtis, former member of the Booker T. Washington Trade Association, remembered the strategies of the Housewives League of Detroit: "The Housewives League was successful in promoting black businesses. These women would go to the merchants and ask for black products that were produced by blacks. If they wouldn't carry them, then they would see that people would not buy there any longer. It was effective." This is a Housewives League bulletin for Fannie Peck Day, about 1945. (BHC.)

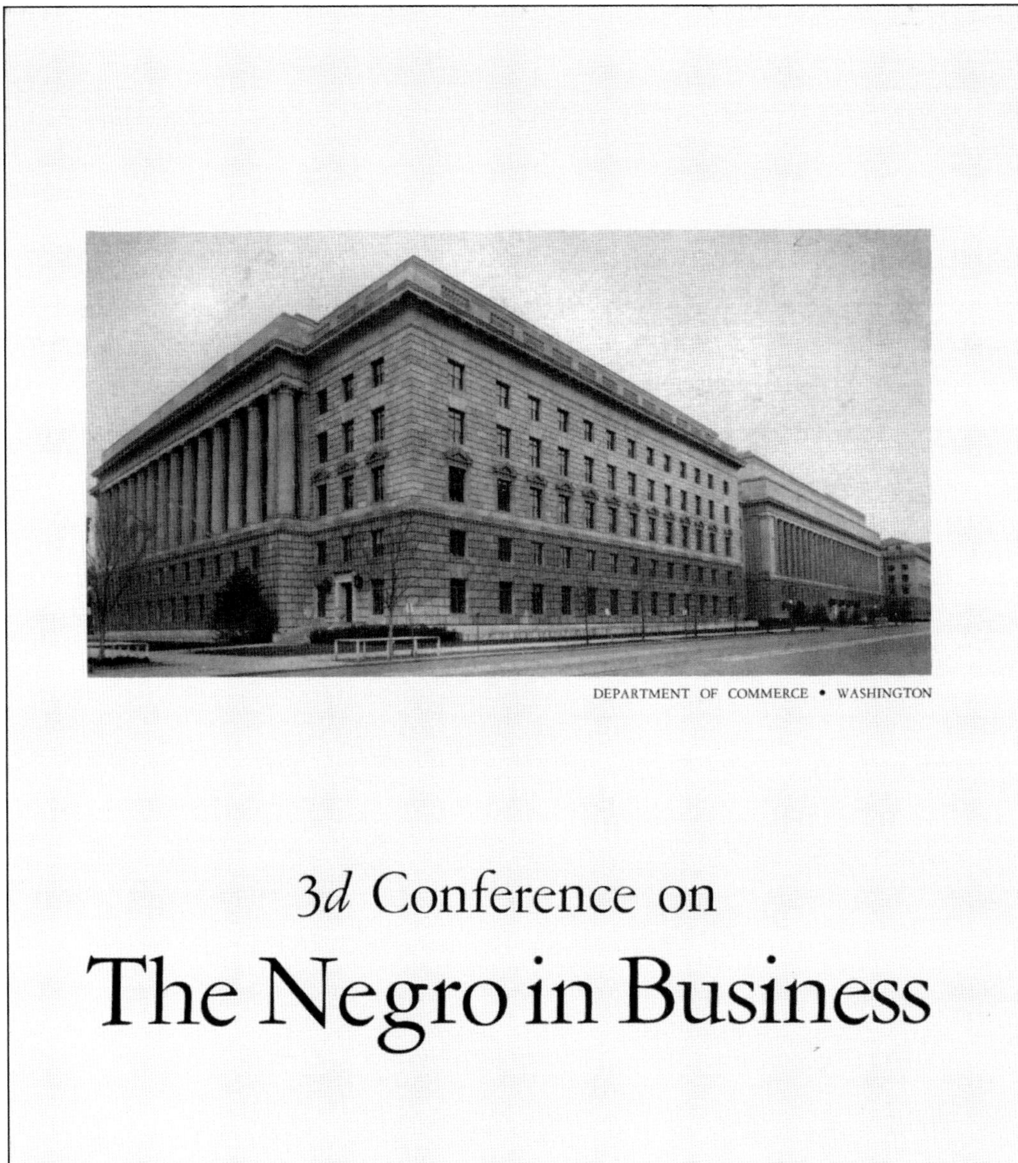

The Booker T. Washington Trade Association and the Housewives League of Detroit were driven by a desire to strengthen the economic power of the black community as a means to build a secure community. They implemented and fostered a self-help philosophy, raised social consciousness, and promoted racial solidarity. Both groups forged alliances with other black institutions to design ways to develop a strong black business community. This is an African American in the business program from about 1948. (BHC.)

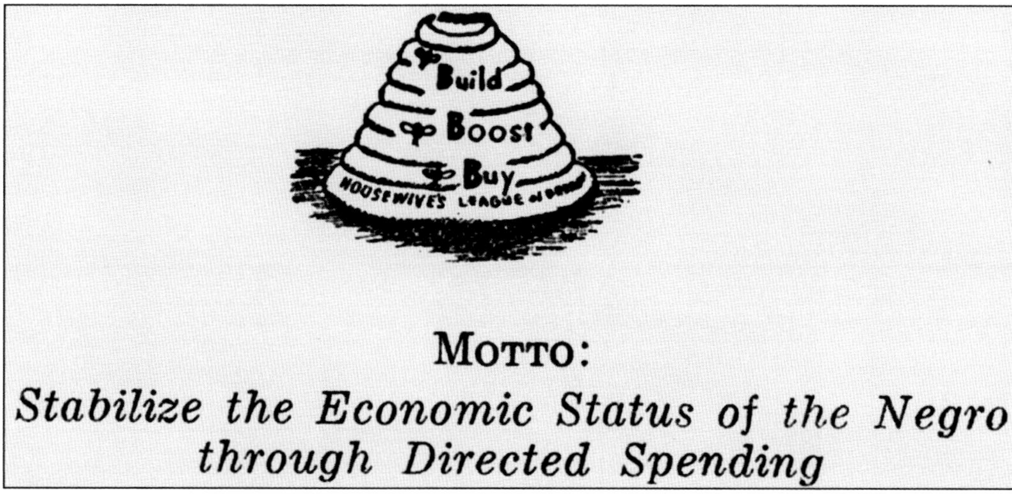

The Housewives League of Detroit became a model of black self-help, implementing programs that assisted black migrants in employment, finances, and other social issues. This is a Housewives League of Detroit Beehive Association program. (BHC.)

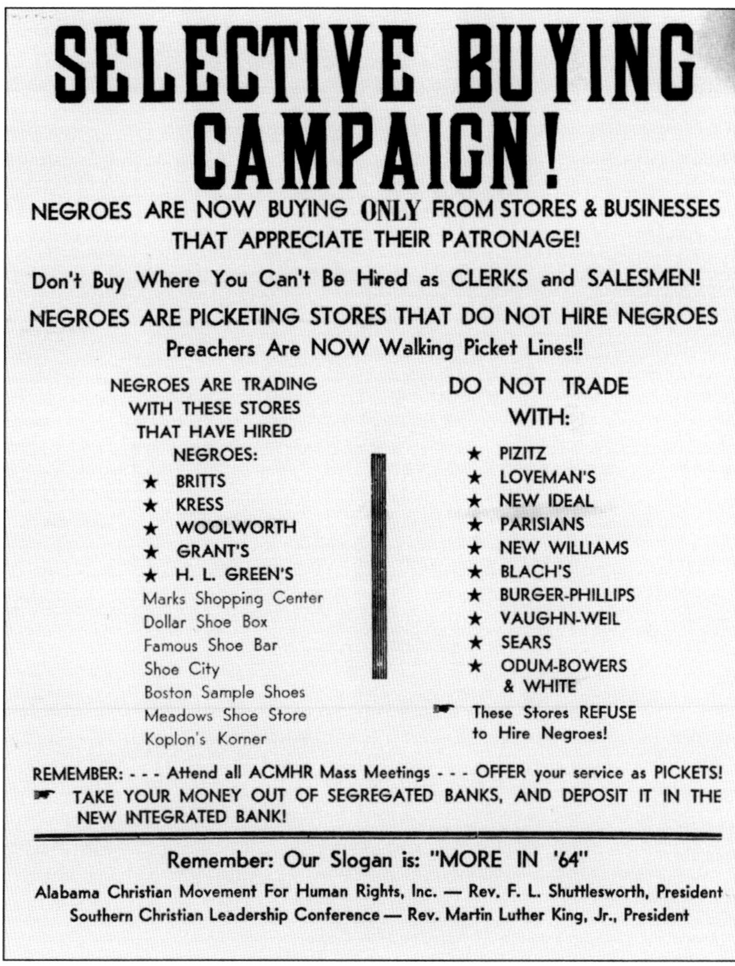

The Housewives League of Detroit's Marcus Garvey–like philosophy ("let's keep our money in our own communities") enabled black consumers in Paradise Valley—Black Bottom's commercial district—to build an economically viable community while establishing "an impressive place for themselves in the state's economy." This is a c. 1964 selective buying campaign flyer. (BHC.)

Declaration of Principles

Constitution and By-Laws

OF THE

BOOKER T. WASHINGTON
TRADE ASSOCIATION

AND THE

DETROIT HOUSEWIVES'
LEAGUE

1937

This is a *c.* 1937 flyer for the Booker T. Washington Trade Association Declaration of Principles. (BHC.)

MEMBER

DETROIT HOUSEWIVES' LEAGUE

An Auxiliary of the Booker T. Washington Trade Association

The League is an Organization of Negro Women formed for the purpose of increasing trade with Negro Business and Professional Men and Women of Detroit. To better inform ourselves on prices of merchandise, family budget etc. There is no financial obligation, no dues, no assessment.

A belief in the future of Negro Business and a desire to assist in every way by patronizing and encouraging the same is all that is necessary to become a member.

Name ....

Address ....

Fannie B. Peck, Pres., Mary W. Winter, Chr. Membership Committee

- -

Branch .... Date ....

I pledge to support the Housewives League and abide by its principles and patronize Negro Business as far as possible.

Name ....

Address ....

Business ....

This is a membership application for the Housewives League of Detroit. (BHC.)

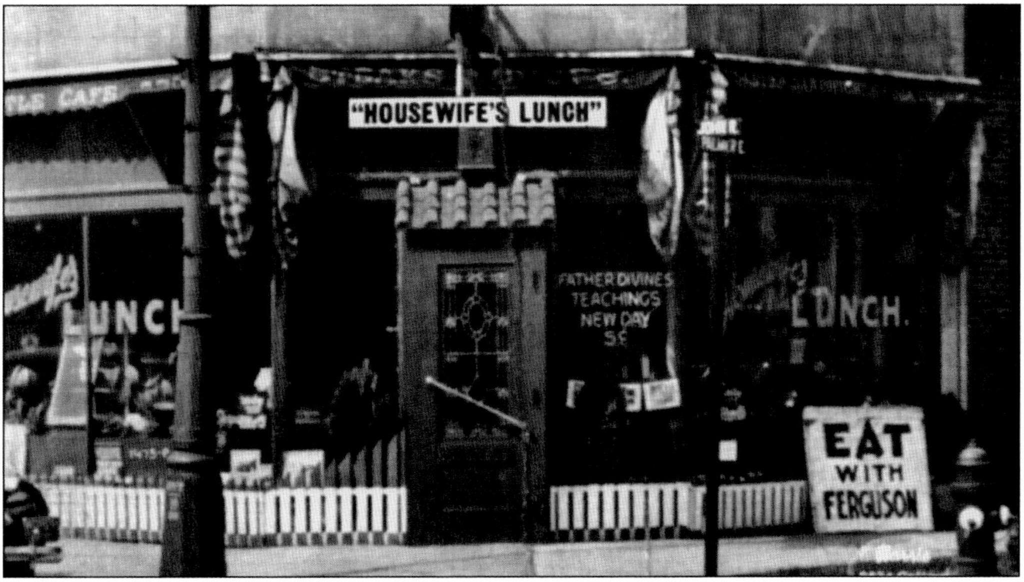

While housing discrimination contained the spread of the black population throughout other areas of the city, a thriving commercial district developed on Hastings and St. Antoine streets. By 1920, blacks owned more than 350 businesses in Detroit, including a movie theater, a co-op grocery, and a bank. The Housewives League of Detroit luncheons were regularly held here at Ferguson's restaurant in Black Bottom. (BHC.)

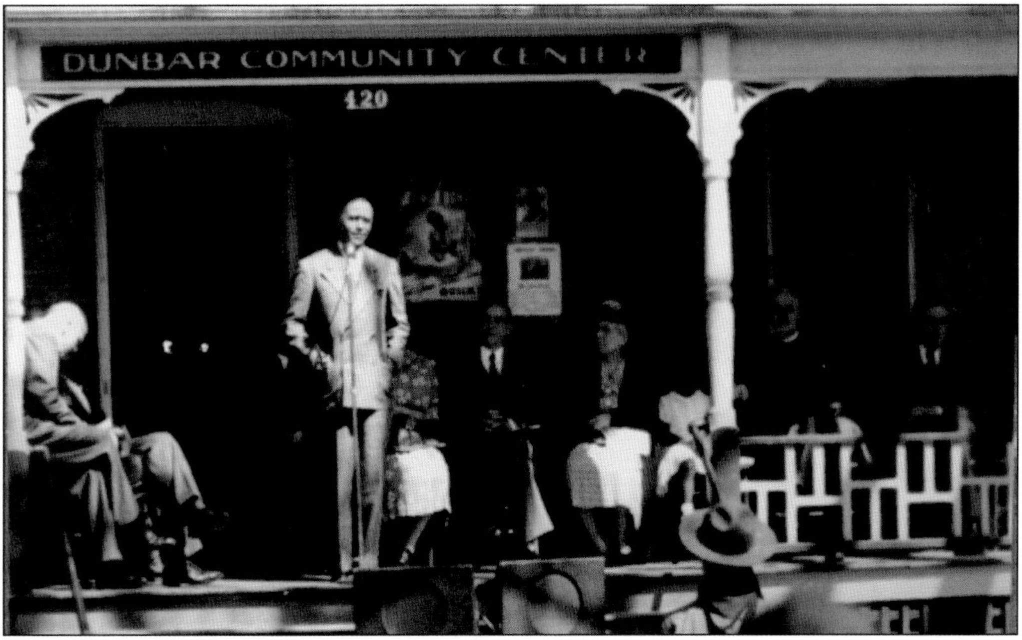

According to *Sands Against the Wind: The Memories of John C. Dancy*, John Dancy used racial uplift ideology to shape the urban league's programs. He opened the Dunbar Community Center in the heart of Black Bottom that served as a baby clinic, job placement office, and cultural center. Dancy also forged a relationship with the Ford Motor Company by placing qualified black workers into factories. This *c.* 1945 photograph shows Dancy lecturing on the Dunbar Community Center porch. (BHL.)

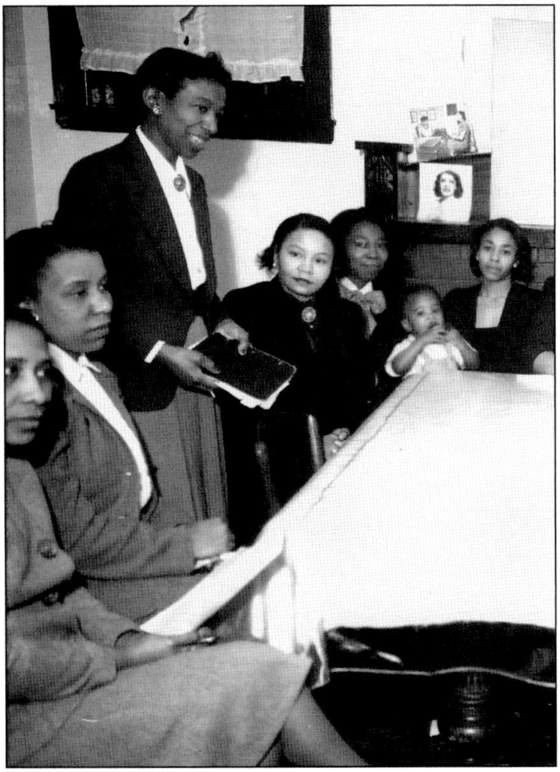

According to the Housewives League of Detroit's Web site, the group designed a consumer-business support model that helped to sustain the economic foundation of Detroit's black population. Based on the knowledge that "housewives controlled 80% of the family's income," the Housewives League of Detroit's strategy of interconnectedness between consumer and business paved the way for black employment opportunities and increased business and consumer education. This is a photograph of a Housewives League of Detroit meeting. (BHC.)

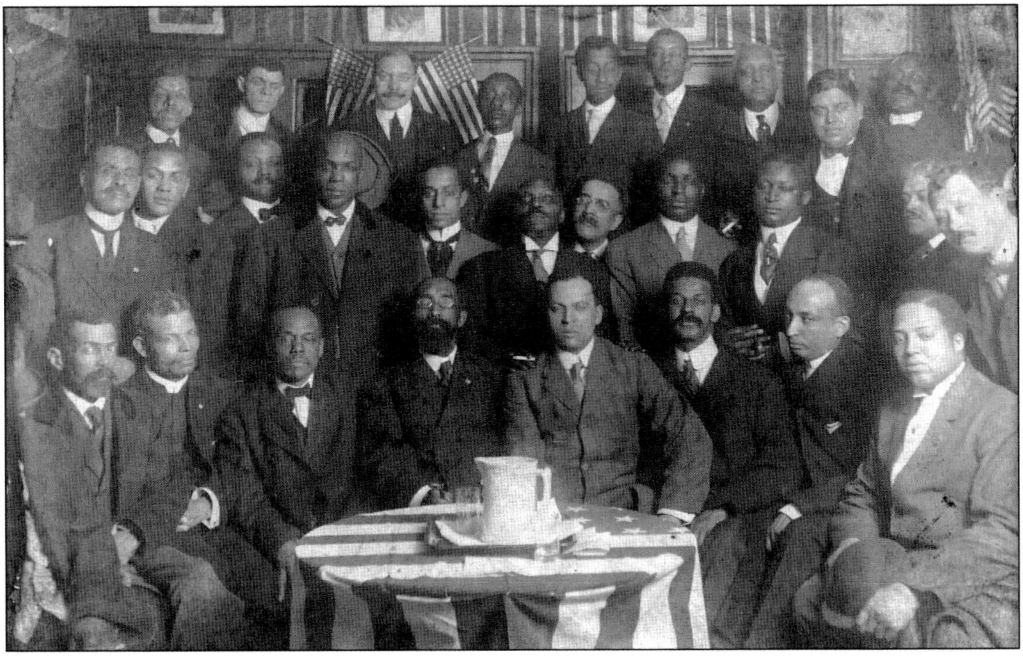

In 1914, when black migrants flocked to Detroit for Henry Ford's $5-a-day offer, Rev. Robert L. Bradby implemented self-help programs and, along with other churches, began social service offices in their churches to aid migrants in finding jobs, food, and recreation. Church officials aided homeless black girls and offered educational facilities staffed with trained teachers. (BHC.)

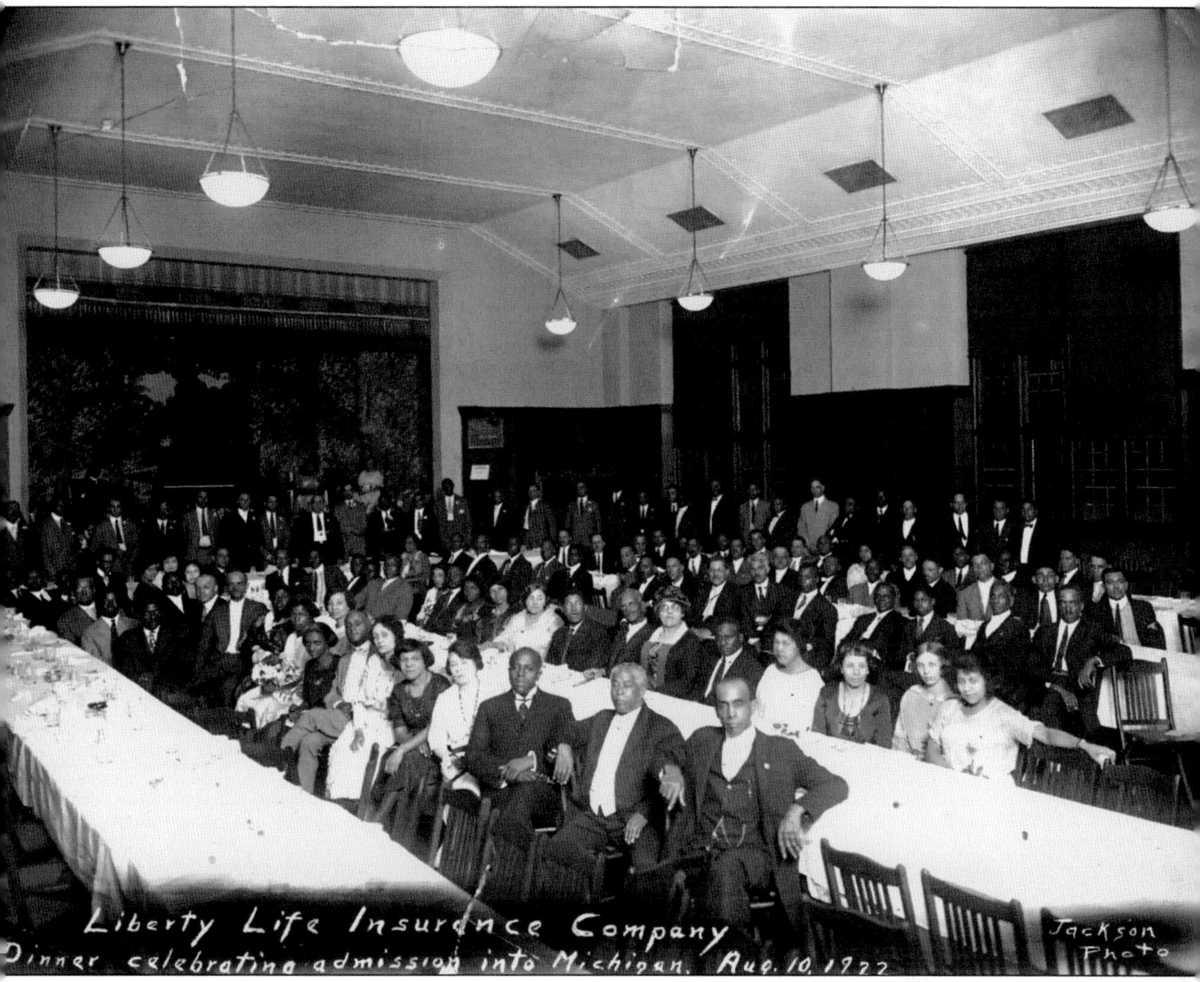

Insurance companies, loan companies, and credit unions all signified social consciousness and self-help in Black Bottom. Also important were the many jobs generated by black insurance companies. By creating jobs and a capital base, black insurance companies helped to keep their dollars in the black community, thus aiding the growth of the black economy. This is a photograph of a Liberty Life Insurance Company gathering. (BHC.)

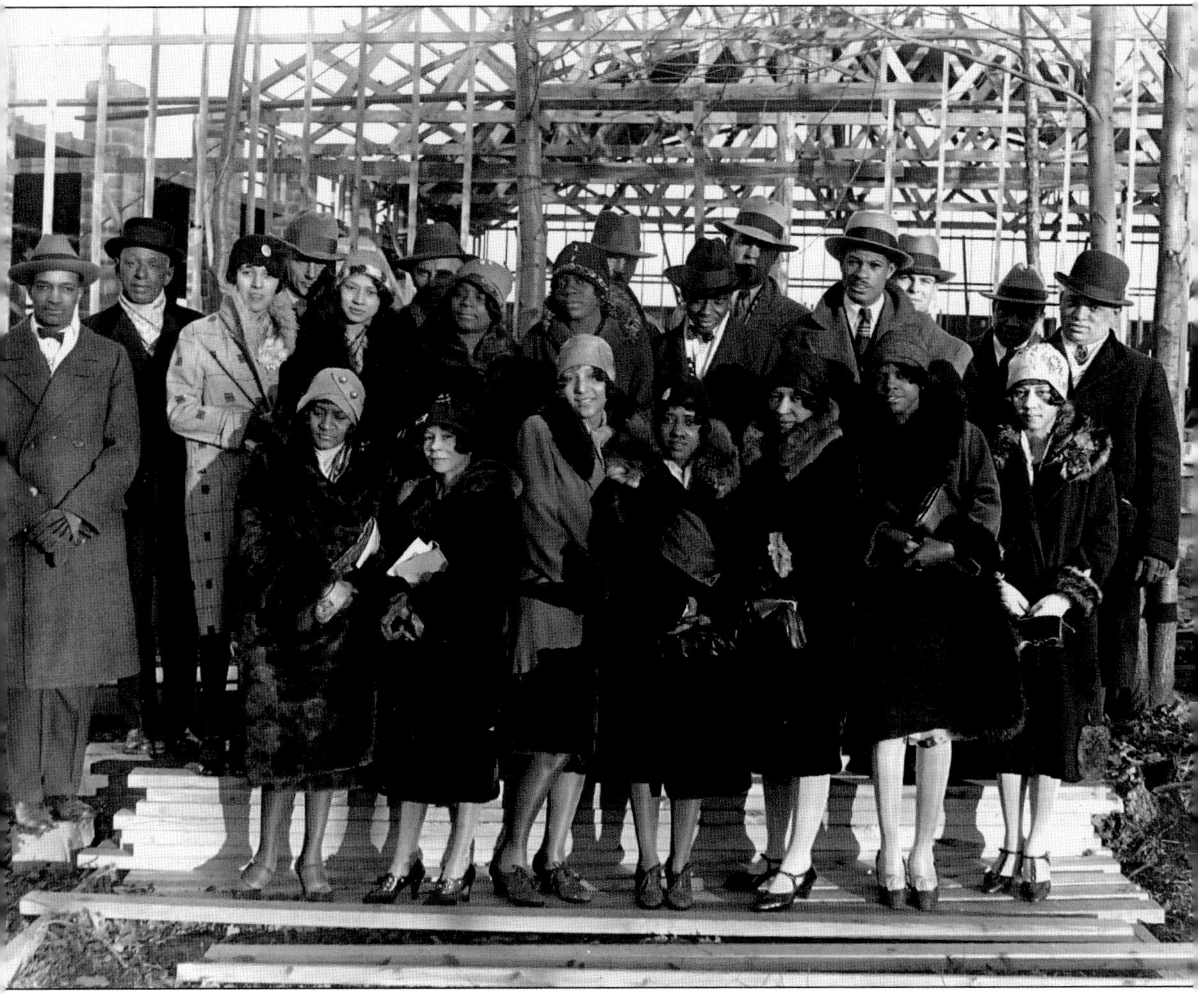

This is a c. 1924 photograph of Nacirema Club members standing in front of a wooden frame structure under construction. Touted as Michigan's first social club for black men, the Nacirema Club gained fame in the 1940s and 1950s for an annual weeklong extravaganza whose highlights were a dance, a racetrack party, a church service, and a moonlight boat ride. And community activities abounded throughout the neighborhood, from informal get-togethers to organized dances. (BHC.)

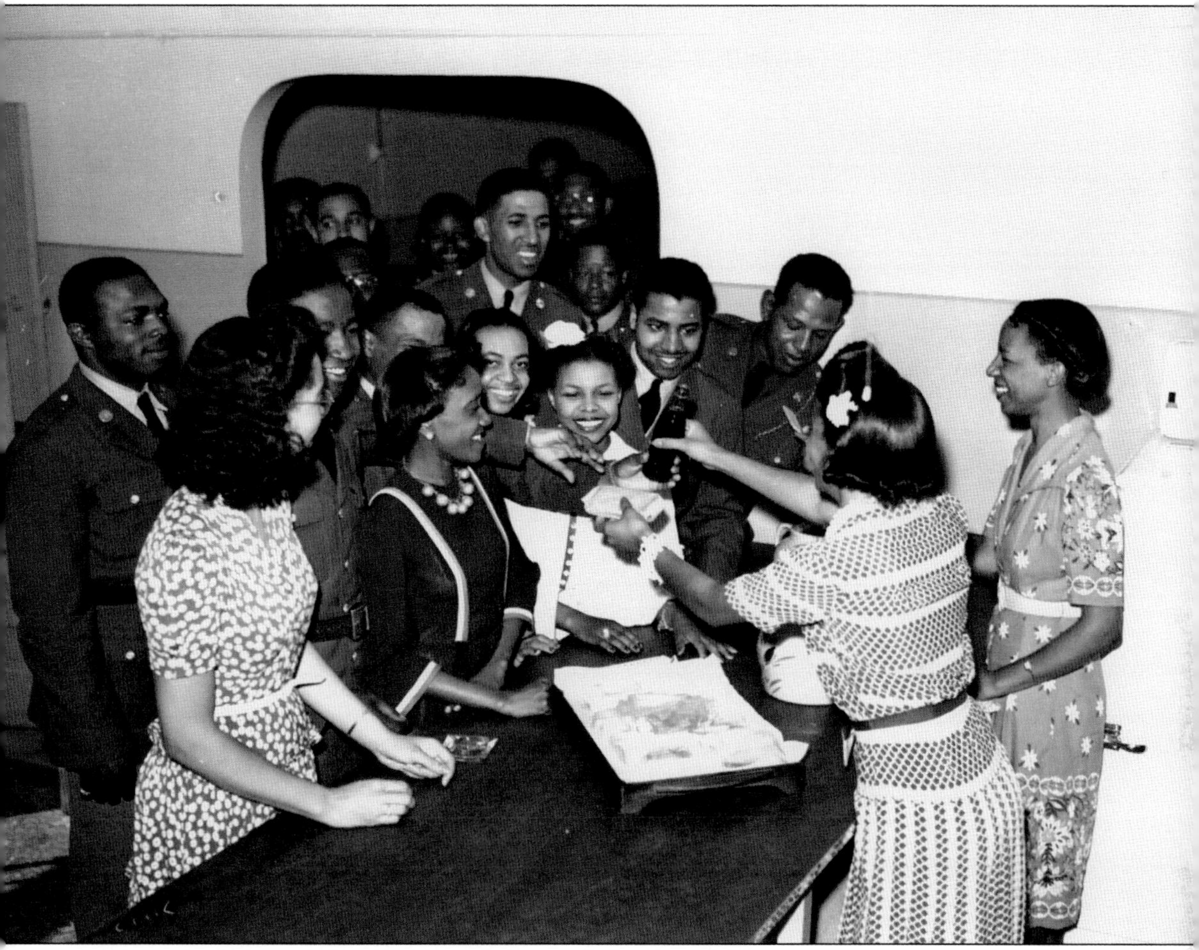

Founded in 1941, the United Service Organization offered supplies as well as social, recreational, welfare, and spiritual facilities to Black Bottom's members of the armed services. The associated agencies include the YMCA, the YWCA, the National Catholic Community Service, the Salvation Army, the Jewish Welfare Board, and the National Travelers Aid Association. Its services discontinued at the end of 1947 but were resumed early in 1949 at the request of Pres. Harry Truman. (WRL.)

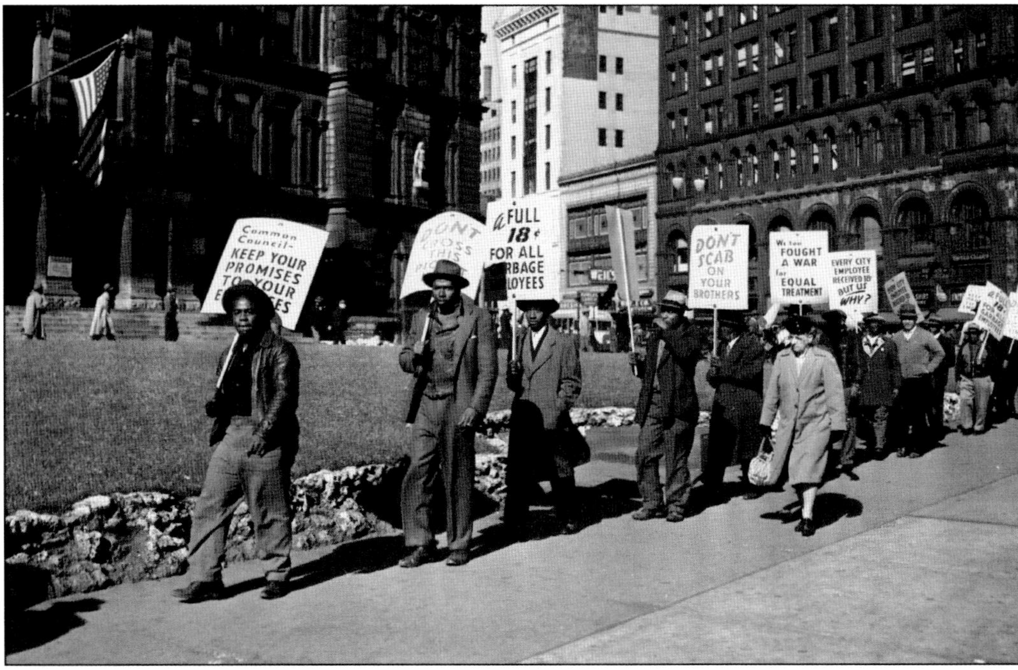

African American men walk in front of the Detroit City County Building carrying signs, one of which reads, "A full 18 cents for all garbage employees." Another reads, "We fought a war for equal treatment." (WRL.)

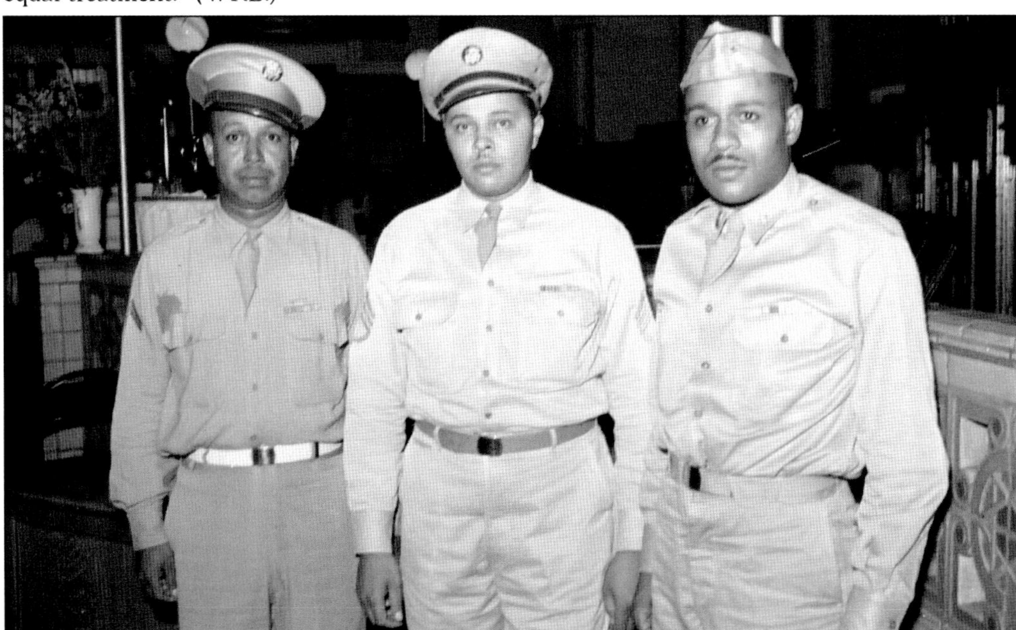

Over 2.5 million black men registered for the draft, and black women also volunteered in large numbers. They served their country with distinction, made valuable contributions to the war effort, and earned high praises and commendations for their struggles and sacrifices. In this image are, from left to right, Cpl. George Davis, Sgt. Crawley Hunt, and Lt. J. M. Lyman. This photograph was taken on July 25, 1943. (WRL.)

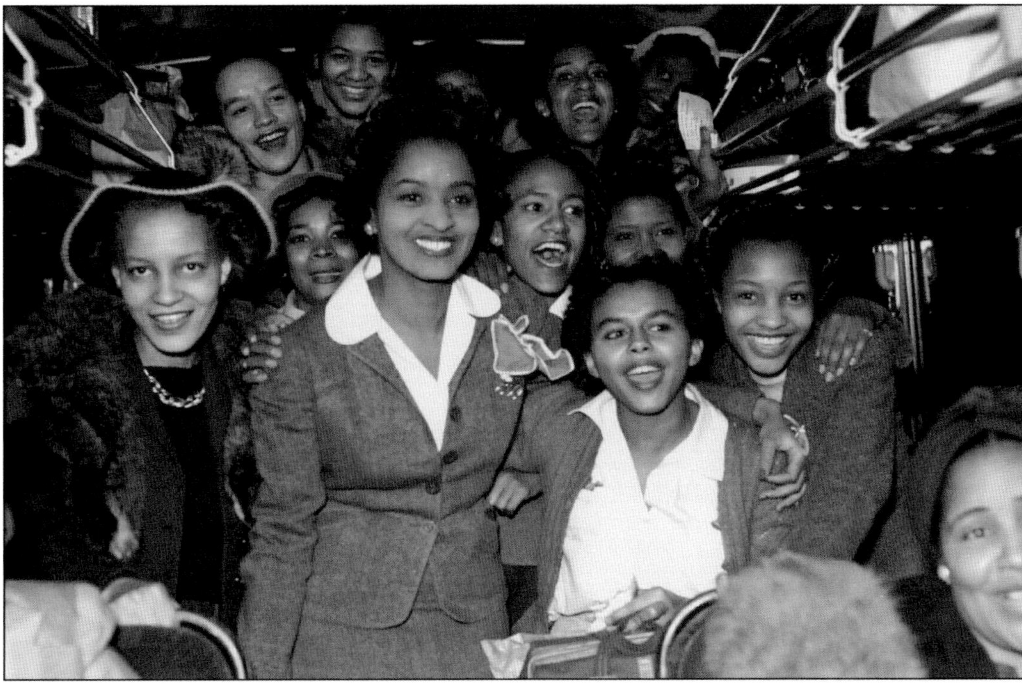

The United Service Organization began in World War II, and it was widely known for providing entertainment to the troops. Some of Hollywood's biggest stars and the country's leading musicians donated their time to entertain U.S. soldiers at home and abroad. The United Service Organization was located at Adelaide and John R. Streets in Black Bottom. In this *c.* 1943 photograph, blacks prepare to leave on a United Service Organization tour to entertain soldiers. (WRL.)

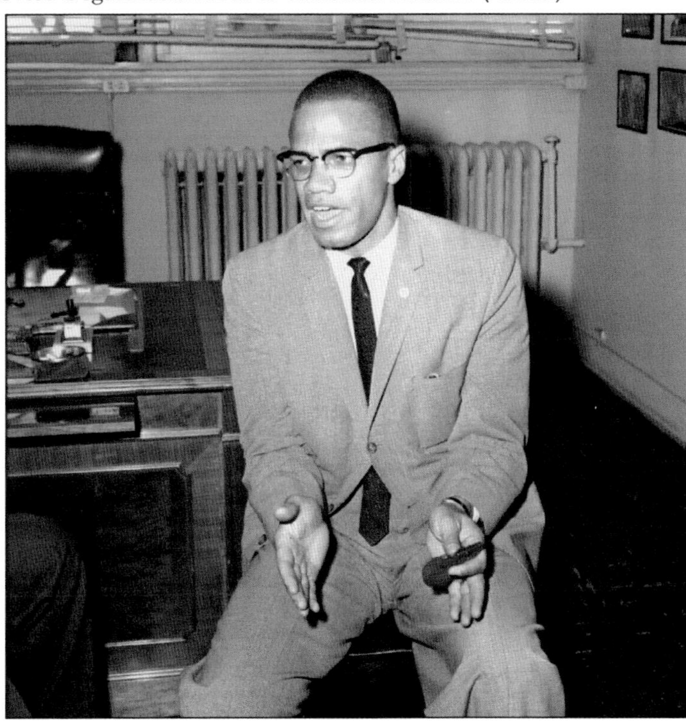

According to Dr. Frank Rashid in *Paradise Valley/Black Bottom*, the Nation of Islam arose in Paradise Valley. While Ford was forced to close factories, Wallace Fard's mosque flourished. In August 1952, Malcolm X was paroled; a new convert, Malcolm X moved to Detroit and eagerly worked to attract new members from the Black Bottom community. In June 1953, Malcolm X, pictured here on June 9, 1962, was named assistant minister of the Nation of Islam's Temple No. 1, located at 3408 Hastings Street. (WRL.)

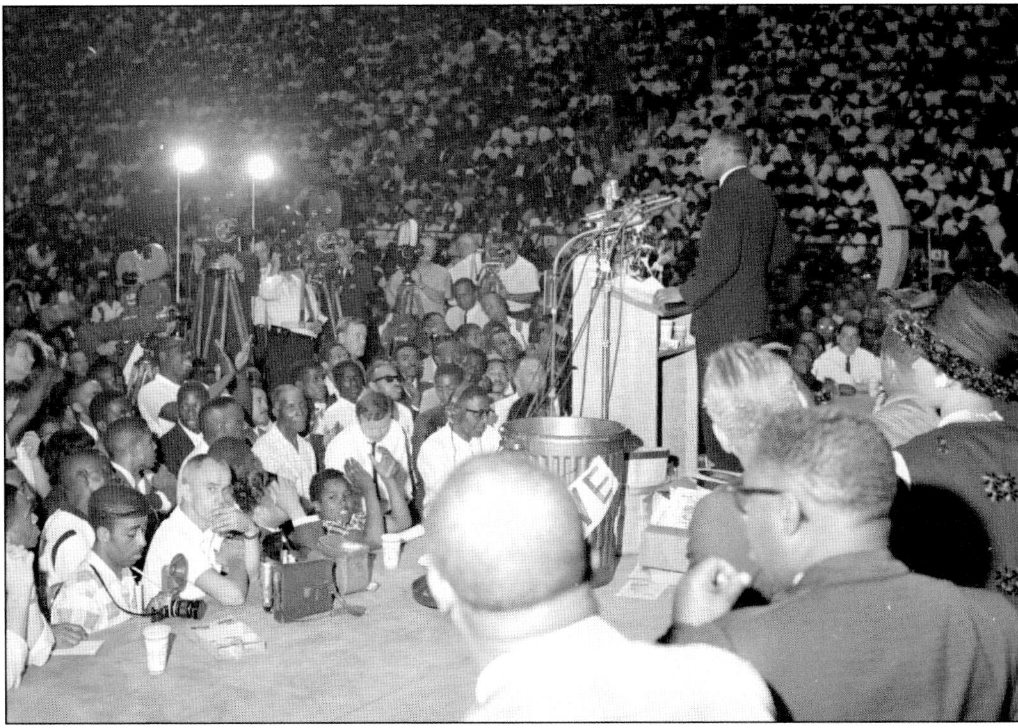

United Auto Worker (UAW) president Walter Reuther and civil rights leader Dr. Martin Luther King Jr. became good friends and allies during the labor movement. When King began planning the Walk to Freedom March that took place in July 1963, Reuther gave King the use of an office at UAW headquarters. In this *c.* 1963 photograph, civil rights leader King is interviewed by reporters. The man on the right is former Detroit television news anchorman Bill Bonds. (WRL.)

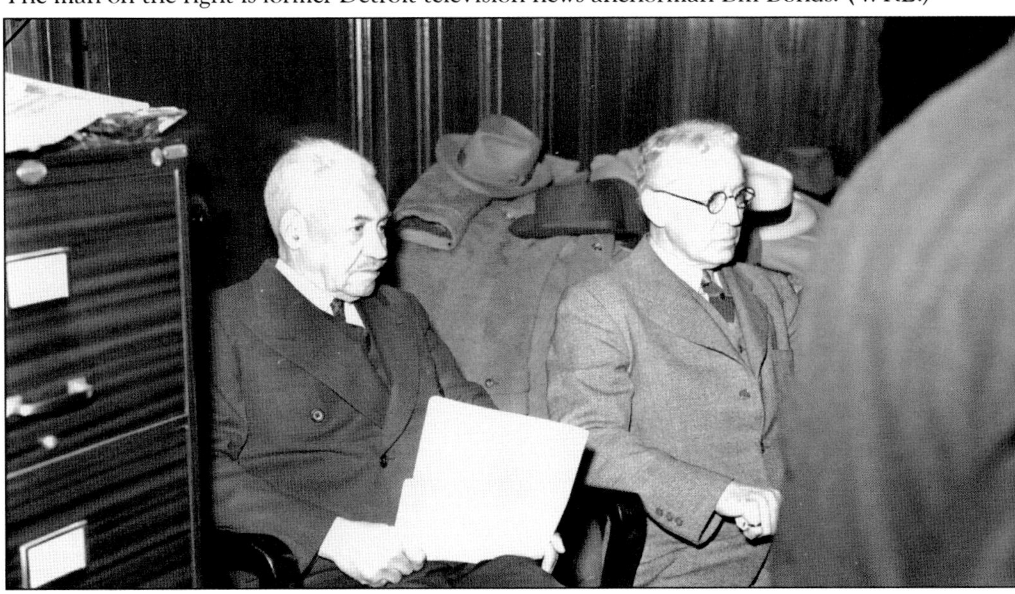

Benjamin B. Pelham was a powerful black Republican. In 1883, he and his brother Robert founded the *Plain Dealer*. This 1950s photograph shows Wayne County accountant Pelham with William E. Dowling. (WRL.)

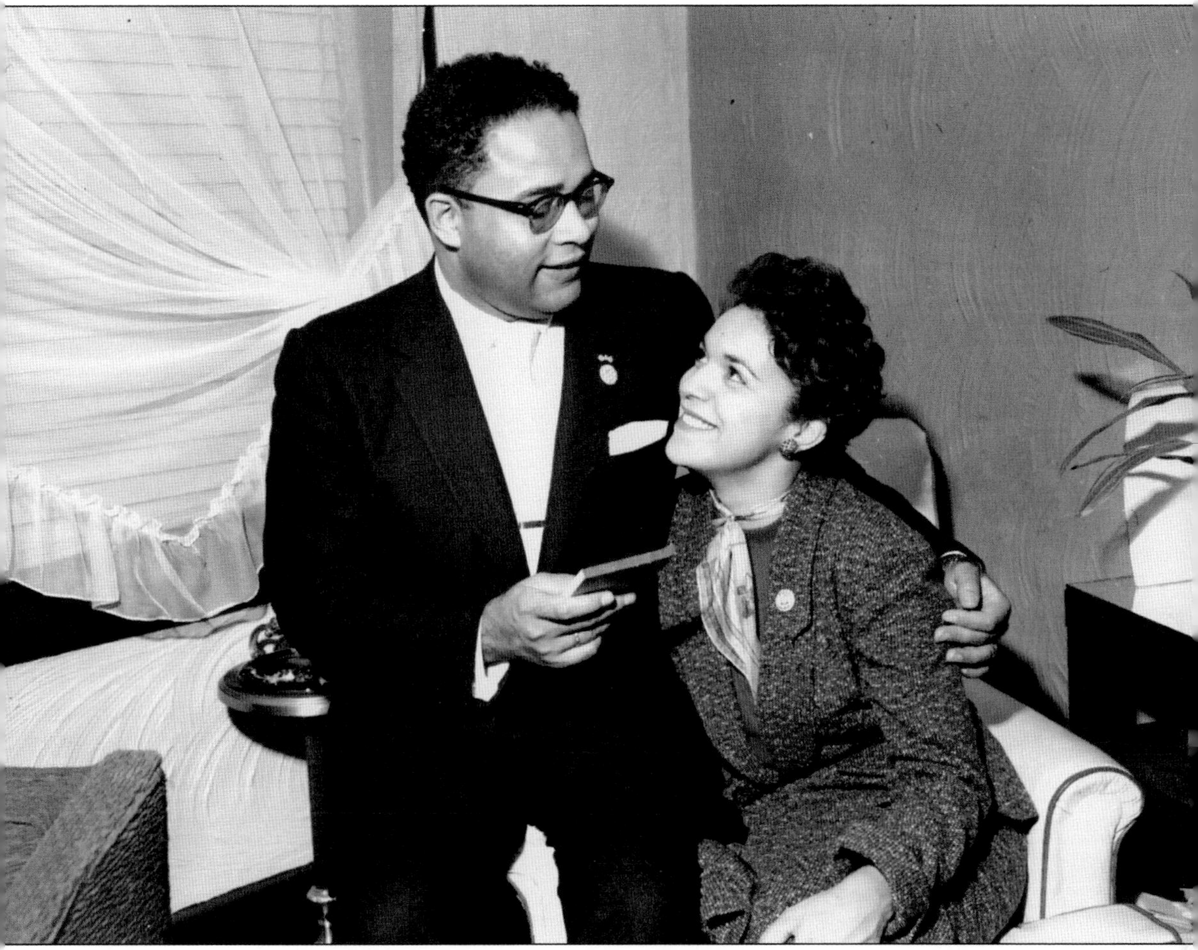

Charles C. Diggs Jr. was the first black Democrat elected to the Michigan legislature. His family lived in Black Bottom. He and Rev. Robert Bradby of Second Baptist Church started a campaign to combat juvenile delinquency in Black Bottom, urging parents to gain control of their wayward children. Diggs organized an antireefer (marijuana) drive to rehabilitate youth. In this photograph, Diggs poses with his lovely wife around 1954. (WRL.)

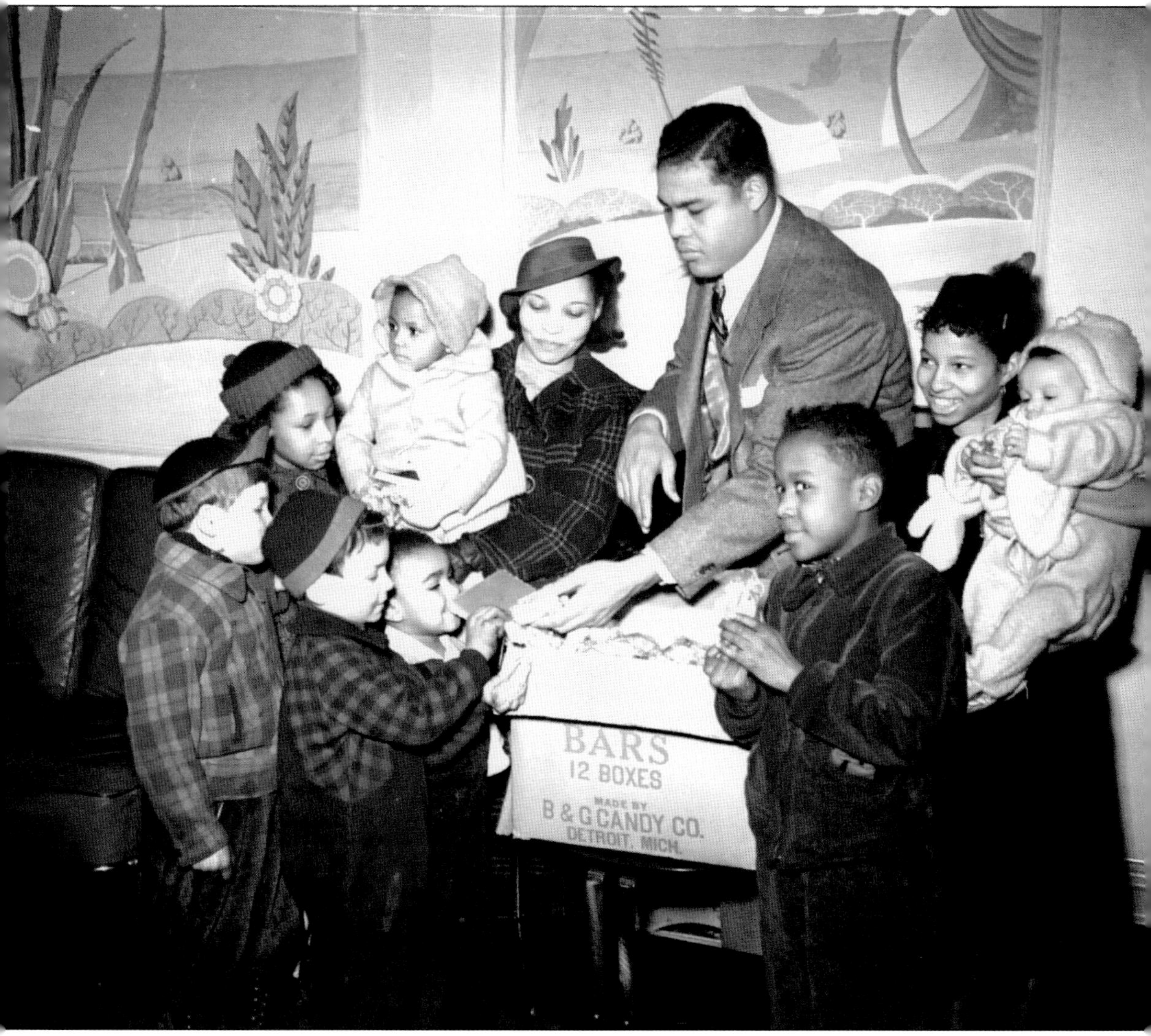

Joe Louis was one of the greatest fighters of all time. But more than that, he was an icon of his time. After his father died, Louis's mother remarried and the family moved to Detroit, settling in Black Bottom. Louis attended vocational schools and took boxing lessons at Brewster's recreational center. Heavyweight boxing champion, Louis was Black Bottom's favorite son. In this photograph, Louis presents needy Black Bottom children with gifts around 1937. (WRL.)

Seven

SOJOURNER TRUTH AND THE RIOTS

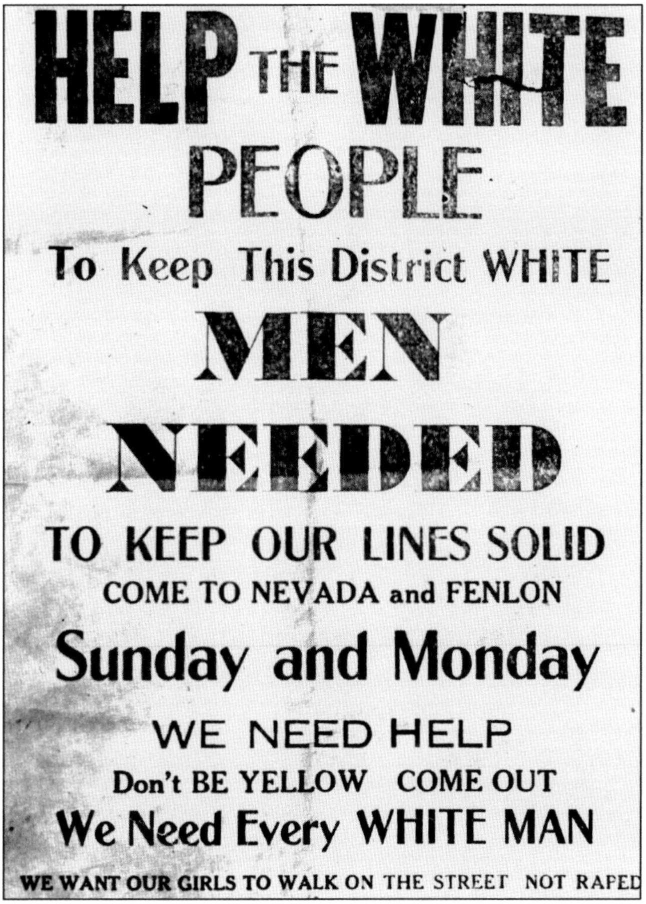

By 1942, the tension of racism and discrimination was at a boiling point. The controversy over blacks' access to a public housing project stirred the public debate. Whites violently protested the inclusion of black war workers in the Sojourner Truth Housing Project and eventually convinced the Federal Housing Administration to restrict the housing project to White families. This photograph was taken around 1943. (WRL.)

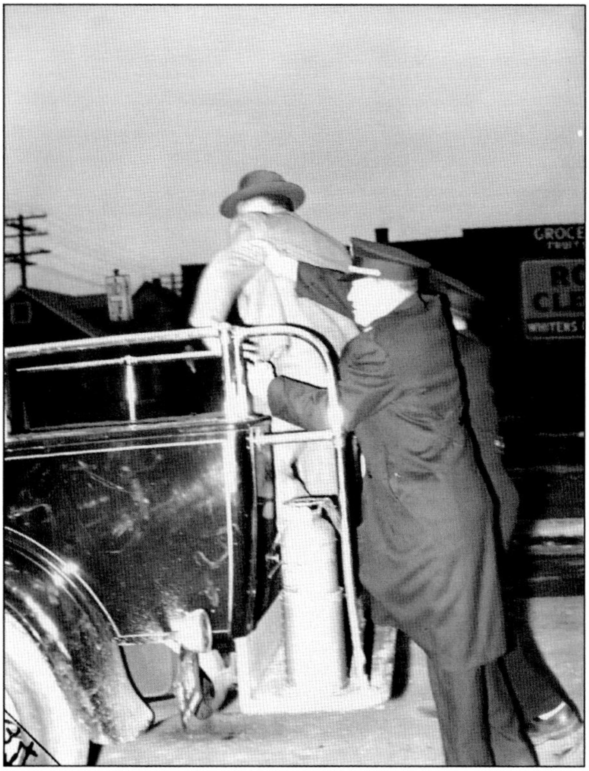

In this *c.* 1942 photograph, uniformed police officers force a man onto the back of a truck in the Sojourner Truth Housing Project. On February 27, with a cross burning in a field near the homes, 150 angry whites picketed the project vowing to keep out any black homeowners. By dawn the following day, the crowd had grown to 1,200 strong, many armed. The police stood aloof some even colluding as the mobs terrorized black citizens. (WRL.)

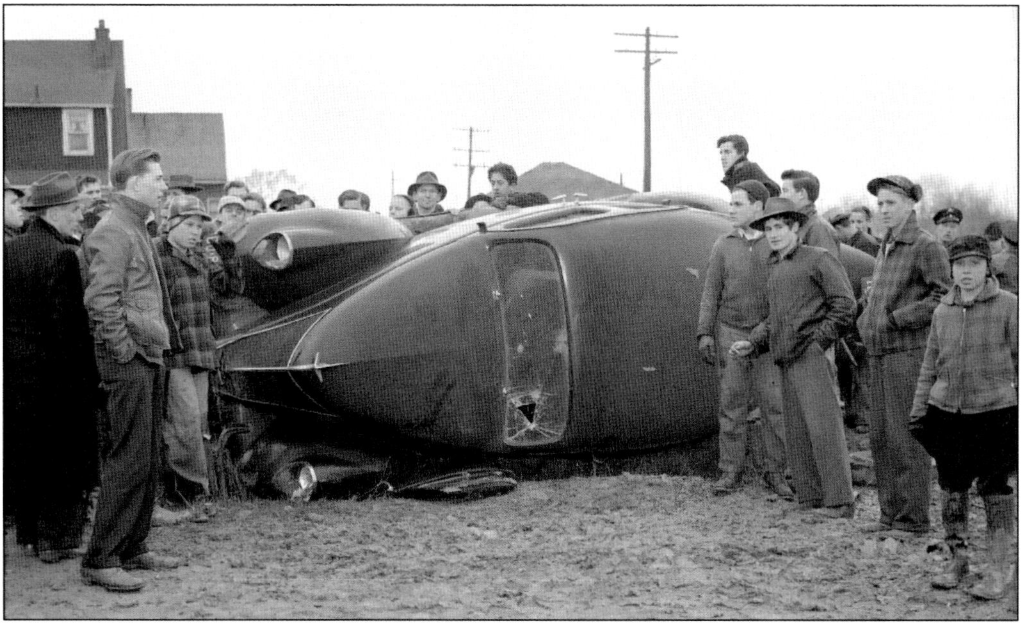

Eleanor Roosevelt supported the Sojourner Truth Homes for blacks. In a PBS interview, Vernon Jarrett talked about the decision to give the homes to blacks: "As a result, the Polish community staged an uprising, which tells you something about what goes on when immigrants come to America. One of the first indoctrinations you have is, to be a true American, is to be opposed to black people." In this *c.* 1942 photograph, men surround an overturned car. (WRL.)

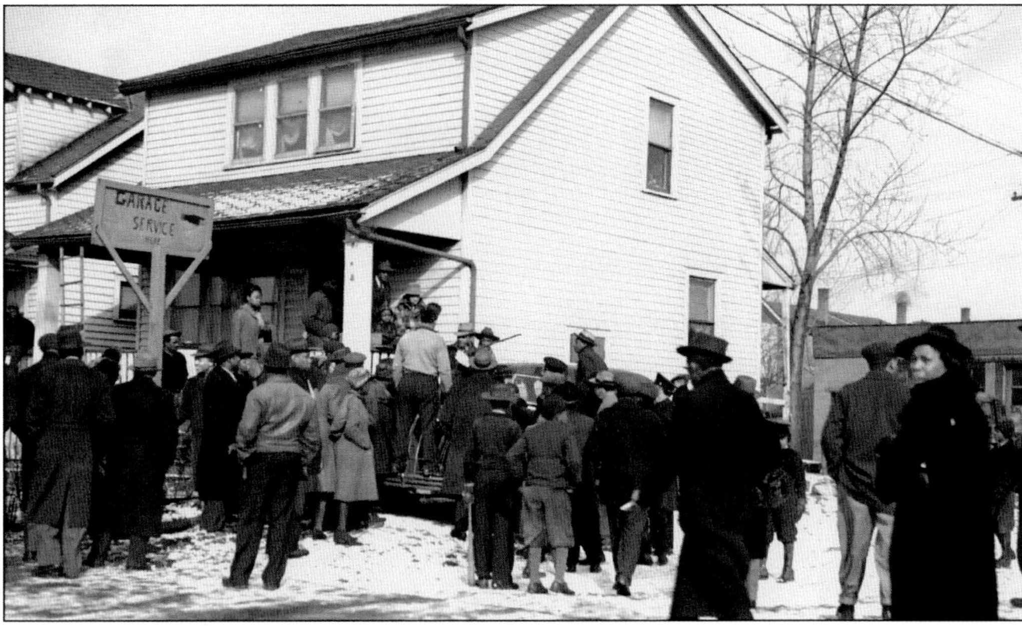

In this photograph, taken on February 28, 1942, a crowd of blacks gather outside a home in Black Bottom to organize against violent white protest against blacks moving into the Sojourner Truth Homes. However, the federal government built the projects in a predominately white neighborhood. In February 1942, there was a protest by 1,200 white workers as black families tried to move into their homes, the protest quickly became violent and resulted in arrests. (WRL.)

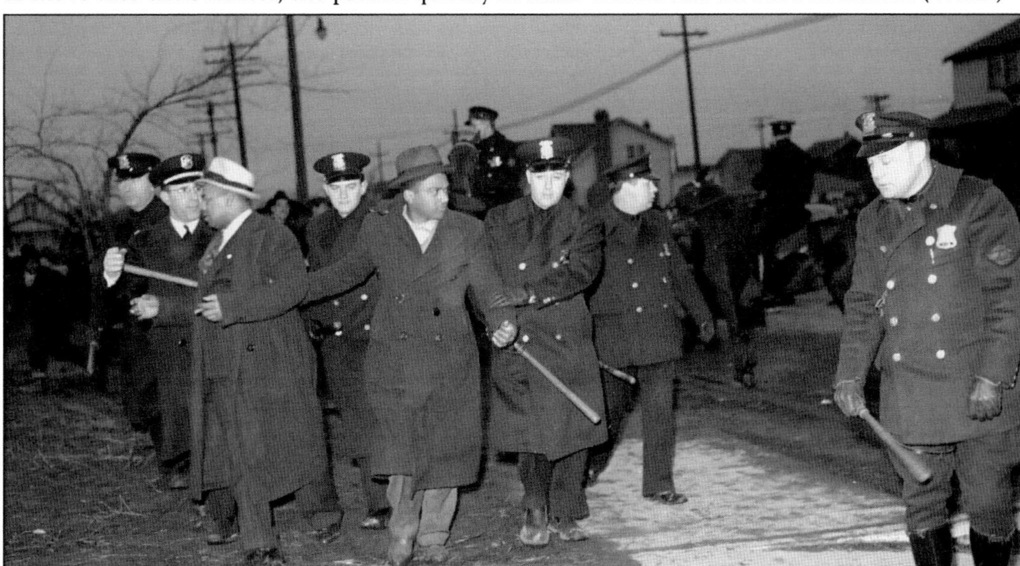

On June 20, 1942, blacks and whites clashed in minor skirmishes on Belle Isle. Two young blacks, angered that they had been ejected from Eastwood Park five days before, went to Belle Isle to even the score. Police began to search cars carrying black passengers to Belle Isle, but they did not search cars driven by whites. Fighting on the island began around 10:00 p.m.; police declared it under control by midnight. More than 200 blacks and whites participated in the free-for-all. In this *c.* 1942 photograph, uniformed officers lead away two black men. (WRL.)

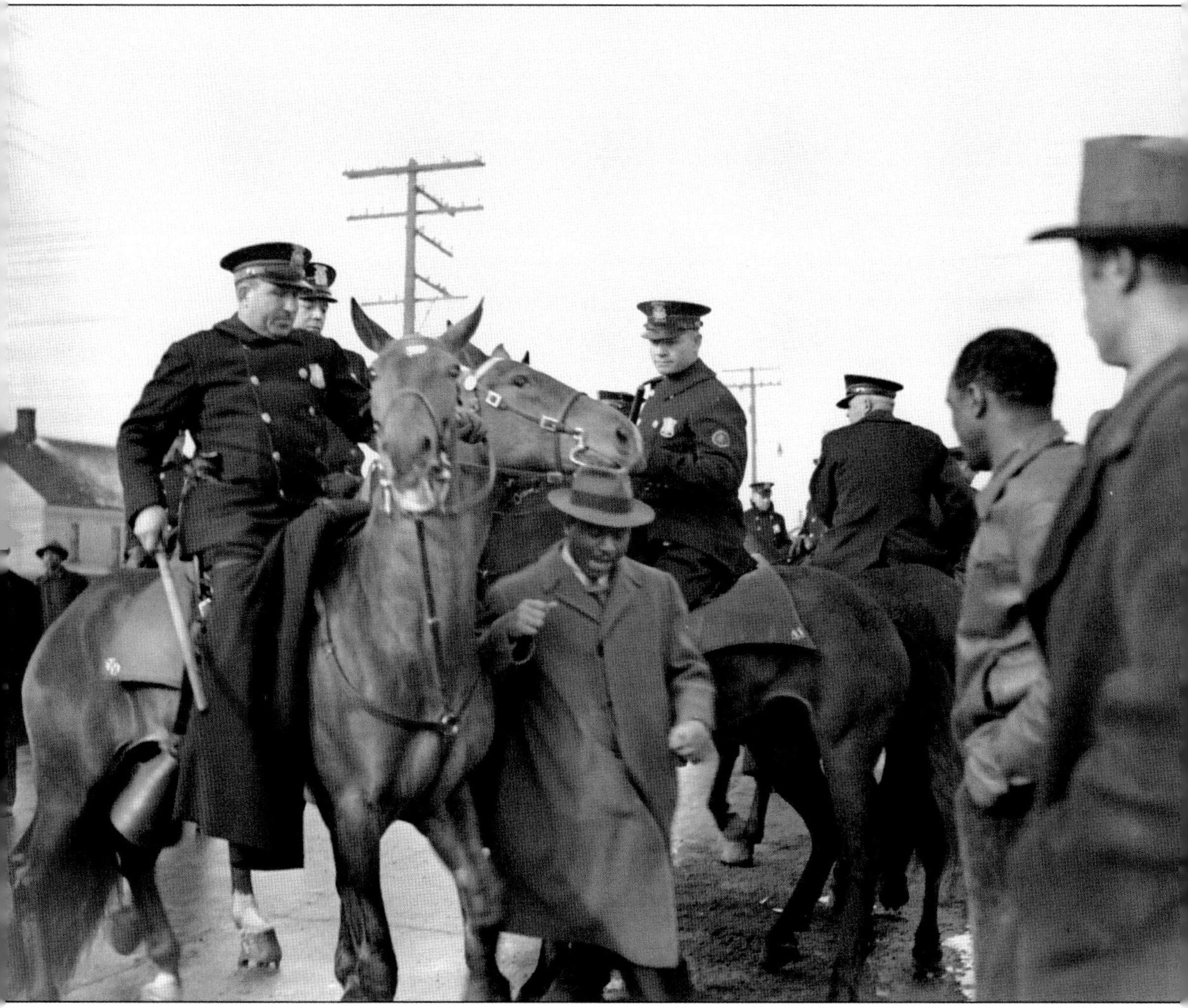

According to Vivian M. Baulch and Patricia Zacharias, by 1943, the number of African Americans in Detroit had doubled since 1933 to 200,000, and racial tensions in the city had grown accordingly. To protest unfair conditions, some blacks had undertaken a "bumping" campaign, walking into whites on the streets and bumping them off the sidewalks or nudging them in elevators. Local and national media anticipated trouble. *Life* magazine called the situation "dynamite." During the ensuing riots, the Detroit Police Department—many white men recruited from the South—was notorious for assaulting innocent, unarmed Black Bottom residents. White policemen even arrested blacks as they were being attacked by violent whites. White police officers stood around watching as white looters and troublemakers vandalized Black Bottom. Angry white crowds moved across Woodward Avenue into Paradise Valley breaking windows, looting stores, and beating blacks. In this *c.* 1942 photograph, police officers push a black man with a horse. (WRL.)

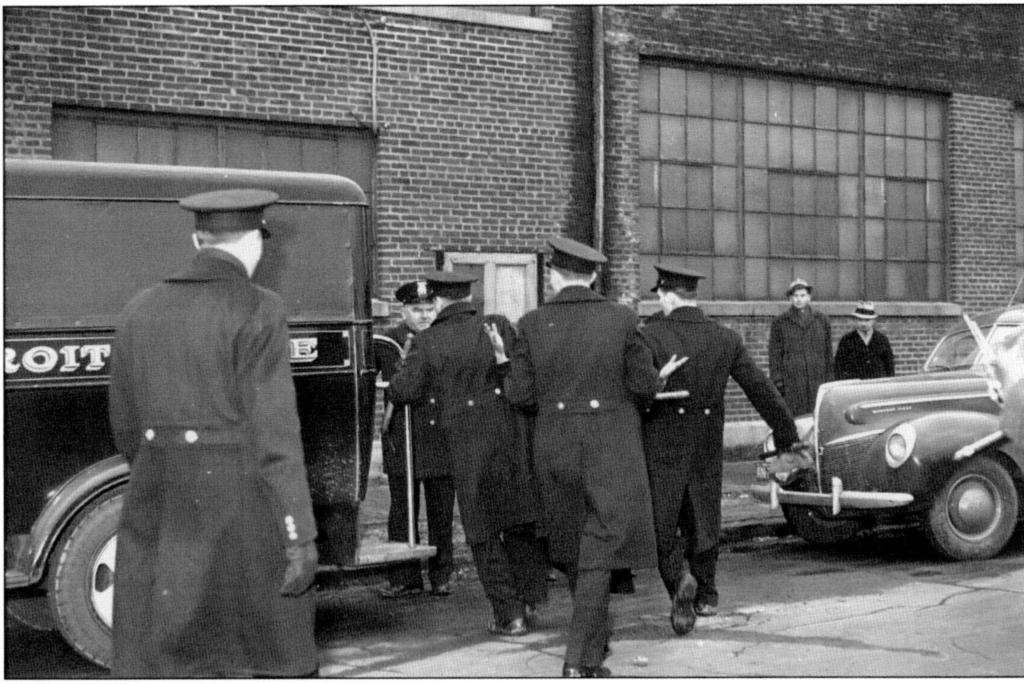

According to Vivian M. Baulch and Patricia Zacharias, "An angry mob of whites spilled onto Woodward near the Roxy Theater beating blacks as they were getting off street cars. At least six Detroit policemen were shot in the melees, and another 75 were injured . . . The virtual guerrilla warfare overwhelmed the 2,000 city police officers and 150 state police troopers." A group of uniformed police officers gathers at the back of a police vehicle. (WRL.)

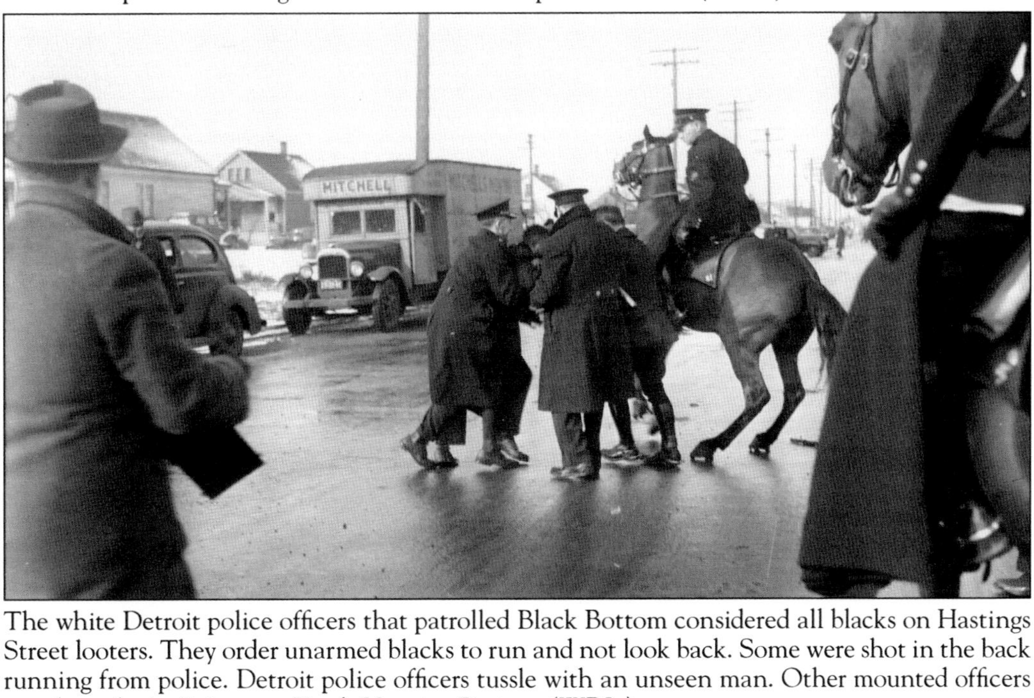

The white Detroit police officers that patrolled Black Bottom considered all blacks on Hastings Street looters. They order unarmed blacks to run and not look back. Some were shot in the back running from police. Detroit police officers tussle with an unseen man. Other mounted officers stand nearby in Sojourner Truth Housing Project. (WRL.)

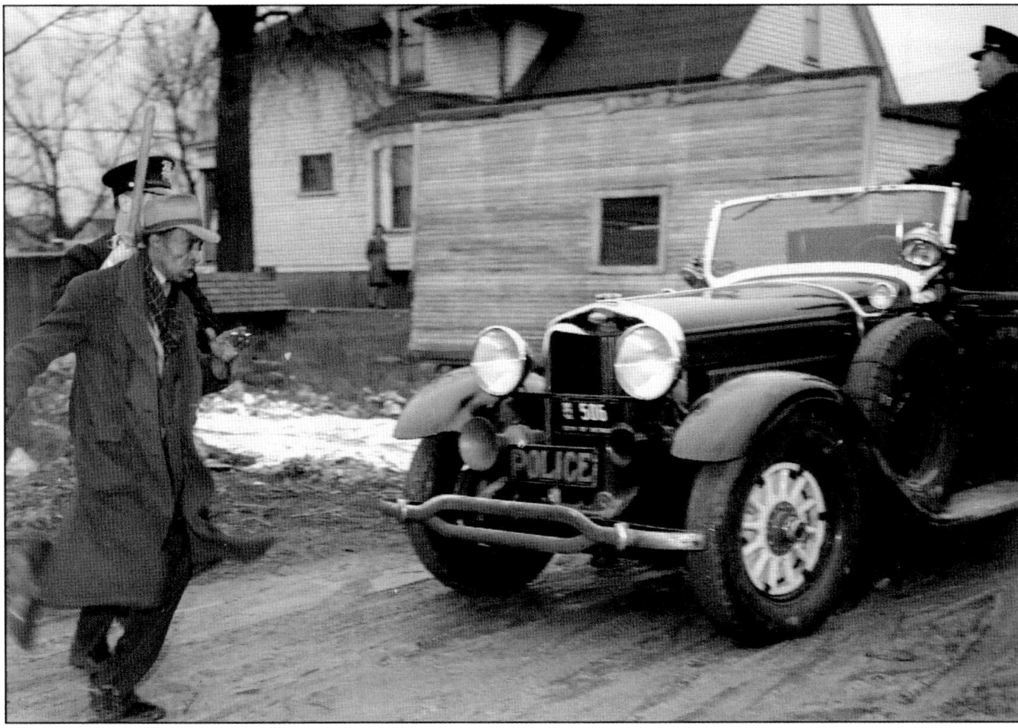

An African American man runs from the violent white melee, in front of a police vehicle. Rampant white brutality from uniformed police officers went unchecked and unregulated. White police officers beat black citizens with nightsticks, utility flashlights, and departmental pistols. (WRL.)

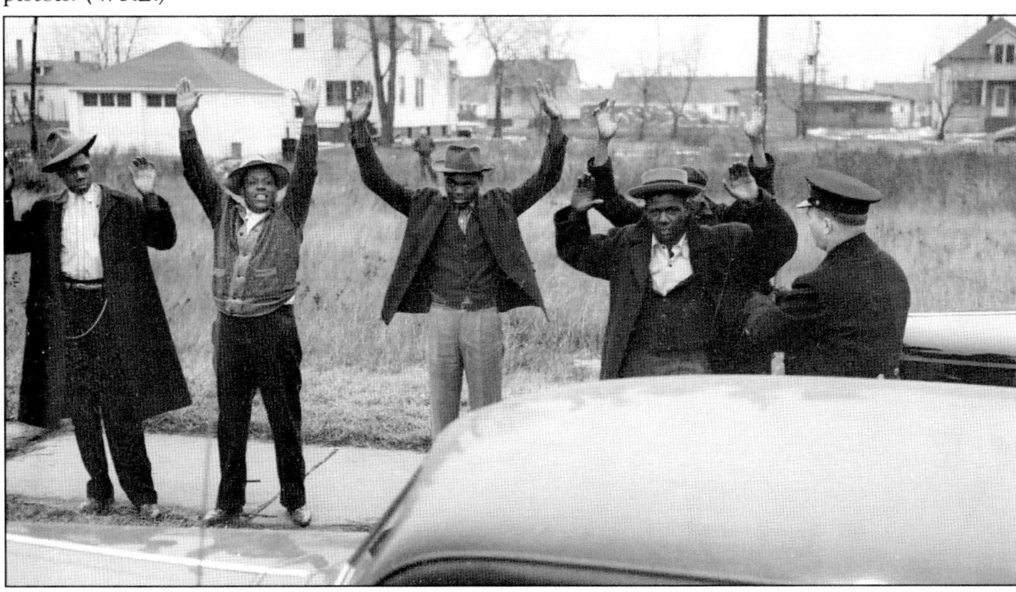

White police officers arrested black men and hauled them down to police headquarters where the innocent men were subjected to more illegal brutality. In this photograph, black men stand on the sidewalk with their hands raised above their heads, with a uniformed police officer facing them in the foreground. (WRL.)

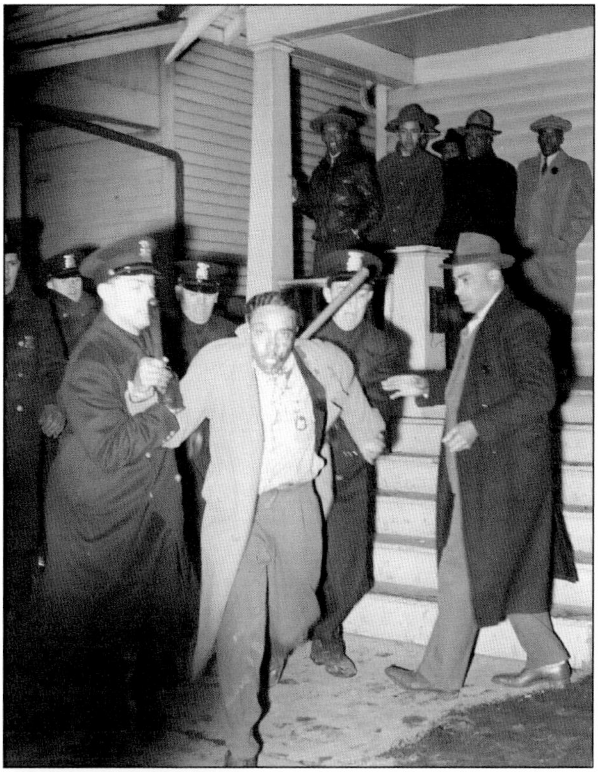

A bloodied black man is led from his home by uniformed officers. Many innocent black men received 80-day jail terms for "disturbing the peace," and some were convicted of bogus charges including concealment of weapons, destruction of property, assault, and larceny. White assailants vandalized and destroyed properties in Black Bottom while police stood by and sometimes assisted. Perversely, the force was criticized for its "restraint" in dealing with the alleged black rioters—only 17 black men were killed by police. (WRL.)

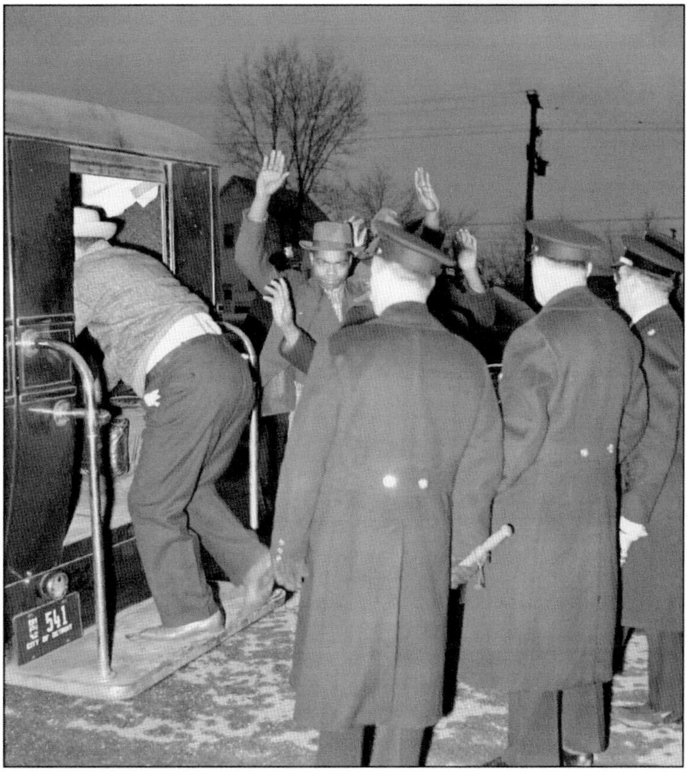

Men are placed into the back of a vehicle. On June 10, 1942, Henry N. Johnson, president of the Detroit Real Estate Board, spoke to the issue of inadequate housing and the slum conditions in which Black Bottom residents lived, telling mortgage bankers that Black Bottom residents should be given "the same opportunity to establish homes as the city's White population, with equal police protection, adequate schools, recreation facilities, garbage collection and other services, Detroit's Negroes . . . would quickly take advantage of it." (WRL.)

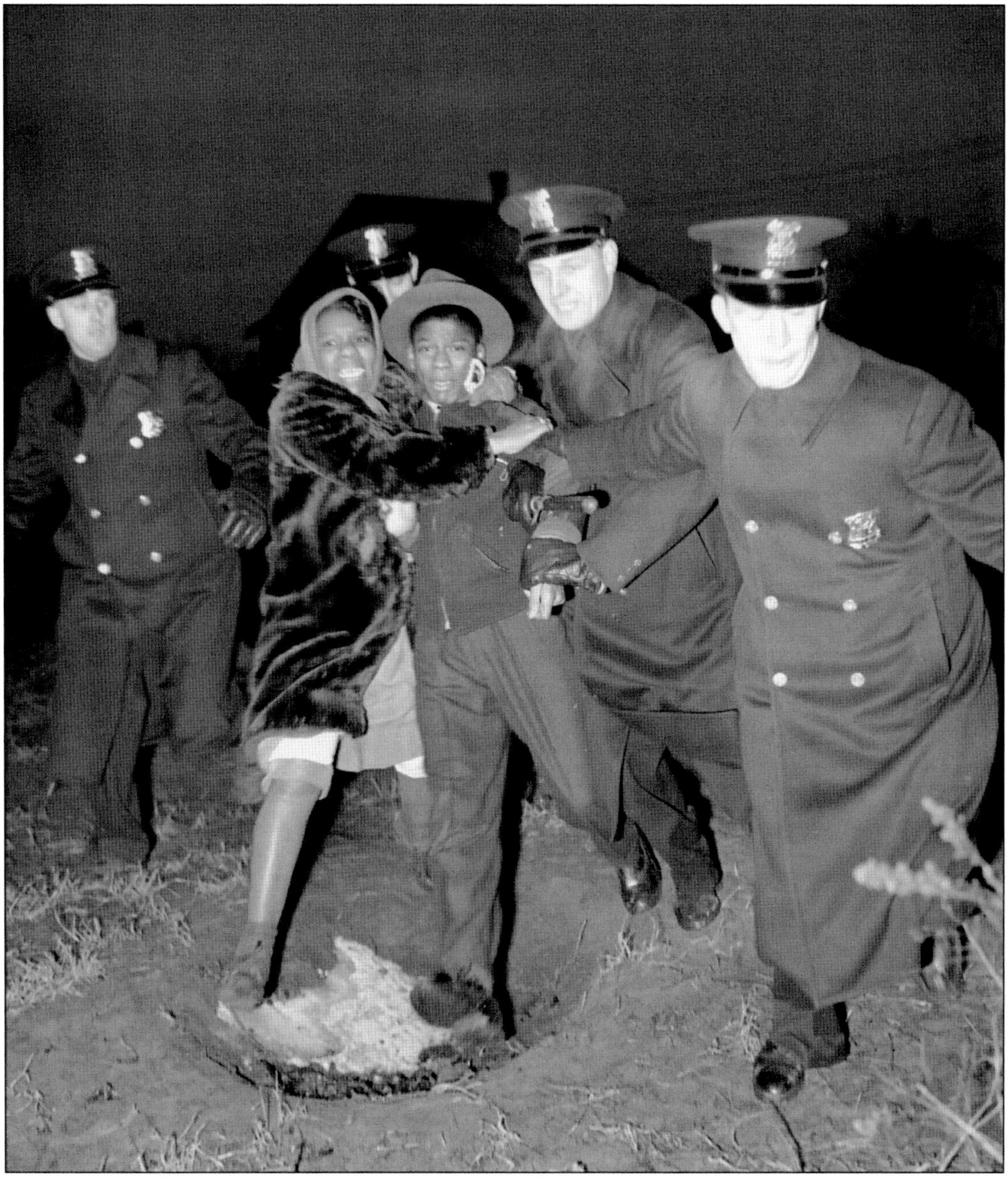

African American men were especially targeted as much by white policemen during the riots, as they had been before the riots. The city's white police department violated African American rights with impunity. When Coleman A. Young became mayor, his first order of business was to hire more black police officers. In this photograph, a woman clings to a young man as uniformed police officers lead him away. (WRL.)

In this photograph, a white woman identified as Dolores Hommer sits back in a chair with a bandage wrapped around her head. She was one of the few whites arrested for racial instigation and violent attacks on blacks in the Sojourner Truth projects riot. Hommer was eventually released and not charged. (WRL.)

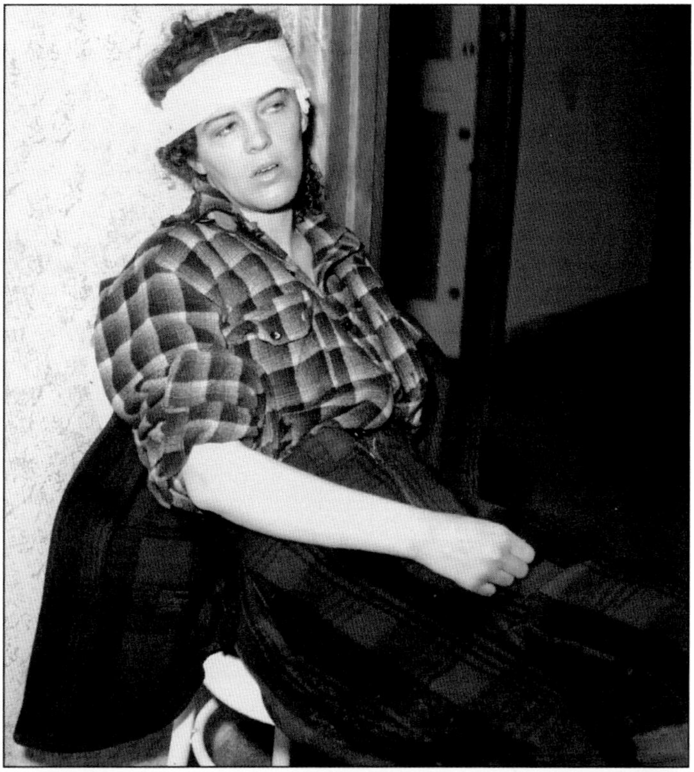

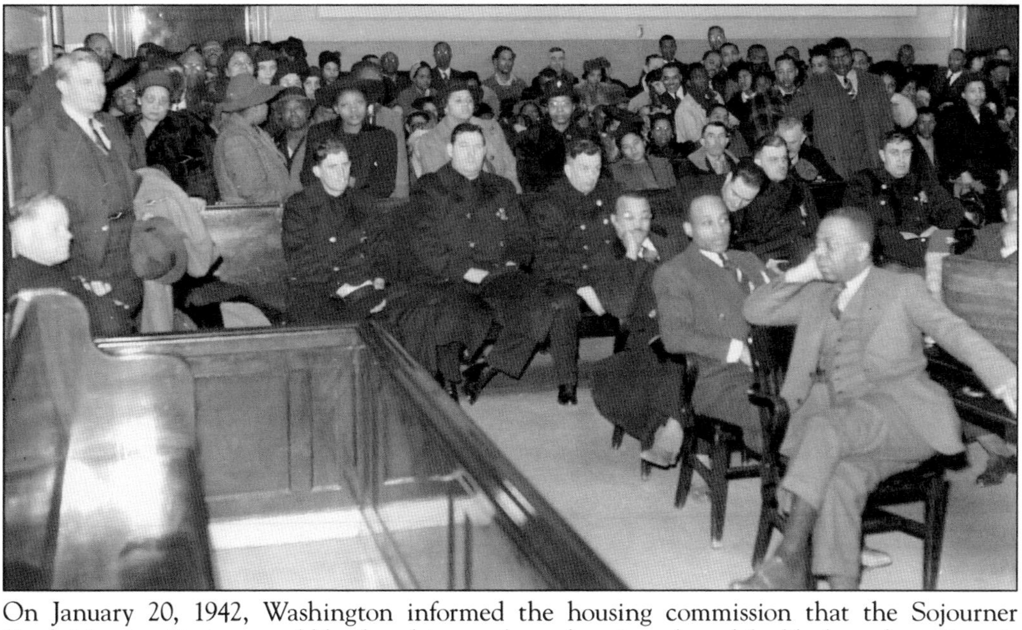

On January 20, 1942, Washington informed the housing commission that the Sojourner Truth Housing Project would be for whites and another site selected for black workers. Detroit newspapers, union leaders, and many other whites campaigned for the government to allow the black workers to move into the homes. The families had given up whatever shelter, they had in anticipation of their new homes; left with no place to go, they were housed with other families in the Brewster homes and other sites. This photograph shows the court proceedings. (WRL.)

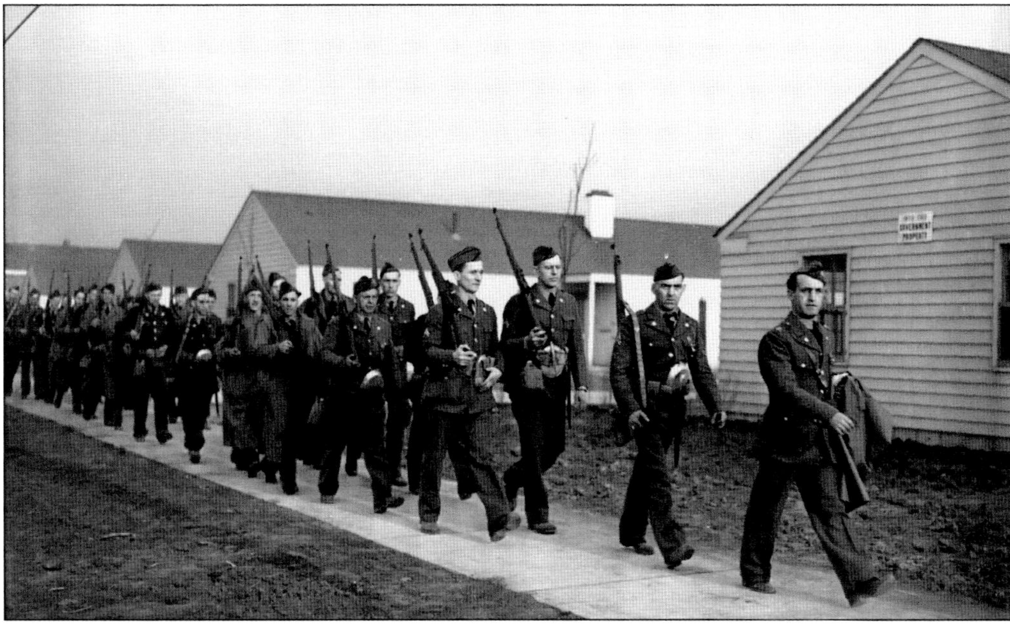

Finally, despite the simmering resentment, black families moved into the Sojourner Truth Housing Project at the end of April. Detroit mayor Edward Jeffries ordered Detroit police and state troops to keep the peace during the move. In this photograph, state troopers guard the Sojourner Truth Housing Project, where whites in the surrounding neighborhood were opposed to black families moving in. (WRL.)

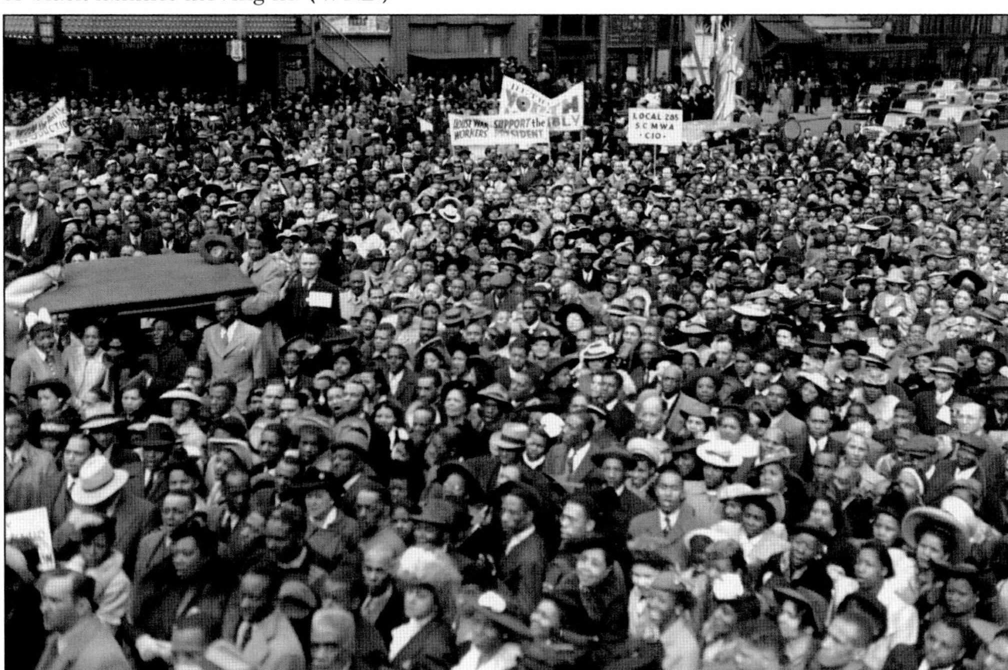

When a suitable site could not be found, the Washington housing authorities agreed to allow blacks into the finished Sojourner Truth Homes. African Americans meet at Cadillac Square to rejoice the victory. (WRL.)

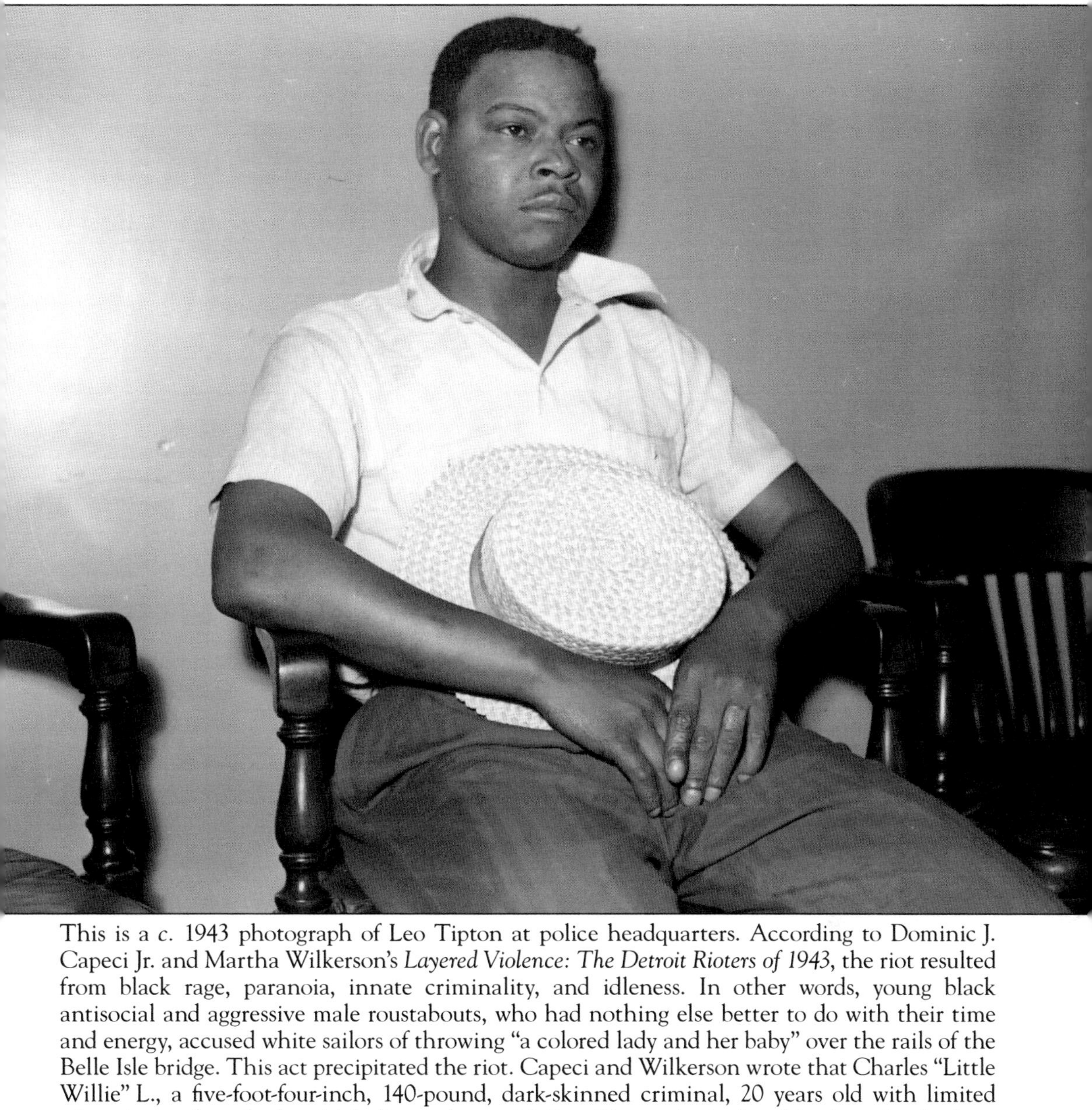

This is a *c.* 1943 photograph of Leo Tipton at police headquarters. According to Dominic J. Capeci Jr. and Martha Wilkerson's *Layered Violence: The Detroit Rioters of 1943*, the riot resulted from black rage, paranoia, innate criminality, and idleness. In other words, young black antisocial and aggressive male roustabouts, who had nothing else better to do with their time and energy, accused white sailors of throwing "a colored lady and her baby" over the rails of the Belle Isle bridge. This act precipitated the riot. Capeci and Wilkerson wrote that Charles "Little Willie" L., a five-foot-four-inch, 140-pound, dark-skinned criminal, 20 years old with limited education and marked racial feelings, along with Leo Tipton, incited and instigated a day-long riot that ended the next day when 4,000 army troops were sent under martial law into the city. Some 35 people lay dead, 530 injured, and 1,300 arrested. Some 20 blacks were given 90-day jail terms for disturbing the peace. No whites were convicted of any wrongdoing. (WRL.)

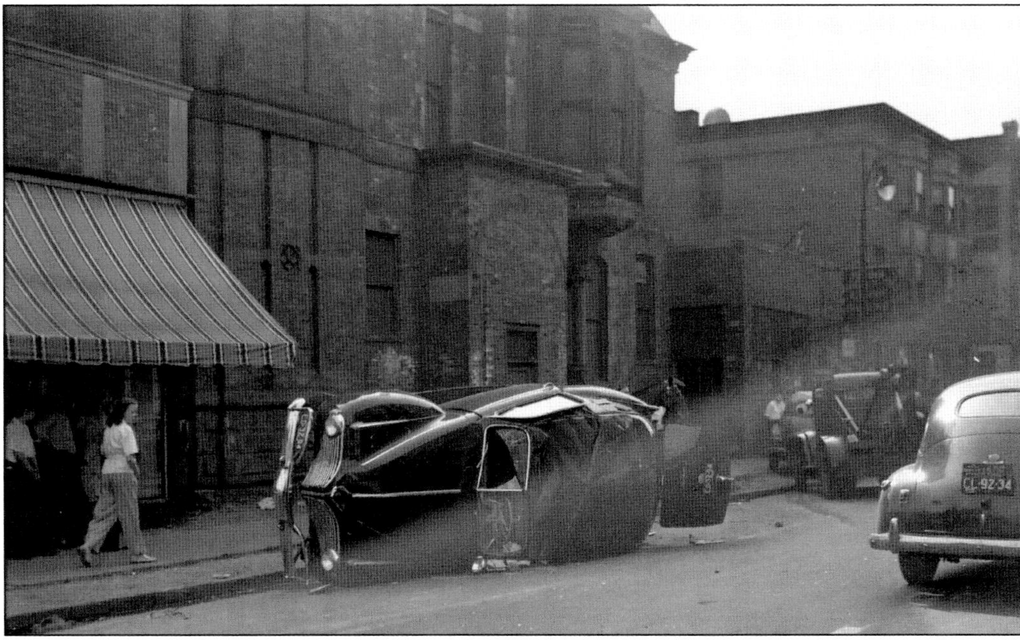

Whenever blacks attempted to expand into new areas, their efforts were often met with white mob violence. Almost a month after the riots, Black Bottom still bore the effects of the riots. Many merchants continued to try to put their businesses (and lives) back together, boarding up broken windows and replacing the vast amounts of merchandise that had been looted during the riots. In this photograph, Polish youths have terrorized Black Bottom. (WRL.)

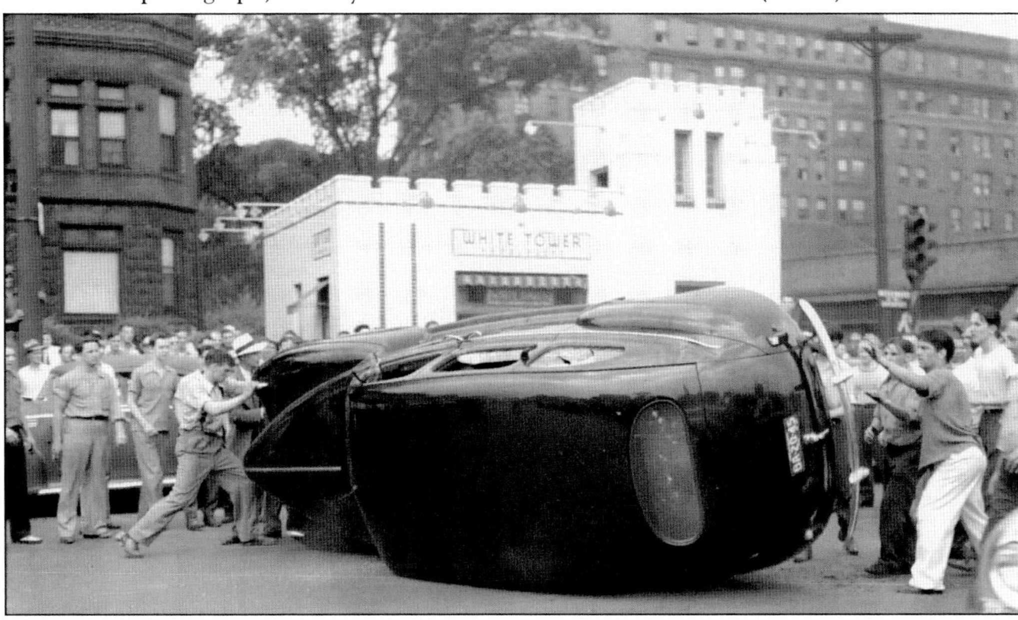

In a PBS interview, Vernon Jarrett recalled the riot of 1943, "It was one of the worst. People unaware of what was going on would have been smashed out of cars and brutalized and killed. And the policemen were, by and large, in favor of the white mob. And then black people began to retaliate, attacking innocent white people. It was just brutal." In this *c.* 1943 photograph, a group of young white men turn a car on its side in front of White Tower Hamburger restaurant. (WRL.)

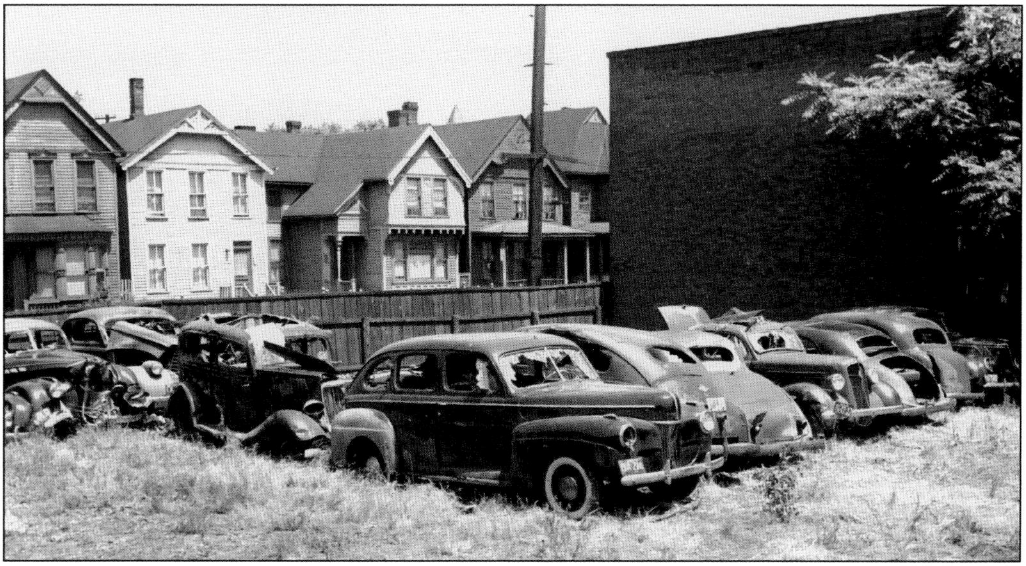

The 1943 race riots destroyed property and cost the city millions. Most of the property damage was reported in Black Bottom. Whites burned black homes, looted profitable businesses in Paradise Valley, and torched overturned automobiles in the face of duplicitous white police officers. In this *c.* 1943 photograph, burned and damaged cars are stored at a makeshift police pound lot in this residential area. (WRL.)

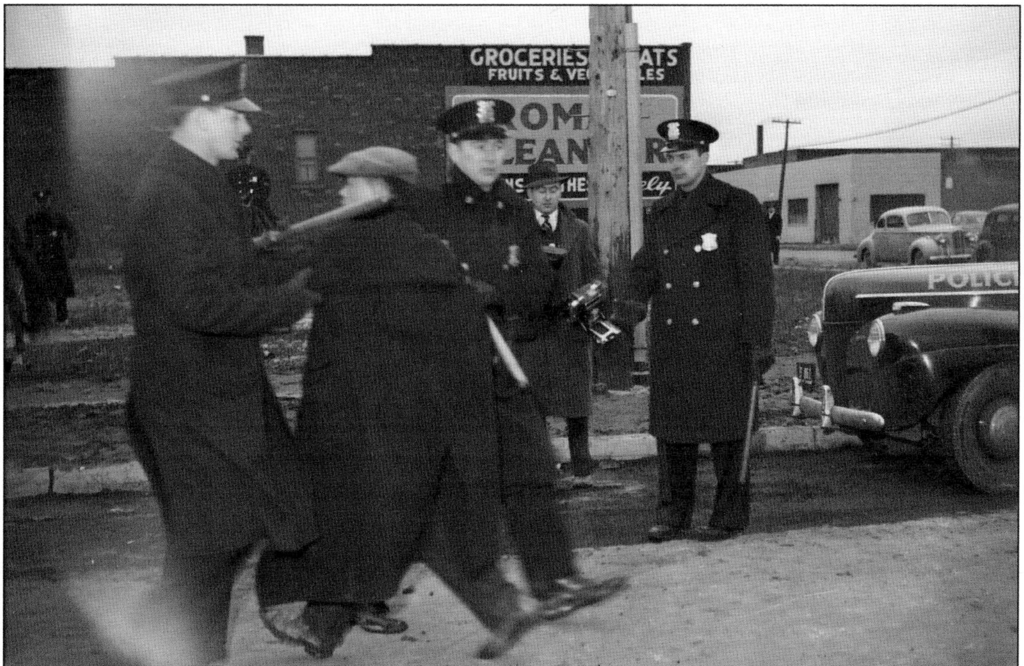

A uniformed police officer holds his nightstick at the neck of a black man in the Sojourner Truth Housing Project. Detroit police officers regularly assisted white mobs in bludgeoning innocent, unarmed blacks during the riots. Federal troops were brought in to quell the riot. The nearly 36 hours of rioting claimed 34 lives, 25 of them black. The majority of the 1,800 arrested for looting were black. Some 13 murders remained unsolved. (WRL.)

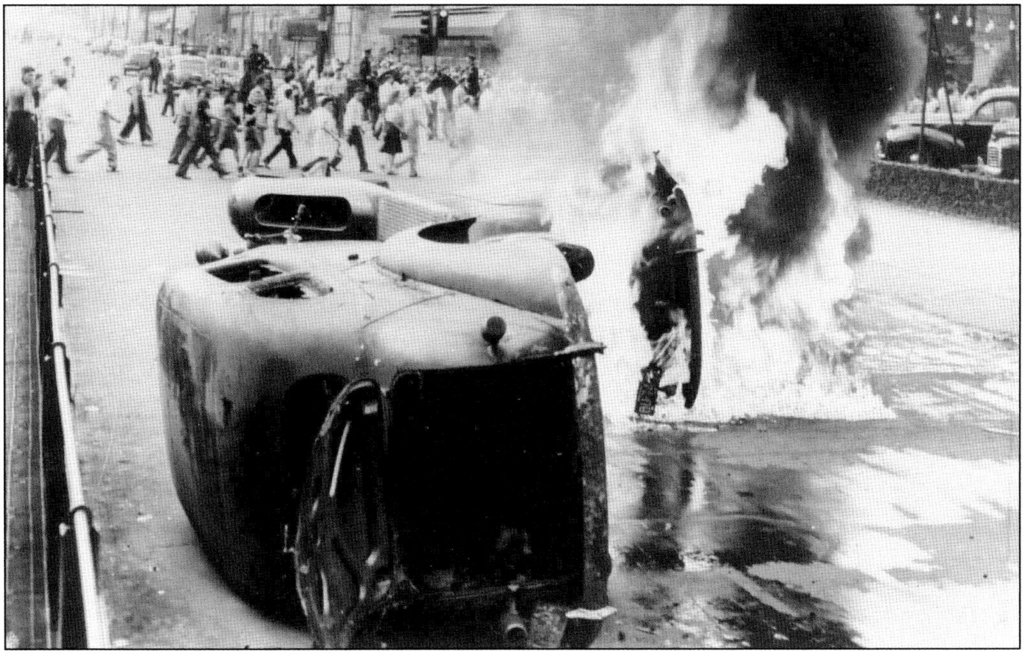

Thurgood Marshall, then with the NAACP, assailed the city's handling of the riot. He charged that police unfairly targeted blacks while turning their backs on white atrocities. He said 85 percent of those arrested were black while whites overturned and burned cars in front of the Roxy Theater with impunity while police watched. "This weak-kneed policy of the police commissioner coupled with the anti-Negro attitude of many members of the force helped to make a riot inevitable." (WRL.)

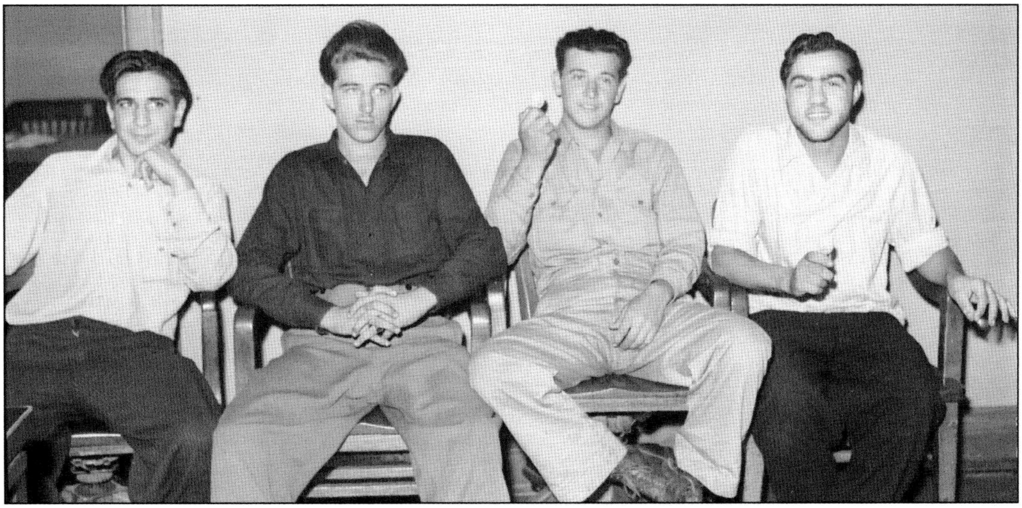

On July 30, 1943, Robert Cattone, Antohny Saraceno, Armando Mastantuono, and Aldo Trani were charged in the racially motivated death of a black man. Sitting at police headquarters, they await arraignment. White men were rarely arrested for attacking blacks and almost always acquitted. Mayor Edward Jeffries praised the force and said he was "rapidly losing [his] patience with those Negro leaders who insist that their people do not and will not trust policemen." The mayor asked Rev. Horace A. White to search for 200 qualified Africans Americans to join the police force. (WRL.)

Eight

Urban Renewal

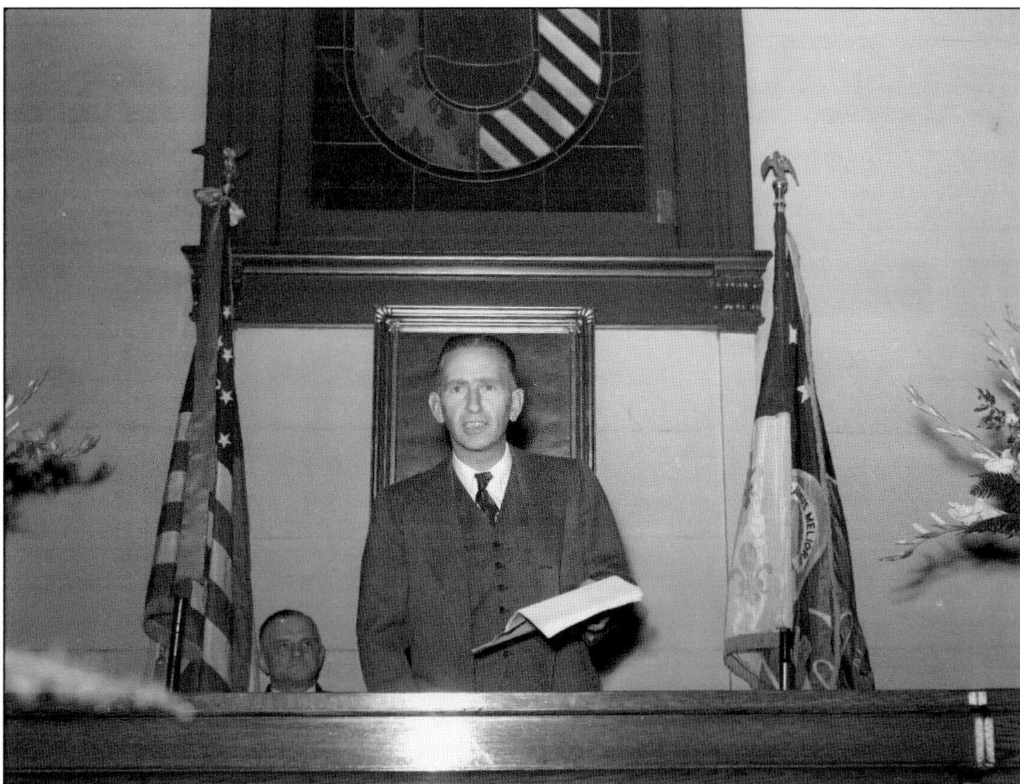

Mayor Jeffries's 1946 Detroit Plan targeted Black Bottom as the ideal site for so-called slum clearance. When the Detroit Plan was issued in its final form in 1951, 140,000 blacks lived in Black Bottom. Black Bottom and Paradise Valley had begun to descend. This is Mayor Jeffries's 1940 inaugural address. (WRL.)

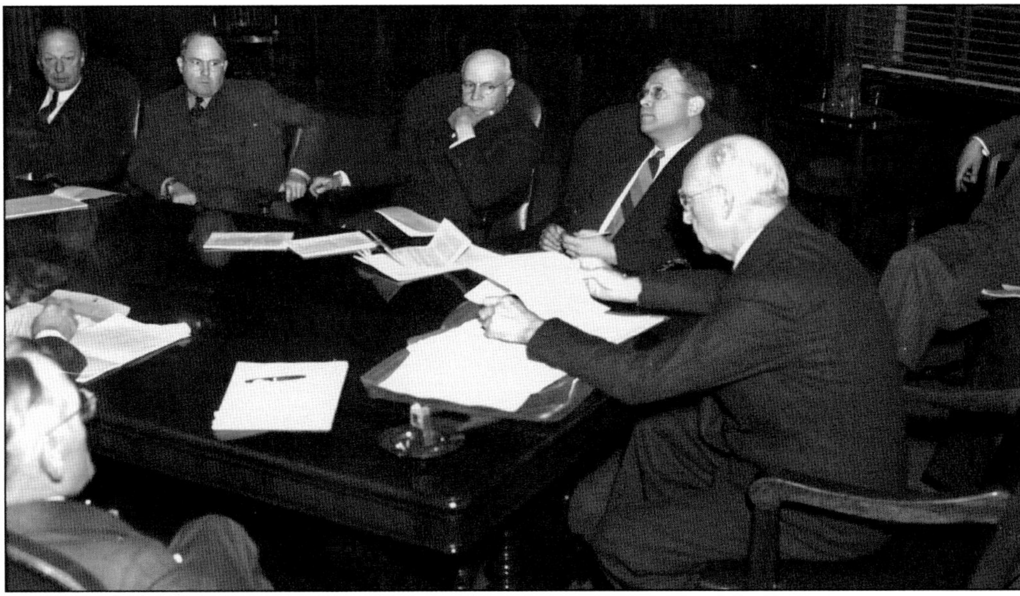

The death knell for the historic community was struck by urban renewal, which transformed Black Bottom into Lafayette Park. As early as 1941, the first concrete plan aiming at ultimate rehabilitation of the area within the Grand Boulevard circle was under consideration by Jeffries's blight committee. In this photograph, rehabilitation committee officials discuss Black Bottom's fate around 1940. Committee members were Charles. L. Biggs, Paul E. Krause, John Miller, Oscar Webber, Donald S. Kiskadden, Charles. A. Lyons, Albert E. Cobo, George Emery, Andrew L. Malott, Edmund Khulman. (WRL.)

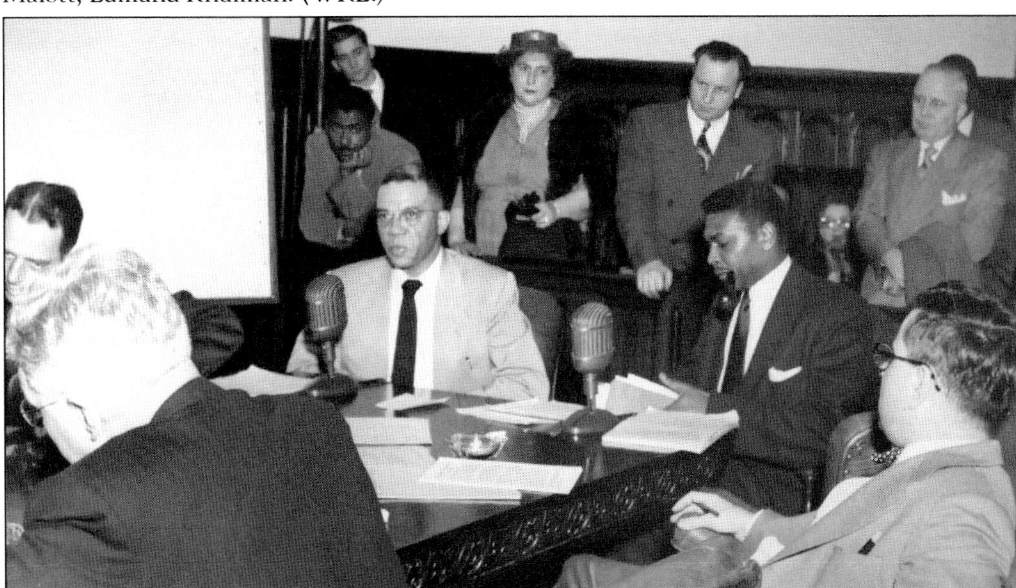

Mayor Edward Jeffries and the Detroit City Plan Commission of 1946 destroyed a community. Black Bottom and Paradise Valley were devastated by highway construction. In this c. 1951 photograph, a meeting including Detroit City Plan Commission president Remus G. Robinson (front, left) and secretary William Price (seated, center), takes place between Detroit Urban League, the City of Detroit, and the common council on the issue of urban renewal and housing. (BHL.)

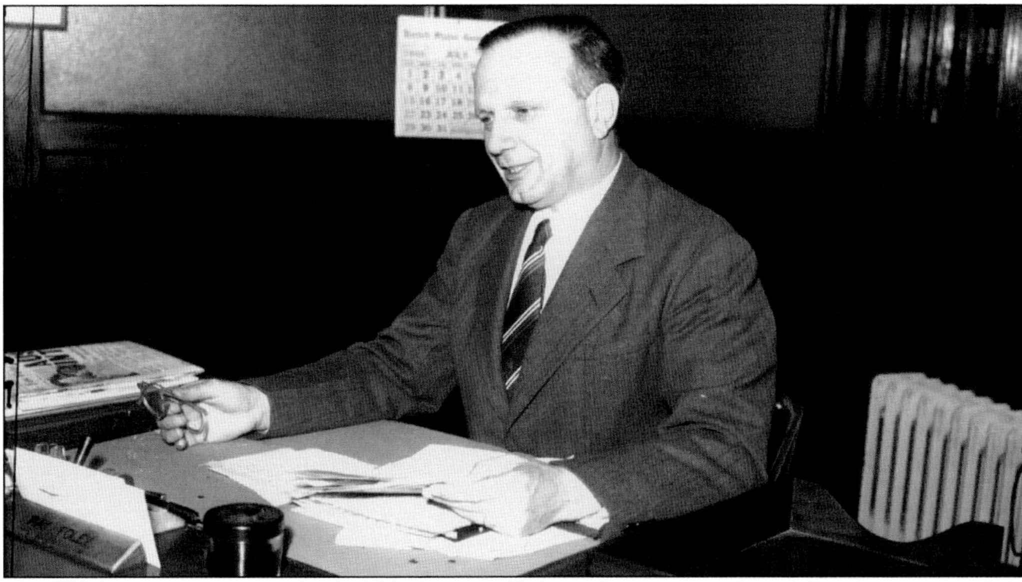

In the early 1940s, the efforts of the Eight Mile Civic Association and local developers gained the attention of Raymond Foley, the Michigan director of the Federal Housing Authority. Thomas Sugrue writes in *The Origins of Urban Crisis*, "Foley, a New Deal Democrat, became the national director of the Federal Housing Authority in the Truman administration. He found the efforts of black neighborhood residents and developers to construct their own homes a compelling cause. Yet Foley's interest in the small black community by no means signaled a new federal commitment to integrated housing . . . Like many social reformers of the New Deal era, he believed in a separate-but-equal philosophy of housing finance." (WRL.)

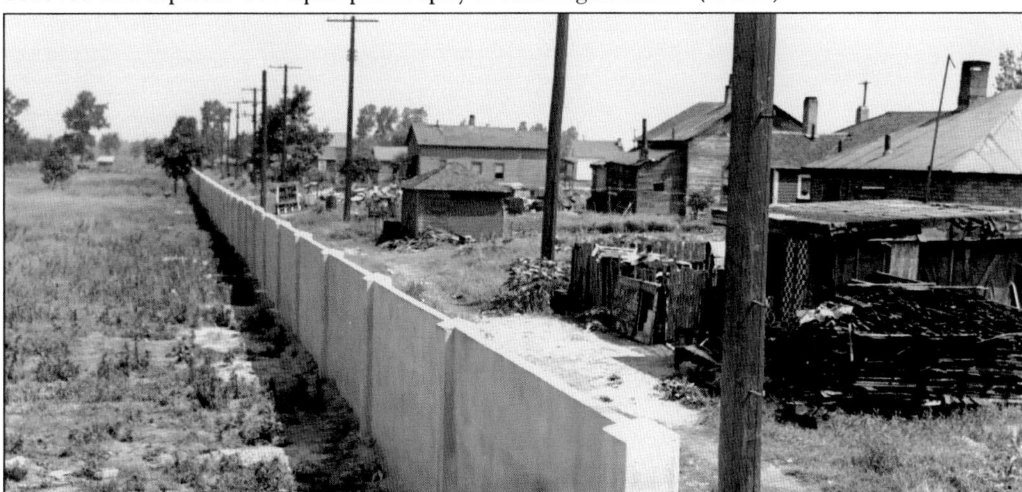

The aftermath of the urban renewal initiative was not much more than a "'no man's land' of deterioration and abandonment." Construction had been delayed and Black Bottom lay dormant. The city did nothing to help business owners or residents relocate. Shopkeepers had no cause to invest in improvements. Condemned buildings were buried under asphalt and cement. Statistics show that by 1950, 423 residences, 109 businesses, 22 manufacturing plants, and 93 vacant lots had been condemned for the first three-mile stretch of the Lodge Freeway, from Jefferson Avenue to Pallister Street. A concrete wall divided white from black; this image is from around 1941. (WRL.)

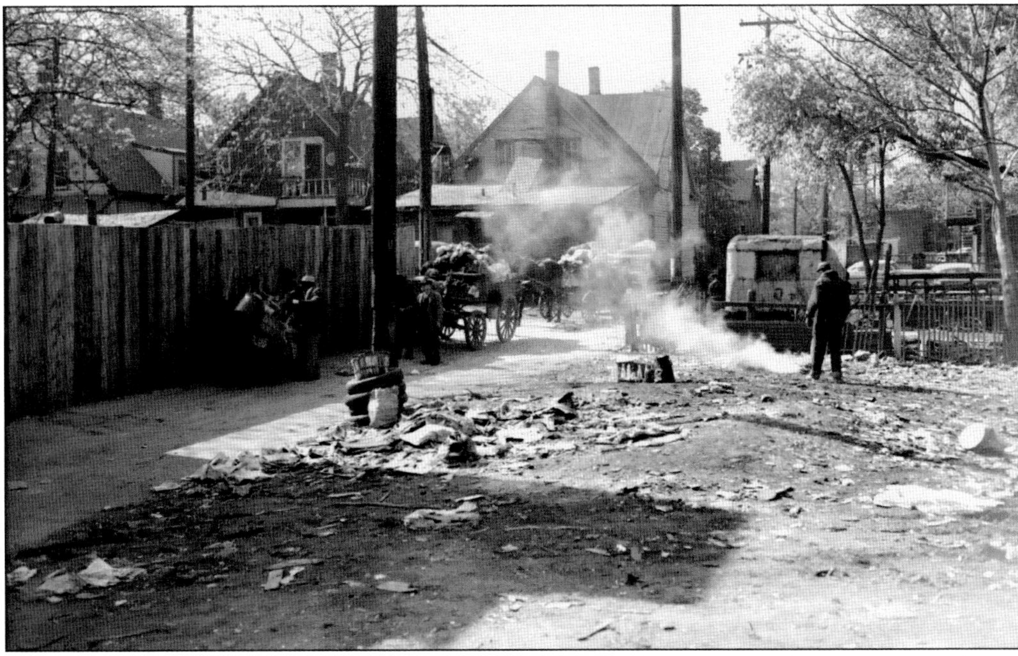

By 1958, the Lodge Freeway had gobbled up 2,222 buildings. Demolition continued with approximately more 2,800 buildings to make way for the Edsel Ford Expressway. While white homeowners were displaced as well, black renters suffered the brunt of the change. Whereas white homeowners were able to relocate, many blacks were left out in the cold. This photograph was taken around 1956. (WRL.)

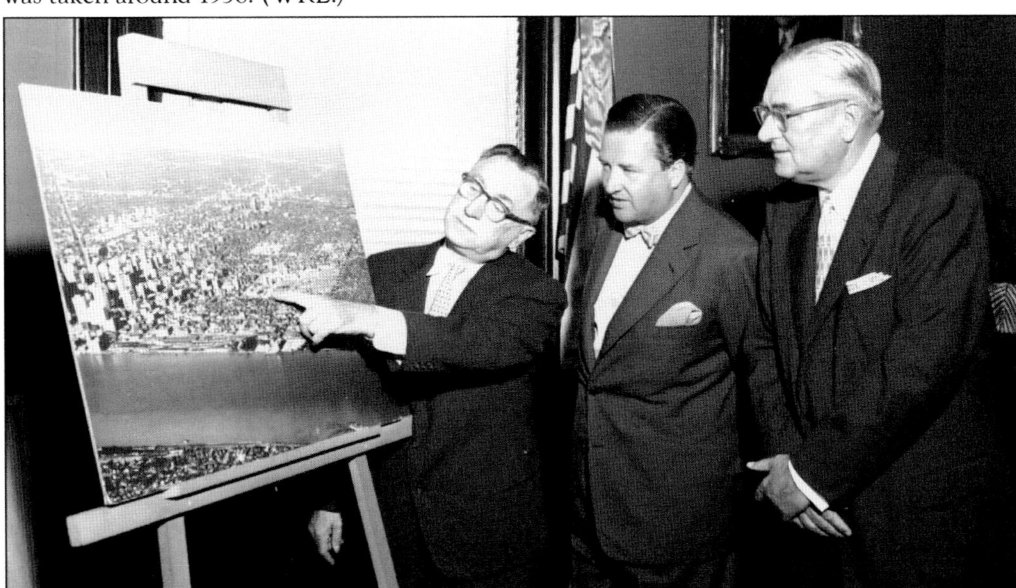

Former Black Bottom resident and businessman Sunnie Wilson believed that, "just like other cities around the country that sought to rid themselves of run-down Black neighborhoods, the take over of Paradise Valley could not be stopped. That's been the White man's philosophy—to move in, move the people out, and let the property sit vacant." In this *c.* 1955 photograph, from left to right, Walter Gehrke, Henry Ford II, and Mayor Albert E. Cobo discuss redevelopment. (WRL.)

The Jeffries Projects—named for the father of Mayor Edward Jeffries—opened in 1953 as a complex of eight separate 14-story buildings. Five more buildings, and additional low-rise housing, were added in 1955. Once a decent and respectable place to live, by the late 1960s, the Jeffries Projects had become a haven for drug dealers and an area with a high crime rate. This photograph was taken on June 18, 1954. (WRL.)

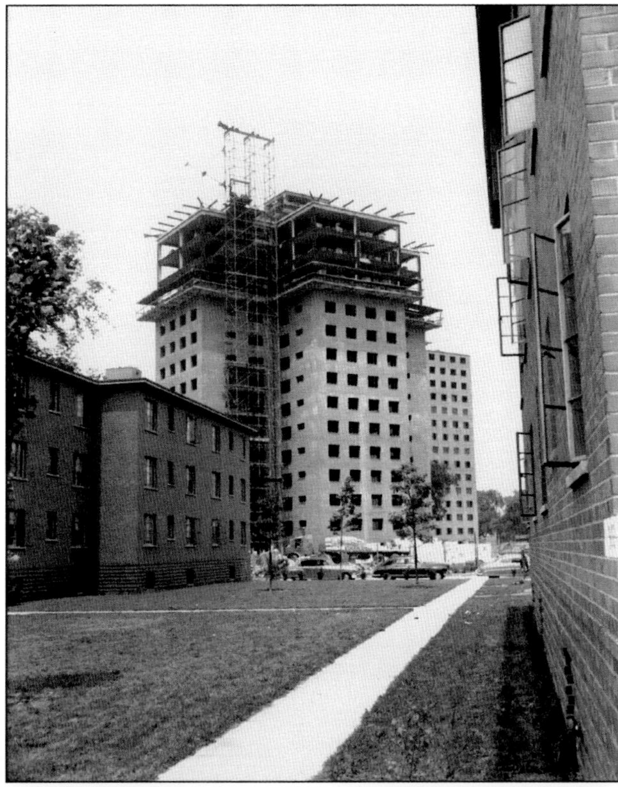

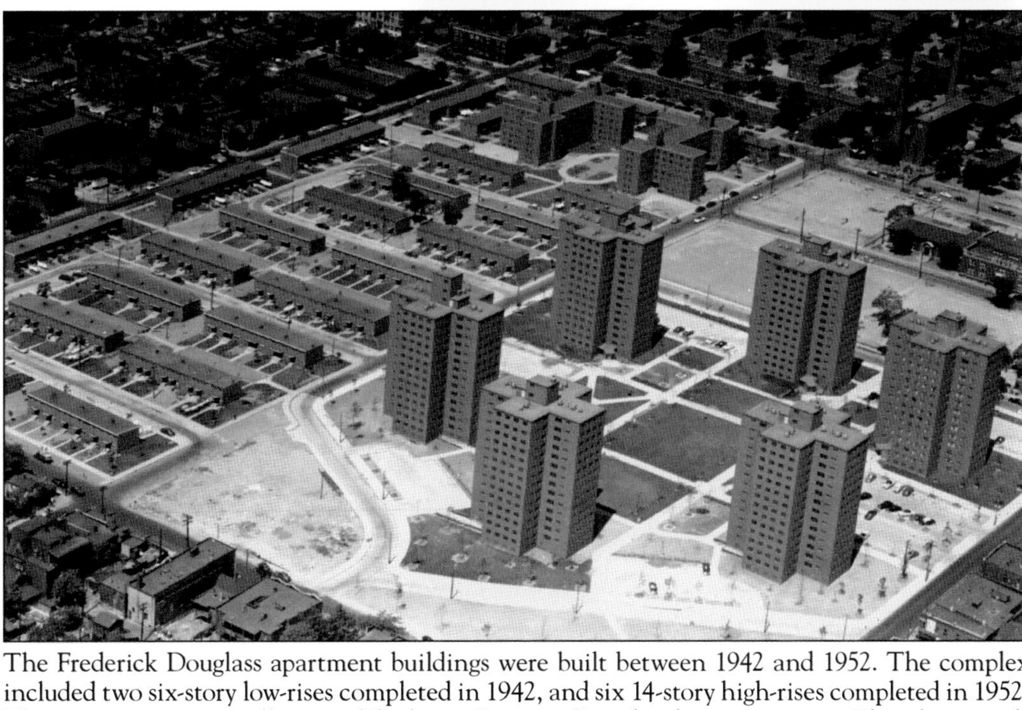

The Frederick Douglass apartment buildings were built between 1942 and 1952. The complex included two six-story low-rises completed in 1942, and six 14-story high-rises completed in 1952. The towers were originally part of the larger Brewster-Douglass housing project. This photograph was taken around 1955. (WRL.)

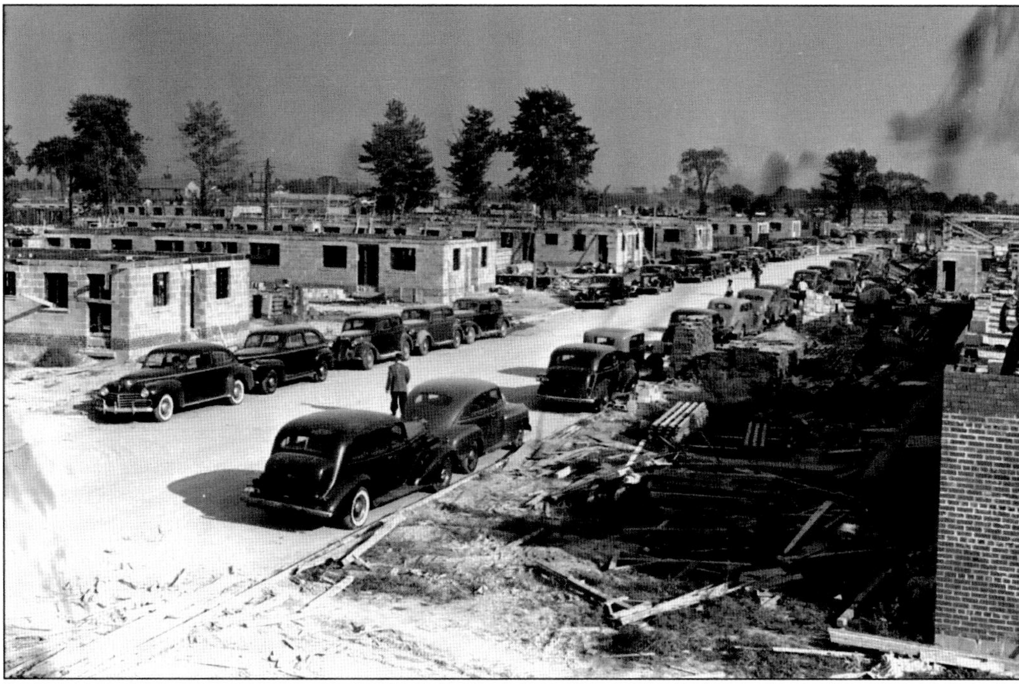

Urban renewal continued to displace Black Bottom residents, sending many to the Herman Gardens. First built in the year 1943, Herman Gardens consisted of 2,144 units of mostly two-story multifamily buildings. The Herman Gardens was home to a few notable individuals such as automobile giant John De Lorean and television judge Greg Mathis. This c. 1941 photograph shows the Herman Gardens under construction. (WRL.)

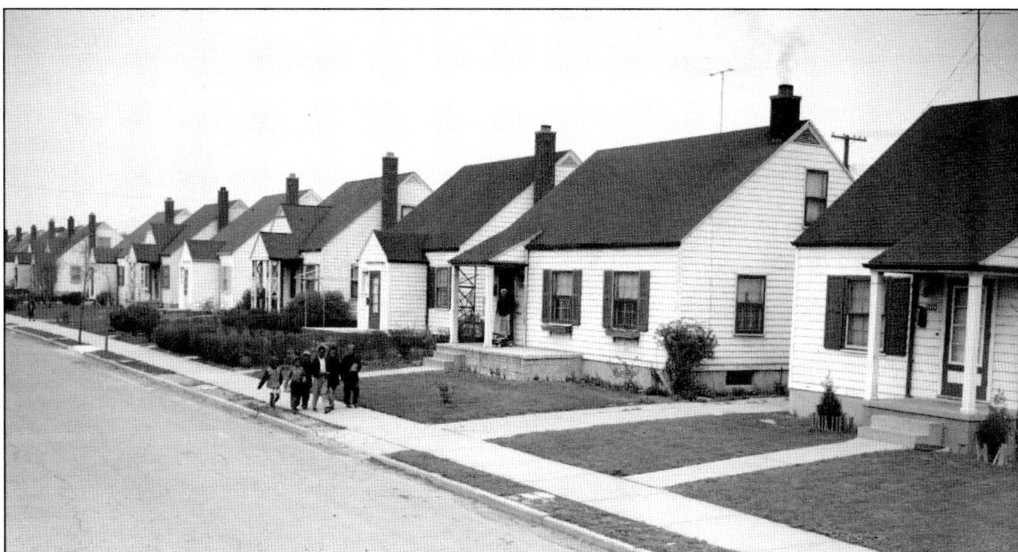

Paradise Valley was obliterated, but the black ghetto simply moved to the Twelfth Street area, forgotten until it became the center of the 1967 riot. Twelfth Street had been the Jewish area; the Jews were now living in Huntington Woods, Southfield, and other suburbs. Middle-class blacks moved to the more prominent neighborhoods of La Salle Boulevard, Chicago Boulevard, Boston-Edison, and Arden Park. Black Bottom was gone. This photograph was taken around 1950. (WRL.)

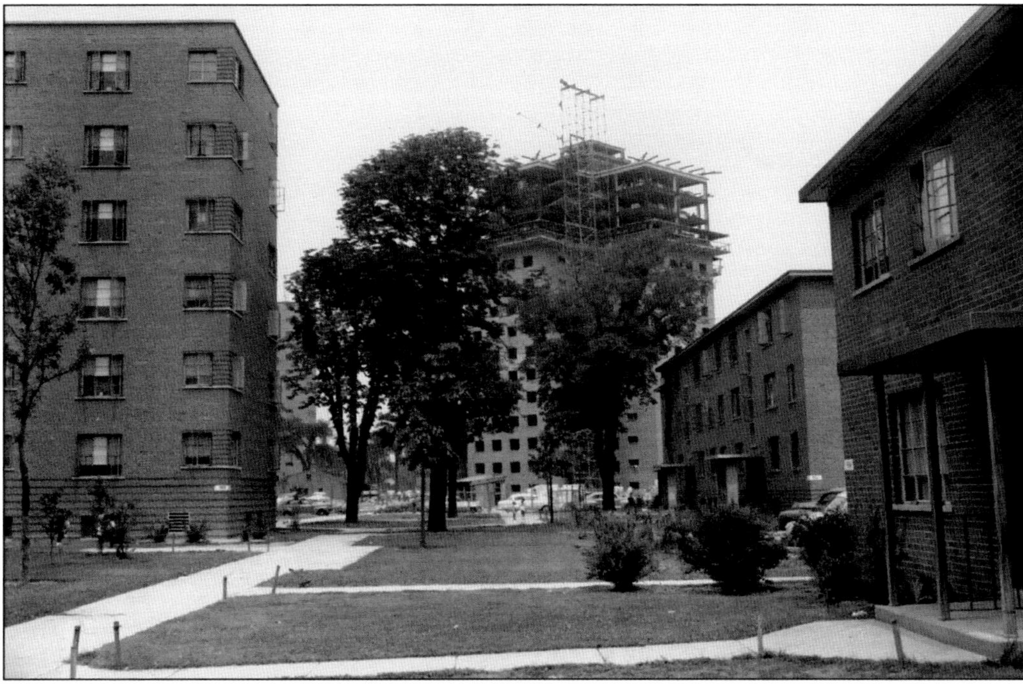

In September 1962, members of the wealthy black elite gathered at Black Bottom's Gotham Hotel for a farewell party for John White. The destruction of the Gotham Hotel symbolized the end of an era. The Gotham Hotel fell, as did many other landmarks in Black Bottom and Paradise Valley, and city officials turned homes and businesses into vacant lots. African American Detroiters were devastated. Some say that racism and segregation made Black Bottom and Paradise Valley, and integration destroyed it. This 1950s photograph shows the Jeffries Projects. (WRL.)

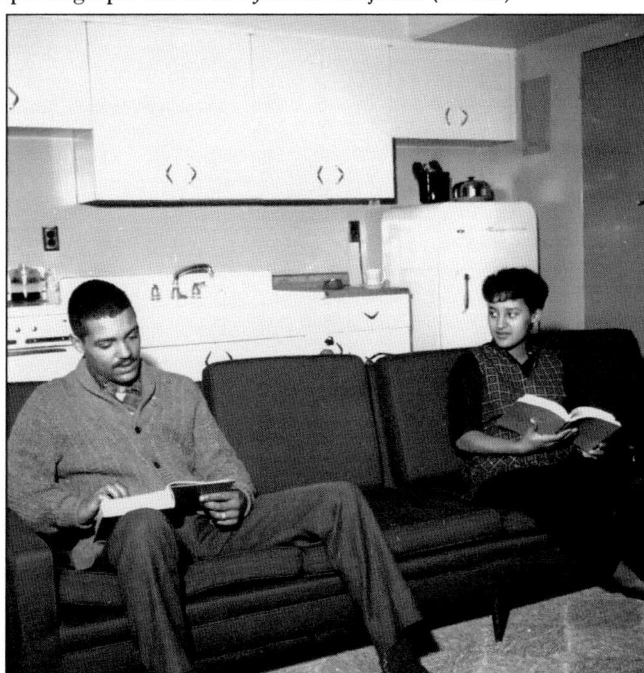

With desegregation, black Detroiters began to spend their money in white-owned establishments. Hastings Street, once a thriving and crowded thoroughfare dotted with African American–owned businesses and clubs, was reduced to rubble. Black Bottom residents could not afford to protest the demolition of their neighborhood. The tight-knit community that had stood as a living example of human will, courage, endurance, and strength under pressure is gone. Memories, photographs, and stories remain. In this photograph, a couple relaxes in their newly furnished home at the Jeffries Projects, around 1960. (WRL.)

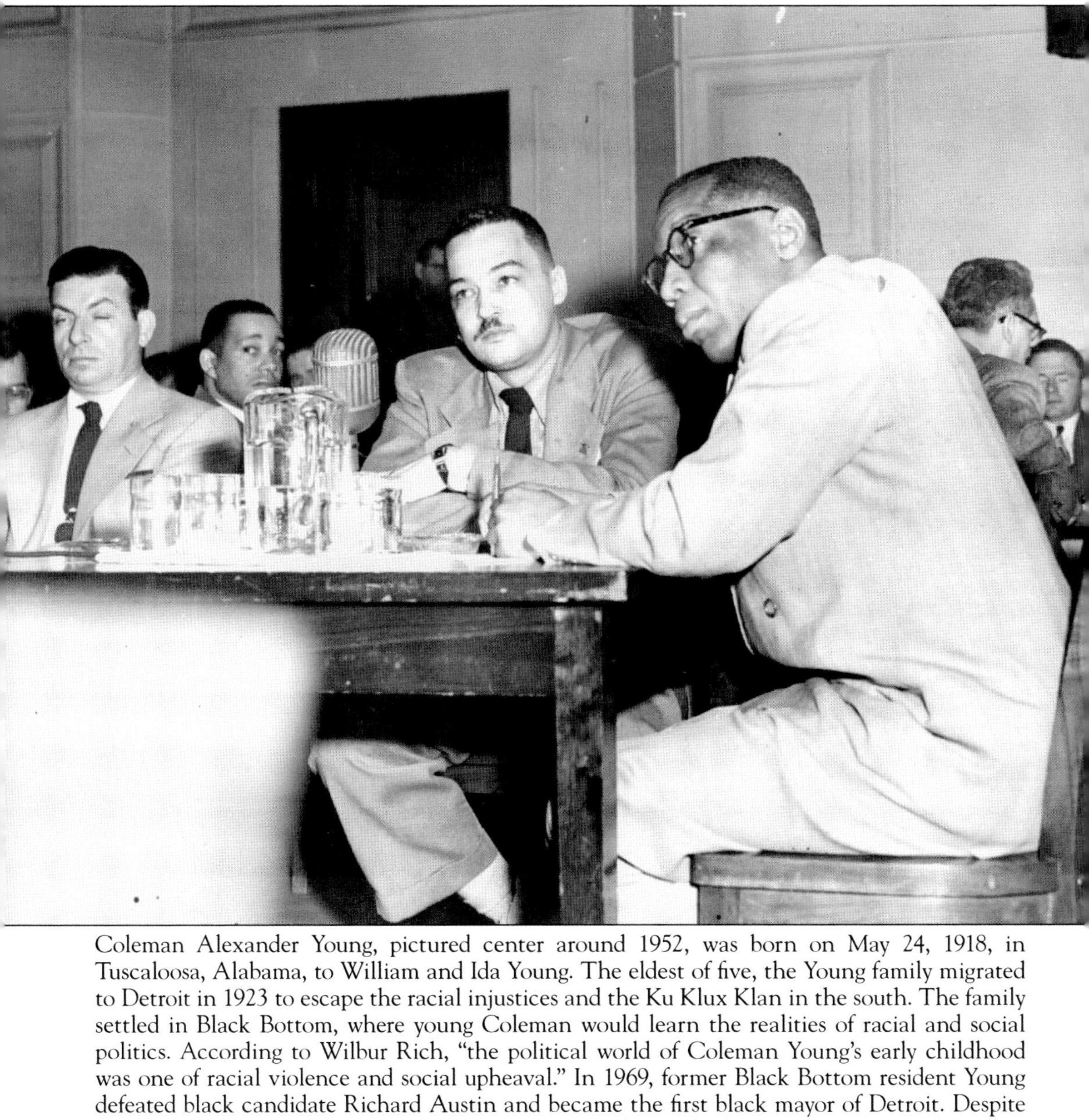

Coleman Alexander Young, pictured center around 1952, was born on May 24, 1918, in Tuscaloosa, Alabama, to William and Ida Young. The eldest of five, the Young family migrated to Detroit in 1923 to escape the racial injustices and the Ku Klux Klan in the south. The family settled in Black Bottom, where young Coleman would learn the realities of racial and social politics. According to Wilbur Rich, "the political world of Coleman Young's early childhood was one of racial violence and social upheaval." In 1969, former Black Bottom resident Young defeated black candidate Richard Austin and became the first black mayor of Detroit. Despite the images that prevailed throughout his tenure, Coleman had a great impact on the newer generation of black politicians. Detroit continued to deal with racial unrest. (WRL.)

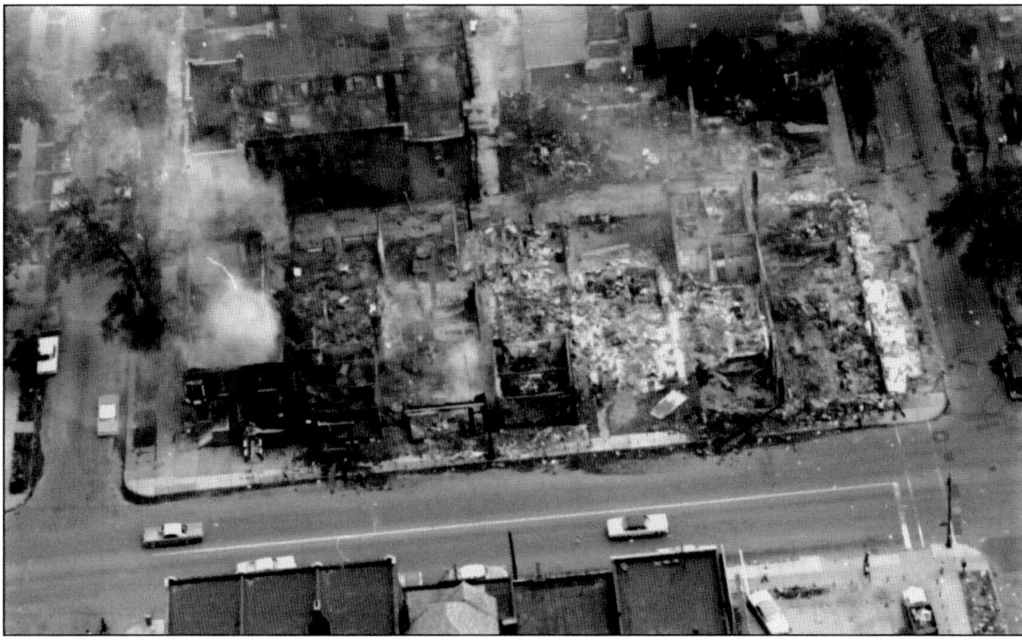

This photograph shows smoke rising from the Linwood area of Detroit during the 1967 riots. According to a Rutgers University Web site dedicated to the riots, "The Detroit Riot of 1967 began when police vice squad officers executed a raid on an after hours drinking club or 'blind pig' in a predominantly black neighborhoods located at Twelfth Street and Clairmount Avenue . . . within 48 hours, the National Guard was mobilized, to be followed by the 82nd airborne on the riot's fourth day, as police and military troops sought to regain control of the city, violence escalated, at the conclusion of 5 days of rioting, 43 people lay dead, 1189 injured and over 7000 people had been arrested." (WRL.)

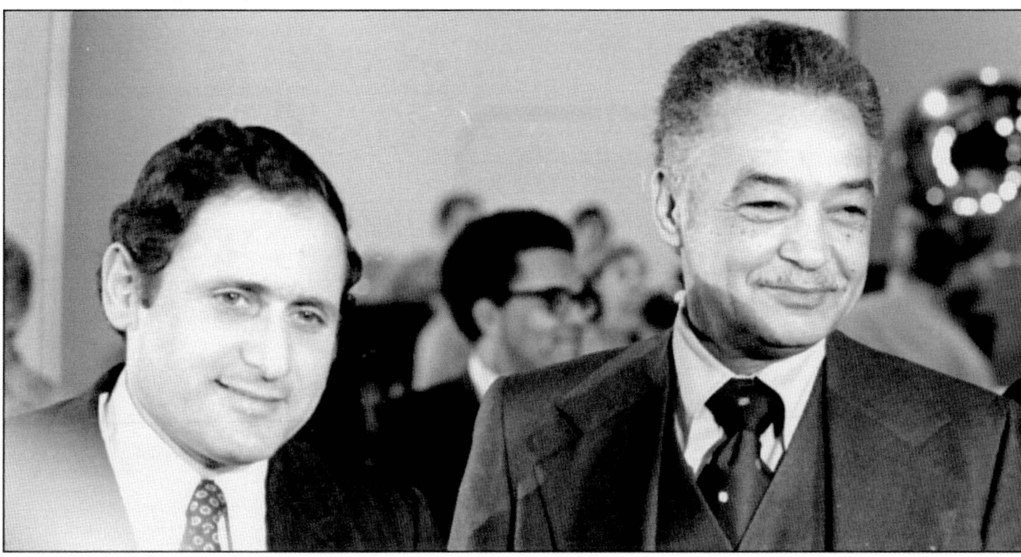

Mayor Young, right, broke down many barriers for African Americans in the political world. Young was successful because he understood the differences between politicking and governing and he was not afraid to tell it like it was. This is a photograph of Young with Carl Levin, taken on Inauguration Day, January 2, 1974. (WRL.)

BIBLIOGRAPHY

Baulch, Vivian M., and Patricia Zacharias. "The 1943 Detroit Race Riots." *Detroit News*, February 11, 1999. http://apps.detnews.com/apps/history/index.php?id=185.

———. "Paradise Valley and Black Bottom." *Detroit News*, August 7, 1996. http://apps.detnews.com/apps/history/index.php?id=174.

Bell, Ernest G. "History of the Black Church in Detroit as a Study in American Public Address." Ph.D. diss., Wayne State University, 1987.

Boyle, Kevin. *Arc of Justice: A Saga of Race, Civil Rights, and Murder in the Jazz Age*. New York: Henry Holt and Company, 2004.

Capeci, Dominic J., Jr. *Race Relations in Wartime Detroit: The Sojourner Truth Housing Controversy of 1942*. Philadelphia: Temple University Press, 1984.

Capeci, Dominic J., Jr., and Martha Wilkerson. *Layered Violence: The Detroit Rioters of 1943*. Jackson, MS: University Press of Mississippi, 1991.

Castellanos, Jorge. "Black Slavery in Detroit." *Journal of Regional History* 6, no. 1 (1982): 54.

Cohassey, John. "Down on Hastings Street: A Study of Social and Cultural Changes in a Detroit Community, 1941–1955." Master's thesis, Wayne State University, 1993.

Current, Gloster. "Paradise Valley: A Famous and Colorful Part of Detroit as Seen Through the Eyes of an Insider." *Detroit Magazine* (June 1946): 32–34.

"Detroit Journal; When Life in the Projects Was Good." *New York Times*, July 31, 1991. http://query.nytimes.com/gst/fullpage.html?res=9D0CE2DC1030F932A05754C0A967958260.

Emmett, J. Scott. "Letters of Negro Migrants of 1916–1918." *Journal of Negro History* 4, no. 3 (1919): 290–340.

Erickson, Cheryl Brent. "Dreamers: The friendship of Dr. Martin Luther King Jr. and Walter Reuther." http://www.uaw.org/events/mlk/02/mlk02.html#_ftn1.

Fry, Charles Luther. "The Negro in the United States—A Statistical Statement," in "The American Negro," sepcial issue, *Annals of the American Academy of Political and Social Science* 140 (1928): 26–35.

Goodwin, Doris Kearns. *No Ordinary Time*. New York: Simon and Schuster, 1994.

Harp, Andrea S., and Alicia Di Rado. "Coleman A. Young: Social and Political Powerbroker." Department of Interdisciplinary Studies, Wayne State University, April 17, 2001. http://www.is.wayne.edu/mnissani/elephant/young.htm.

Haynes, George Edmund. *Negro Newcomers in Detroit*. New York: Arno Press and *New York Times*, 1969.

Hicks, Mary. "The Coverage of World War I by the Radical Black Press, 1917–1919." *Iowa Historical Review* (2007): 57–82.

Hunter, Gary Jerome. "'Don't Buy Where You Can't Work': Black Urban Boycott Movements During the Depression, 1929–1941." Ph.D. diss., University of Michigan, 1977.

Johnson, Charles S. "Incidence Upon the Negro." *American Journal of Sociology* 40, no. 6 (1935): 737–745.

Katzman, David M. *Before the Ghetto: Black Detroit in the Nineteenth Century*. Chicago: University of Illinois Press, 1973.

Landon, Fred. "The Negro Migration to Canada after the Passing of the Fugitive Slave Act." *Journal of Negro History* 5, no. 1 (1920): 22–36.

Latzman, Elaine Moon. *Untold Tales, Unsung Heroes: An Oral History of Detroit's African American Community, 1918–1967*. Detroit: Wayne State University Press, 1994.

Mays, Benjamin E. *The Negro's Church*. New York: Institute of Social and Religious Research, 1933.

"Michigan: Decline in Detroit." *Time*, October 27, 1961. http://www.time.com/time/magazine/article/0,9171,873465-1,00.html.

Moore, Peggy A. *Paradise Valley Days: A Photo Album Poetry Book of Black Detroit, 1930's to 1950's*. Detroit: Detroit Black Writer's Guild, Inc., 1998.

Murage, Njere Wa. "Organizational History of the Detroit Urban League, 1916–1960." Ph.D. diss., Michigan State University, 1993.

Palmer, Dewey H. "Moving North: Migration of Negroes during World War I." *Phylon* 28 no. 1 (first quarter, 1967): 52–62.

Patterson, Joyce Shaw. "Black Automobile Workers in Detroit, 1910–1930." *Journal of Negro History* 64, no. 3 (1979): 177–190.

Reid, Ira De A. "A Critical Summary: The Negro on the Home Front in World War I and II." *Journal of Negro Education* 12, no. 3 (1943): 511–520.

Sugrue, Thomas. *The Origins of the Urban Crisis*. Princeton, NJ: Princeton University Press, 1996.

Talley, Scott. "Black Bottom Was Tops." *Michigan Chronicle Online*, July 16, 2008. http://www.michronicleonline.com/articlelive/articles/2919/1/Black-Bottom-was-Tops/Page1.html.

Thomas, Richard W. *Life for Us Is What We Make It: Building Black Community in Detroit, 1915–1945*. Bloomington, IN: Indiana University Press, 1992.

Trotter, Joe William, ed. *The Great Migration in Historical Perspective: New Dimensions of Race, Class, and Gender*. Bloomington, IN: Indiana University Press, 1991.

Trotter, Joe William, and Earl Lewis. *African Americans in the Industrial Age: A Documentary History, 1915–1945*. Boston: Northeastern University, 1996.

Washington, Forrester B. "Deluxe Summer Camp for Colored Children." *Journal of Negro Life* 9 (1921): 303–306.

Weaver, Robert C. "Detroit and Negro Skill." *Phylon* 4, no. 2 (second quarter, 1943): 131–143.

White, Horace. "Who Owns the Negro Churches?" *Christian Century* (February 1938): 176.

Wilson, Sunnie, and John Cohassey. *Toast of the Town: The Life and Times of Sunnie Wilson*. Detroit: Wayne State University Press, 1998.

Wolcott, Victoria W. *Remaking Respectability: African American Women in Interwar Detroit*. Chapel Hill, NC: University of North Carolina Press, 2001.

Wood, L. Hollingsworth. "The Urban League Movement." *Journal of Negro History* 9, no. 2 (1924): 117–126.

Wye, Christopher G. "The New Deal and the Negro Community: Toward a Broader Conceptualization." *Journal of American History* 59, no. 3 (1972): 621–639.